The Half-Life of Deindustrialization

CLASS : CULTURE

SERIES EDITORS
Amy Schrager Lang, Syracuse University, and Bill V. Mullen, Purdue University

RECENT TITLES IN THE SERIES:

Sherry Lee Linkon, *The Half-Life of Deindustrialization: Working-Class Writing about Economic Restructuring*

Mark W. Robbins, *Middle Class Union: Organizing the 'Consuming Public' in Post–World War I America*

Marie A. Failinger and Ezra Rosser, Editors, *The Poverty Law Canon: Exploring the Major Cases*

M. Michelle Robinson, *Dreams for Dead Bodies: Blackness, Labor, and the Corpus of American Detective Fiction*

Benjamin Balthaser, *Anti-Imperialist Modernism: Race and Transnational Radical Culture from the Great Depression to the Cold War*

Clarence Lang, *Black America in the Shadow of the Sixties: Notes on the Civil Rights Movement, Neoliberalism, and Politics*

Andreá N. Williams, *Dividing Lines: Class Anxiety and Postbellum Black Fiction*

Liam Kennedy and Stephen Shapiro, Editors, The Wire: *Race, Class, and Genre*

Mark W. Van Wienen, *American Socialist Triptych: The Literary-Political Work of Charlotte Perkins Gilman, Upton Sinclair, and W. E. B. Du Bois*

John Marsh, *Hog Butchers, Beggars, and Busboys: Poverty, Labor, and the Making of Modern American Poetry*

Matthew H. Bernstein, Editor, *Michael Moore: Filmmaker, Newsmaker, Cultural Icon*

Lorraine M. López, Editor, *An Angle of Vision: Women Writers on Their Poor and Working-Class Roots*

Carole Srole, *Transcribing Class and Gender: Masculinity and Femininity in Nineteenth-Century Courts and Offices*

Pamela Fox, *Natural Acts: Gender, Race, and Rusticity in Country Music*

Clarence Lang, *Grassroots at the Gateway: Class Politics and Black Freedom Struggle in St. Louis, 1936–75*

Fran Leeper Buss, Editor, *Moisture of the Earth: Mary Robinson, Civil Rights and Textile Union Activist*

The Half-Life of Deindustrialization

Working-Class Writing about

Economic Restructuring

Sherry Lee Linkon

UNIVERSITY OF MICHIGAN PRESS · ANN ARBOR

Published in the United States of America by the
University of Michigan Press
Manufactured in the United States of America
⊗ Printed on acid-free paper

2021   2020   2019   2018   4   3   2   1

A CIP catalog record for this book is available from the British Library.

Library of Congress Cataloging-in-Publication Data

Names: Linkon, Sherry Lee, 1959– author.
Title: The half-life of deindustrialization : working-class writing about
    economic restructuring / Sherry Lee Linkon.
Description: Ann Arbor : University of Michigan Press, 2018. | Series: Class :
    culture | Includes index. |
Identifiers: LCCN 2017052937 (print) | LCCN 2018007547 (ebook) |
    ISBN 9780472123704 (e-book) | ISBN 9780472053797 (paperback) |
    ISBN 9780472073795 (hardcover)
Subjects: LCSH: Deindustrialization—United States—History. | Industrial
    policy—United States. | Working class—United States—Economic
    conditions. | United States—Economic conditions—20th century. | United
    States—Social conditions—20th century. | BISAC: HISTORY / United
    States / 20th Century. | BUSINESS & ECONOMICS / Economic
    History. | LITERARY CRITICISM / American / General.
Classification: LCC HD5708.55.U6 (ebook) | LCC HD5708.55.U6 L56   2018
    (print) | DDC 338.973—dc23
LC record available at https://lccn.loc.gov/2017052937

COVER PHOTOS: (*front*) *Clairton Coke Works, Pennsylvania*; and (*back*) *Train
Hopping Couple, Conway Yard* by Michael S. Williamson, courtesy of the
photographer.

*Dedicated to the memory of my parents, Helene and Gordon,
and to the future of my granddaughter, Francesca*

Acknowledgments

Writing a book involves many hours of solitary labor, but it is never a solo act. This book grew out of discussions with students in my Working-Class Studies courses, and its development was supported by two universities and numerous colleagues and friends. The Center for Working-Class Studies at Youngstown State University provided an intellectual home for many years. Conversations with three of its affiliates—Salvatore Attardo, Christopher Barzak, and James Rhodes—helped me begin to envision this project early on. Patty LaPresta made sure I had the time and focus to do "my own" work by effectively managing the collaborative work of the center. My thinking was also shaped by conversations with visiting speakers at the center, especially Dale Maharidge and George Packer, as well as with local colleagues outside the university, including Tyler Clark, John Slanina, and Hannah Woodroofe.

When I moved to Georgetown, I was fortunate to find another circle of Working-Class Studies colleagues. Carolyn Forché, Pamela Fox, Joe McCartin, Lori Merish, and Patricia O'Connor offered friendship and support that helped me feel at home at Georgetown. I also appreciate the comradeship of the terrific team at the Kalmanovitz Initiative for Labor and the Working Poor. I found a writing comrade in Christine Evans, whose friendship and faith in the power of art inspired me through much of this project. Amy Goldstein was a research fellow at Georgetown early in my time there, and discussions of her work on how Janesville, Wisconsin, was responding to a major plant closing reminded me that the process of deindustrialization is still active and fresh in many places. The commitment and extraordinary competence of my colleagues in the Georgetown University Writing Program—Matthew Pavesich, Maggie Debelius, David Lipscomb, and Karen Shaup—helped me balance research and writing with the program's needs. I also found support in the English Department, led by Kathryn Temple and Ricardo Ortiz. The Lannan Center for Poetics and Social Practice funded a research assistant, Tyler Laminack. English and American Studies colleagues, including participants in an English Department works-in-progress session and in the Americas Initiative, organized by John Tutino, offered valuable advice on drafts. Sandra Hussey, Melissa Jones, and Maura Seale at Lauinger Library made sure I had access to sometimes obscure books and materials. In more practical terms, a sabbatical and summer research award from Georgetown enabled me to complete the manuscript.

As the book developed, I presented a series of papers about deindustrialization literature at Working-Class Studies Association conferences, where I also spent many hours in informal conversations with colleagues whose work inspired me and whose enthusiasm provided essential encouragement. My thanks to Jim Catano, Nick Coles, Joseph Entin, Michele Fazio, Fred Gardaphe, Larry Hanley, and Christine Walley. I am also deeply grateful to Paul Lauter for providing advice and support throughout my career and for serving as a scholarly and professional role model. While University of Michigan Press editor LeAnn Fields deserves particular thanks for her support for and advice on this project, I also want to express my appreciation for her larger contribution to Working-Class Studies by developing the series in which this volume appears. Her commitment and insight have helped to shape and to promote this field. I am also grateful to Jenny Geyer, Kevin M. Rennells, and Anne Taylor at the Press for their work on shepherding this book through the publication process. Special thanks to the extraordinary Michael Williamson for the beautiful cover photos.

Many years ago, after an especially uncomfortable interaction with a famous working-class writer, I swore I would never again write about living authors. This project not only required me to break that oath, but it also changed my mind. I did not have the opportunity to interact directly with most of the writers discussed in this book, but four of them have been especially generous. I had known Jim Daniels and Christopher Barzak for many years, so I was not surprised—but I am nonetheless grateful—that they were willing to answer my many questions about their work, and I appreciate their encouragement of this project. I have never met either Dominique Morisseau or Lynn Nottage, but both trusted me with copies of their as-yet unpublished plays. Their work was incredibly important to this project, and I am deeply grateful for their willingness to share it.

This book would not exist, plain and simple, without Jack Metzgar, Tim Strangleman, and John Russo. All three read and critiqued every chapter of this book multiple times. Thanking Jack for his fierce and formative arguments, his insightful editing, and his enthusiastic cheerleading has become a tradition in Working-Class Studies, and I am grateful to join (again) the long list of scholars who rely upon him. As someone who spends a lot of time editing my colleagues' work, I especially appreciate having a true critical friend in Jack, someone I trust to help me hone arguments and polish sentences. If I don't always take his advice, the error is mine, but his wisdom is—as he occasionally reminds me—almost always right. Tim's contribution to this book was even more crucial. We were writing in tandem, two very different books on deindustrialization, and that made the process into an extended conversation. Tim also pointed me to many of the conceptual sources that shaped this book. A few times he literally sent me books he thought I needed, all the way from England. That Tim's own writing on deindustrialization is cited here so many times reflects the depth of his influence on this project. For academic writing to be a shared, interactive experience is in itself a gift, and I am thankful to have found such a generous intellectual brother.

I have been lucky to have John Russo as my "partner in all things" for many years now. The work we have done together laid the groundwork for this project, and John's influence is as important to this book as it has been in everything we have written together. We have often commented that we make each other better, and there is no doubt I am a better scholar (and a better person) because I have spent years talking through ideas and experiences with John. I depend on his knowledge, insight, and political commitment, not to mention his everyday presence and assistance. He challenges me all the time, but he also believes in me. I am grateful for his love and wisdom every day.

Anyone working on a big project needs the support of friends and family who see you not as a scholar but just as a person. I wrote most of this book during summers in Youngstown, where Ellen and Sascha Lamb, Hunter Morrison, Barbara Orton, and Sharon Stringer cheered me on but also helped distract me from the labor. In D.C., I have been productively distracted by Michael Coventry, Chuck Fant, Pam Fox, Vicki Gray, John and Denise MacGaffin, Mark Popovich, Bert Quint, and Hope Zoss. The last months of work on this book coincided with a particularly difficult period in my life, and I am deeply grateful to my family—Neal and Julie Linkon, Carey and Josh Pickus, Alex Russo, Lara Quint, and my lovely granddaughter, Francesca—for their love and support. Finally, I am grateful to my parents, Helene and Gordon Linkon, who did not live to see this book completed. They taught me to work hard, to value family and community, and to believe that I could make a difference. After many years of wishing that I would have babies, my father finally accepted that, as he put it, my books were my children. Although, as Dad would say, with a little more effort this book would have been perfect, I would like to think my parents would have been proud of this last "grandchild" of their lifetimes.

Contents

Preface

I finished the first complete draft of this book just a few days after Donald J. Trump accepted the Republican Party's nomination as its candidate for the 2016 presidential election. Trump's support from the white working class sparked a national discussion about the many Americans, especially those without college degrees, who had been left behind by economic restructuring. While some commentators charged these voters with gullibility or racism, others emphasized their resentment over being ignored by the nation's leaders and denigrated by the media, the educated elite, and public discourse more generally. While it would be another six weeks before Hillary Clinton would label many of these people as "a basket of deplorables," it was already clear that many Americans, especially professionals who lived in large coastal cities, were at best puzzled by the support for Trump and at worst dismissive and even judgmental of those who found him inspiring. At the same time, many in the white working class were all too aware of how they were seen, and they were excited by a candidate who, despite his wealth and power, shared their impatience at political correctness and their anger at politicians for not doing enough for "real" Americans.

The election made visible a cultural divide that has deep roots and a long history. Karl Marx would tell us that class difference and conflict are inherent in capitalism, and historians argue that the working class was created as part of the Industrial Revolution. In the postwar era, as industrial unions bargained contracts that enabled many workers to live middle-class lifestyles, the divisions seemed less absolute. Yet despite the pride they took in their productive labor, home ownership, and hard-won stability, working-class people still recognized that they were seen as lesser in a society that prized upward mobility. Long before corporations began relocating their factories in search of cheaper labor, many steelworkers and autoworkers encouraged their sons (and sometimes their daughters) to aspire to "something better"—jobs that would pay more, demand less of a worker's body, and allow a sense of pride in having pulled oneself up, not by bootstraps but by a mix of effort and talent. Even as many hoped that their children would lead easier and more prosperous lives, working-class people felt what Richard Sennett and Jonathan Cobb called "the hidden injuries of class." The shame of not moving up the class ladder mixed but also sometimes conflicted with pride and a strong sense of community. They wanted their children to become middle class, but they also felt a real sense of loss when grown children left their families, neighborhoods, and ways of life behind.

For those in the middle and upper classes, meanwhile, the working class was at once admired and denigrated. Working-class people were seen as genuine, down to earth, tough, and intuitively wise, but they were also often portrayed in popular culture as fools. A growing faith in meritocracy encouraged middle-class and elite people to assume their own superiority. They deserved their higher incomes, independence, and influence because they had the ability and determination to succeed, and they had made smart choices. Working-class people had certain virtues, but they either had not followed the right path or did not have the qualities necessary for success. When factories shut down and thousands of workers lost their jobs, many elite observers either ignored the injuries of economic displacement or dismissed them as self-inflicted. If only unions had not demanded such high wages, they might say, or if only workers had made smarter choices, like going to college instead of into the mill when they turned eighteen. Even those who didn't blame workers for the loss of industrial jobs dismissed deindustrialization as part of a "natural" process of "creative destruction" and insisted that the economic changes that emerged in the 1970s would eventually bring better jobs—at least for those who were willing to retrain, move, or make other changes to accommodate the new order.

Despite this long history, many expressed surprise and confusion about the class divide that seemed to emerge during the 2016 election, and dozens of articles and television interviews offered explanations (ignoring the support Trump also garnered from middle-class and elite voters; some exit polls show that he won, albeit narrowly, in every income bracket above $50,000). Some defined the divide in terms reminiscent of the Occupy Movement, noting the growing gap between the wealthy and the struggling but also that many of those who once fit comfortably in the middle now felt anxious about their own and their children's economic prospects. Others focused on education, explaining that those holding college degrees—especially from more elite schools—had better opportunities to construct comfortable, stable lives and more power in shaping public policy, while those without degrees lacked opportunities but were making their voices heard in this contentious campaign season. Still others mapped the divide geographically, noting that urban voters leaned to the left while rural voters were more conservative. And, of course, as many noted, the divide reflected a long history of racial segregation and discrimination as well as resentment by some whites (of all social classes) toward the cultural attention and perceived advantages given to people of color in recent decades. In the effort to explain the 2016 election, commentators cited all of these elements and more.

In trying to understand a cultural divide that many had not previously noticed, journalists and general readers turned to experts, including several social scientists who had, in recent years, published studies that diagnosed the cultural decline of the white working class. For example, Charles Murray's 2012 book, *Coming Apart: The State of White America, 1960 to 2010*, argued that the white working class had lost its moral compass, turning away from the values and habits of middle-class culture such as stable marriages, church attendance, and long-term employment. Andrew Cherlin's 2014 *Labor's Love Lost: The Rise and Fall of the Working-Class Family in America* tied falling rates of marriage among the working class to their economic decline. In 2015, Robert Putnam's *Our Kids: The American Dream in Crisis* and Allison J. Pugh's *The Tumbleweed Society: Working and Caring in the Age of Insecurity* offered more sympathetic and nuanced views, linking the social and psychological challenges of the working class less to moral failure than to economic decline. By the time investment lawyer turned political commentator J. D. Vance published *Hillbilly Elegy: A Memoir of a Family and Culture in Crisis* in 2016, his narrative of working-class dysfunction should have been familiar. But the book's popularity and Vance's rise as a pundit suggest that the story was still fresh for many readers, who were looking for insight into white working-class voters. Others may have found the book appealing because it reinforced assumptions that working-class people are to blame for their problems.

As someone who had been studying the social costs of deindustrialization for almost two decades, and who lived for most of that time in the heart of the Rust Belt, I found all of this attention at once affirming and frustrating. On the one hand, I was pleased that the not-so-hidden injuries of class in the post-industrial era were finally being recognized. Working-Class Studies, the field that my colleagues and I helped establish in the early 1990s with conferences and an interdisciplinary center at Youngstown State University, had long argued that American culture should pay more attention to working-class people and their perspectives. On the other hand, I was frustrated that so many people seemed surprised to discover that the working class was still struggling with the effects of deindustrialization. By 2016, both the challenges facing the working class and the difficulty many educated, privileged people had in understanding working-class people were, for me, old and familiar patterns.

I began studying working-class communities and the effects of deindustrialization in the mid-1990s, in part because I wanted to understand my students, most of whom were the children or grandchildren of steelworkers and autoworkers. Many had been born around the time that steel mills in Youngstown and the surrounding Mahoning Valley began to close, disrupting the lives of individuals and the prosperity of the community. Many were going to college because they had no other options. One of the most iconic local steel mills was slated for demolition in 1995, while near downtown, the building designed to house a museum commemorating the city's defining industry had finally opened. In that context, John Russo and I began examining the stories that people told about Youngstown, especially how they linked labor with community identity. In our 2002 book, *Steeltown USA: Work and Memory in Youngstown*, we traced a shift from a communal sense of pride as an industrial city that, as Bruce Springsteen put it in his song about Youngstown, "built the tanks and guns that won this country's wars" to a conflicted mix of insecurity and resentment after deindustrialization, when residents realized that, as Springsteen sings at the end of the song, they had helped make steel company leaders "rich enough to forget my name."

One of the results of deindustrialization, we argued, was the "politics of resentment," which had generated fierce support for a bombastic, arrogant, entertainingly blunt white guy with bad hair and questionable ethics, Jim Traficant. Mahoning Valley voters reelected him eight times before he was convicted of bribery and racketeering and expelled from Congress. We also wrote about local resentment toward Bill Clinton, who, like so many other politicians, had won strong support from Youngstown voters in part by promising to address their problems. Within a few years, Clinton had helped pass the North American Free Trade Agreement, welfare reform, and the war on drugs. Twenty years later, the politics of resentment was still a powerful force in the valley. In the 2016 Republican primary, more than 21,000 people who had not been registered to vote and another 6,000 who had been registered as Democrats joined the local Republican Party. While John Kasich won the statewide vote, Trump won in the Youngstown area by 13 percentage points. An important shift had occurred, but it did not represent a new trend. Rather, as Youngstown's story suggests, what we saw was an acceleration of a pattern that had begun long ago.

During the summer of 2016, Russo and I wrote a series of op-eds, adding our analysis to the national discussion about how working-class voters viewed Clinton and Trump. Most of our pieces appeared on the Moyers and Company website, a project that grew out of a lively dinner conversation with Kathy Kiely, an editor for Moyers who grew up in Pittsburgh and shared our interest in working-class life and deindustrialization. At one point in that discussion, Kiely wondered aloud whether there weren't some novels that could help us make sense of contemporary working-class attitudes. I told her about this book and explained that a whole genre of such literature was emerging, going back to the late 1990s and still growing. A few weeks later, in my first piece for Moyers, I recommended several deindustrialization novels as must-reads for anyone wanting to understand white working-class voters. As I argued there, deindustrialization literature provides insight that neither journalism nor social science can offer, because it tells stories not merely about but also from the perspective of working-class people. Janet Zandy phrases this powerfully, describing working-class literature as writing "from the skin of a worker." From inside someone's skin, we not only learn about their experiences but also gain access to their ways of seeing and feeling. That perspective might help readers see working-class people not as "deplorables" or deluded fools or angry mobs but as human beings whose lives and attitudes deserve consideration, even if we disagree with their politics.

Deindustrialization literature also reminds us of two important insights that public discussions about the 2016 election missed. The first is that, while the working class has often been divided along racial lines, it also includes people of color. Although the genre has, so far, generated more writing by whites than by writers of color, like all working-class literature, as Zandy argues, deindustrialization literature is not white writing— because the working class is not only white (91). Even more important, working-class people do not live entirely segregated lives. Narratives about deindustrialization suggest that workers' relationships, including strong interracial bonds, are often disrupted when plants close. Commentators too easily assign racism and xenophobia to the white working class, but deindustrialization literature offers a more complex and nuanced view of the intersections and tensions between class and race.

Second, deindustrialization literature reminds us that working-class culture involves much more than loss and resentment. These narratives reveal the struggles of the working class in recent decades, but they also show the resilience of individuals and communities in the face of long-term economic decline. Deindustrialization and the broader economic restructuring of which it is one element represent significant challenges to working-class culture, and the social costs of these changes have been enormous. Yet, as deindustrialization literature shows us, working-class people continue to search for meaning in their labor, for connections to one another, and for ways to survive and make a difference.

Deindustrialization literature takes us inside working-class lives, and that is where we must begin if we want to make sense of public life, including our shared political landscape. I did not write this book to explain the 2016 election, of course, and I doubt that most of the writers whose stories, poems, essays, and films I discuss here saw their work as commentaries on electoral politics. They write about deindustrialization for its own sake, as do I, because it matters, to us and to the people whose lives have been shaped by its long-term effects. Indeed, part of the power of deindustrialization literature is that, in tracing those effects, it insists that we see only a small slice of working-class culture in the way people vote. At the same time, working-class frustration helped to determine the undeniably significant outcome of an unusual and portentous election, and this will in turn influence public policy and civic life for years to come. Working class or not, we are all living in the half-life of deindustrialization.

Introduction

The Half-Life of Deindustrialization

"Just get over it." Residents of deindustrialized communities hear this refrain often, as officials from local economic development agencies urge people to stop being obsessed with the past. After all, they say, the mills closed forty years ago. "The steel industry isn't coming back," they explain, as if anyone expected it to. "This isn't your grandma's city," they say, as if that were news to anyone. Such warnings insist that clinging to memories of the industrial past keeps communities from embracing new opportunities—high-tech development, fracking, call centers, small-scale specialty manufacturing—and from accepting new realities— shrinking populations, more part-time employment, low wages, jobs that demand more training. If people would just let go of the past, some imagine, they would be better prepared for the future.

Meanwhile, in these same communities, neighbors remember helping each other scrape by as one factory after another closed starting in the late 1970s. They gather every summer for ethnic festivals to eat pizza or pierogies, dance to one of the many variations of polka music from familiar local bands, and catch up with old friends. They take their grandchildren downtown and show them where the local department store used to be. They drive from their suburban homes back into the city every Sunday to go to the church where they and their parents were baptized. Their memories were forged long ago through the shared experiences of working-class life—hard work, neighborhood bars, ethnic churches, and persistence. They also remember the pain of losing good jobs. Many still resent that, as Bruce Springsteen sings in the voice of a Youngstown steelworker, they made the owners "rich enough to forget my name." Old friends left in search of new jobs, but they stayed because this was home. They watched the community deteriorate, and that, too, strengthened their connections with other people and with the place itself.

For those who grew up after the plants closed, the shared memories may be less sweet, but they hold people together nonetheless. Like their parents, they take pride in their cities' toughness, but for them grit is not about hard, dangerous work but about living through tough times. They remember overhearing their parents' anxious conversations about how to pay the bills, but they also recall listening to family stories around the dinner table and exploring abandoned factories and office buildings in the middle of the night. Their bonds formed in Catholic school and Little League baseball or while collecting discarded tools from the old mills. Some went off to college and came back, while others took jobs in big box stores or local schools. They don't want to make steel or mine coal, and while they may be excited about a new coffee place or high-tech business moving into downtown, they also fight to preserve the façade of a long-empty movie theater or to save an old church from demolition. They embrace signs of recovery, but like their parents and grandparents, they value the past, even the parts they know only from stories. They want opportunity and a sense of community, and many believe that a better future can be built on past strengths.

For these communities, deindustrialization is not an event of the past. It remains an active and significant part of the present. Like toxic waste, the persistent and dangerous residue from the production of nuclear power and weapons, deindustrialization has a half-life. Its influence may be waning, slowly, over time, but it remains potent, and it cannot simply be forgotten or ignored. In its half-life, deindustrialization may not be as poisonous as radioactive waste, though high rates of various illnesses as well as alcoholism, drug abuse, and suicide suggest that it does manifest itself in physical disease.[1] Equally important, though, the half-life of deindustrialization generates psychological and social forms of disease, as individuals and communities struggle with questions about their identities and their place in a global economy that has devalued workers and their labor. This struggle can seem like an obsession with the past, with what has been lost. Working-class people (and scholars who write about them) have been accused of being foolishly nostalgic for a past that will never return. More accurately, I would argue, they (and we) are wrestling with the contrast between the memory of an era when being a worker had social value and the difficult reality of a present in which wages have stagnated, jobs have become more tenuous, and workers feel they have lost status and power in society at large and especially in conflicts between capital and labor.

While some have denigrated working-class attachment to the past as "smokestack nostalgia," moving beyond the past is not simply a matter of letting go of idealized memories. Four decades after what historian Stephen High describes as the "tsunami" (996) of deindustrialization hit in the 1970s and 1980s, the economic and social damages of that era continue to affect working-class people and American culture more broadly. As Jefferson Cowie and Joseph Heathcott argue in their introduction to *Beyond the Ruins: The Meanings of Deindustrialization*, deindustrialization was not a discrete historical event of the 1970s, nor did it affect only the displaced workers, their families, or their communities. Plant closings and job losses were just the beginning; the effects of deindustrialization persist and expand across decades and generations. After forty years of decline, deindustrialized communities still hope for recovery, and individuals still struggle with the loss of economic stability, social networks, and self-efficacy. While economic restructuring brought increasing productivity and profits to corporations, for most workers, across races, working-class and middle-class alike, it has brought stagnant incomes, growing inequality, and a sense of powerlessness. For many Americans, and especially for the industrial white working class, the economic and political shifts that underlie economic restructuring seem distant and obscure. People experience the effects in immediate and personal ways, and many place the blame not on capitalism and its valuing of profit and investor interests but on other workers—immigrants, women, people of color—who seem to have benefited, or at least not been hurt as much, by a changing economy. While this blaming of the other has been most visible among white working-class people, the loss of solidarity also affects people of color, for whom the economic losses of deindustrialization were even greater than for whites. Workplace solidarity, an often hard-won sense of commonality that linked workers across race, ethnicity, gender, and sexuality, is harder to come by when the workplace itself is disrupted. Solidarity emerges from shared experience, rooted in daily interaction and collaborative labor. Neoliberalism undermines this, but for many, the larger forces involved remain abstract and distant. The lived experience of the half-life is concrete and immediate.

Those who urge residents to "just get over it" imagine a clean cultural slate, but even if erasing the past would enable deindustrialized communities to envision and create better futures—and it is not clear that it would—such erasure is simply not possible. The conditions of the present include the remnants of the past, material and social. This may be especially clear in deindustrialized communities, where people live every day with the tangible evidence of the past, in buildings where people once worked and in empty lots where neighbors' homes once stood. Memory remains in social relations as well. Although social networks fray when some people leave the area, those who remain often feel even more deeply tied to each other, in part because they draw on shared memory to remind themselves of why they stayed. They tell each other stories about the way things used to be and how they changed. These stories create and maintain social relationships, but they also function as cultural interpretations that explain and evaluate what happened and the way things are in the present. Memory and narrative enable and reinforce each other, and they in turn shape the way people understand themselves and their social worlds. Memory provides the basis for, but is also made usable through, narrative. Stories about the past also emerge within the context of the present. As Mieke Bal explains, "ordinary narrative memory fundamentally serves a social function: it comes about in a cultural context whose frame evokes and enables the memory" (x). The past and the present are thus interconnected, even, we might say, mutually dependent. The past, in the form of stories but also social and physical structures, remains significant because of its social function—as part of identity formation, social connections, and material experience—in the present.

And while working-class people often remember the pride and prosperity associated with industrial work, and some no doubt look back on the postwar era as if it were the norm rather than "the great exception," as Cowie calls it, their memories also include struggle and conflict. They remember labor battles and shutdowns, fights within unions and among workers for access to better jobs for women and people of color, and the pain of watching the old mill be torn down and long-time neighbors lose their homes. Their past includes difficulty, loss, and betrayal as well as pride and confidence. For those who were born in the late 1970s and early 1980s, the most vivid past involves the forty years of decline that followed the closings. Deindustrialization did not displace them. It defined them. They grew up in families and communities that were struggling to adapt to economic and social losses, and they came of age in a constrained economy that offered limited opportunities. For them, working-class life involved the memory of not only stability or solidarity but also their own experiences of precarity and uncertainty. Their stories make visible the often hidden injuries of deindustrialization: the lack of good work, the fracturing of communal identity, the difficulty of becoming an adult in a time and place that offer few options and limited stability.

I define this period, starting in the 1980s and continuing well into the twenty-first century, as the half-life of deindustrialization, because that phrase foregrounds the struggle with loss and change that has been so central for working-class people in the United States during this period. Some have described this era as "postindustrial" and "post-Fordist," but both terms suggest that we have moved beyond earlier conditions. The continuing economic and social effects of deindustrialization suggest that we are not yet "post" anything. Yes, the global economy now relies more on the exchange of services and information than on manufacturing, but even in the American cities and towns that we most identify with deindustrialization, people still make things. In Youngstown, Ohio, for example, 50,000 people lost their jobs when the steel industry contracted, and health care and education now dominate the local economy. Yet local mills continued to make basic steel until well into the twenty-first century. The GM Lordstown plant employs about 4,500 workers, and small factories continue to operate in the region. Even in purely economic terms, Youngstown is not postindustrial, nor are other cities like it. In cultural terms, the community still values its industrial identity, and images of gears, brawny men holding sledgehammers, and smokestacks still appear regularly in local advertising and art. "Post-Fordist" better captures the change in working conditions, since even union jobs no longer offer the kind of stability, wages, or benefits that industrial labor once provided. Although post-Fordist is more accurate than postindustrial, both terms suggest a clear break between past and present, even as they define the present in terms of its relation to the past. Adapting Raymond Williams's concept of a residual structure of feeling, in which the culture "formed in the past" remains "very much alive in the present, still active in the cultural process," sociologist Tim Strangleman has suggested that contemporary working-class culture reflects an "industrial residual structure of feeling" (2016, 471). In order to fully comprehend the effects of the economic, social, and cultural disruptions of deindustrialization, he argues, we need to be "more attentive to continuities and more subtle change" (479). The relationship between the past and the present is messy and evolving, and our language should reflect that.

"The half-life of deindustrialization" better captures the liminality of this era. In physics, half-life refers to the time it takes for a substance to lose half of its activity, and it has been used most often to talk about the decay of radioactive materials. The half-life measures the slow decline of toxicity, highlighting its persistence as well as its dangers. These implications apply usefully to deindustrialization, which is both toxic and still active in the lives of many working-class Americans. Like radioactivity, deindustrialization may be losing influence over time, but it has not yet dissipated, and its continuing effects are problematic. Like the diseases caused by exposure to radiation, the injuries of deindustrialization are shared, as we see in the varied social costs of deindustrialization that scholars have identified as common across locations: population decline, the deterioration of buildings and infrastructure, toxic waste, long-term unemployment, mental and physical health problems, rising rates of addiction and suicide, distrust of institutions, and political resentment. As with radiation disease, many who survived the unnatural disaster of deindustrialization are damaged, and those damages are often passed down to their children and grandchildren. We see evidence of the half-life of deindustrialization not only in the slow social and physical decline of working-class communities but also in internalized uncertainties, as people try to adapt to economic and social changes. We cannot predict just how long it will take for the influence of deindustrialization to dissipate, but the half-life of deindustrialization clearly extends well into the twenty-first century.

The continuing effects of deindustrialization are especially significant for the working class, because the changes they experience affect the very core of working-class experience, identity, and culture. The challenges have been most visible for white workers, in part because many had such a strong investment in identities rooted in industrial labor, but as we will see, the half-life also affects workers of color and, perhaps even more important, the possibility of class solidarity across differences of race and gender. The half-life also affects working-class people across time. While workers were immediately and directly harmed by shutdowns and the loss of jobs, relationships, and homes, the effects of deindustrialization include longer, slower, subtler but perhaps even more significant changes as people respond to fundamental shifts in the underlying structural conditions that formed the working class. These shifts may well reshape working-class culture itself. Historian Ira Katznelson argues that the working class emerged in the nineteenth century as people "had to make sense of and deal with a cluster of fundamental changes in the organization of production, conditions of work, community organization, and politics." Those changes were "massive and multi-faceted," and they "provoked basic changes in language, consciousness, and institutions—in short, in the symbolic and organizational aspects of culture." The "webs of significance" that Katznelson suggests make up working-class culture reflect the challenges the working class faced at the time, conditions that "suspended" them "between very hard and jagged economic, social, and political rocks" (22). Today's working class faces a comparable set of fundamental changes, and as Strangleman suggests, the two historical shifts function as bookends framing the industrial era (2016, 467). In both periods, people had to adapt to significant structural changes, which in turn generated cultural shifts, though the economic and social conditions of the early twenty-first century seem at once especially "hard and jagged" and more abstract. Under global capitalism and neoliberalism, the forces affecting working-class lives involve not only new material conditions of labor, including its location and the growing presence of computers and robotics that make some forms of industrial work less manual and more technical, but also new social and political conditions. Within the United States and around the globe, anti-union ideologies and policies together with debates over the effects of trade agreements disrupt the possibility of solidarity, and efforts to organize workers around a sense of transnational working-class identity falter in the face of growing nationalism. In response to the damages of deindustrialization, today's working class is weaving its own "webs of significance," revising if not entirely remaking working-class culture in the process.

The Half-Life of Deindustrialization explores this shift, focusing on how working-class people experience and interpret changes that are as "massive and multifaceted" as the rise of industrialization. What emerges most clearly from this exploration is an understanding that, in social and cultural terms, the transition from one economic period to another is not immediate or absolute. Rather, in the half-life of deindustrialization, as in the beginning of the industrial era, expectations and ideas from the earlier era continue to shape people's responses to emerging conditions. As working-class culture adapts to economic restructuring, the memory of industrial work and the cultural values and ways of living associated with it still have influence, as does the memory of deindustrialization itself. It is not yet clear what a postindustrial working-class culture will look like, but as with the industrial working class, it is taking shape in response to both the conditions of the present and the memory of the past. While capturing culture as it changes is challenging, we would do well, as Strangleman argues, to resist the temptation to define history in terms of neat breaks and to focus, instead, on process and continuities (2016, 479). Put simply, if we want to understand the emerging postindustrial working class, we must examine the liminal period of the half-life of deindustrialization.

A number of social scientists have taken up that challenge, using largely qualitative methods to study contemporary working-class life and perspectives. Some have interviewed young white working-class men in coal and steel towns in England to learn about how, in the absence of work that fits their models of masculinity, they turned to violence and drinking. Others have tracked the life patterns of younger working-class men and women, white and black, noting how economic change shifts gender roles but also feeds racial resentment. Still others consider the changing uses and meanings of industrial spaces or efforts to preserve the memory of industrial work. While such research often relies on interviews in which people tell stories about their lives, and some of it explicitly examines the kinds of stories people tell, few social scientists have acknowledged the emerging body of literary narratives that addresses the same social territory and themes. *The Half-Life of Deindustrialization* treats that literature, especially the growing body of writing and creative media work focused on the lives of younger adults in deindustrialized places, as a lens through which to trace cultural change.

Much of this work is being produced by and focuses on the children and grandchildren of autoworkers, steelworkers, and miners. These narratives explore the reconstruction of working-class culture and identity in the absence of good work, amid the deterioration of both material and social environments, and under the influence of a significant if sometimes contentious relationship with the past. Writing about contemporary life in deindustrialized areas highlights the lived experience of the half-life, emphasizing how characters' situations and choices are shaped by shifts that are at once social and cultural. These are stories of individuals, with particular personal and family histories and positions, but they are also social narratives, reflecting the contingency of contemporary labor and the disruptions of working-class communities, as well as the ways that working-class culture is responding to these changes.

Perhaps most important, these narratives represent subjectivity, exploring the effects of deindustrialization and economic restructuring through individual stories. Deindustrialization literature reminds us that, although large-scale social and economic forces shape individual lived experiences, most people do not see their daily lives through the lens of the global movement of capital or neoliberal politics. Rather than think about the ideologies or actions of those with power, who often seem either disembodied or simply distant, people see the abandoned house next door and the run-down neighborhood bar and empty factory down the street. This personal, local perspective frames contemporary capitalism in terms of memory and loss, often without any overt political consciousness. This displacement from the political to the personal is part of the power of capitalism, yet it is also central to the lived experience of working-class people. Simply put, if we want to understand the cultural influence of economic restructuring, we must attend to its emotional, intimate, everyday effects. Through stories, poems, essays, and films, the literature of deindustrialization makes those effects visible. It explores how working-class people perceive and respond to the changes occurring around and being imposed on them. These texts make clear that people do not "just get over" deindustrialization. They live with it, and they work through it. By offering representations of subjectivity, literature functions as a Geiger counter for the half-life of deindustrialization.

Deindustrialization literature is a thematic and temporal genre. Like most working-class literature, these texts reveal how economic forces affect the lived daily experience and social interactions of working-class people, but its contemporary setting and recognition of large-scale economic shifts make this genre distinct. Most of this work was published after 2000, a decade or more after the closings, and it focuses not on those who were displaced when plants closed but on those who are still living with the effects of those closings. Deindustrialization literature is a distinctly working-class genre, even though some of its core texts were written by and focus on the somewhat more middle-class children and grandchildren of industrial workers. Like working-class literature across the past two centuries, deindustrialization literature focuses on daily life as seen from working-class perspectives, or, as Janet Zandy so memorably phrases it, from within "the skin of a worker." Work remains an important theme in this genre, as does the way economic conditions shape people's relationships, identities, and everyday experiences of the world. Like working-class literature as a whole, deindustrialization literature reflects the diversity of working-class experience, including varied ways of being working class and writing by and about men and women of all races. Working-class literature has always been a literature of struggle, and that remains true for deindustrialization literature as characters struggle to find meaning, build relationships, and construct meaningful adult lives in the context of economic and social uncertainty.

Few of these works have received critical attention beyond a few reviews, and *The Half-Life of Deindustrialization* aims to correct that oversight by identifying some of the genre's most notable works and articulating its central themes and insights.[2] Deindustrialization literature emerged from cultural responses to the shutdowns that began in the 1970s, but its growth over time reflects the continuing influence of the half-life. The earliest examples of the genre include poetry, memoir, and commentary produced by worker-writers responding to the loss of their jobs but also describing the experience of industrial work. Much of that writing appeared in local and regional publications such as the Pittsburgh-based *Mill Hunk Herald* and the San Francisco newsletter *Working Classics*.[3] Writing about work also gained attention within academic publishing during that period because of efforts by writers and scholars interested in, and in many cases coming from, the working class. For example, the Feminist Press published *Women Working*, one of the first anthologies of writing about work, in 1979. At a time when the most visibly displaced workers were men, the collection offered a counter-narrative. As editors Nancy Hoffman and Florence Howe note in their introduction, looking at women's writing about work not only allowed them to "restore women writers to American literature" (xv) but also corrected the long-standing notion that only men's identities were defined by work (xvi). In 1990, Zandy expanded this vision with her anthology *Calling Home: Working-Class Women's Writings* and Nicholas Coles and Peter Oresick offered the first of two collections, *Working Classics: Poems on Industrial Life*, followed by *For a Living: The Poetry of Work* in 1995. Between 1990 and 2014, more than a dozen anthologies of writing about work appeared, many clearly designed for classroom use. While few of these projects defined work solely as industrial labor, and some included pieces from two centuries or more of American writing, it is clear that the economic restructuring that cost many workers their jobs and led some social scientists to predict "the end of work" also generated critical and creative interest in working life.

While late twentieth-century writing about work and its loss provides the foundation for deindustrialization literature, writing about the longer-term effects of deindustrialization began to appear around 2000, with narratives about younger characters who were, like many of the writers themselves, growing up amid the economic and social devastation of shutdowns. I first began to notice this work in the early 2000s, when I read Tawni O'Dell's *Back Roads*, a 1999 novel set in a western Pennsylvania coal town. While Oprah's Book Club focused on the family drama of the novel, I was struck by the way the protagonists' experiences were shaped by economic decline. Although much of the story focused on incest and domestic violence, it also highlighted the struggles that eighteen-year-old Harley faced in trying to support his family on what he earned working two part-time jobs. This was the first time I had encountered a fictional character who faced the economic and social constraints that shaped the lives of many of the first-generation students I taught at Youngstown State University. Like some of my students, Harley had modest expectations for his future, and he felt at once bound to and frustrated by his family and his community, which were both suffering the effects of deindustrialization. I then read O'Dell's second book, *Coal Run,* in which—as we will see—economic decline and the memory of industrial labor play even more central roles. That led me to start looking for more examples. At first, they seemed rare and elusive. Using library databases and Amazon's search tool, I found a few short story and poetry collections. Small press series, like Made in Michigan and Bottom Dog Press, led me to a few more. In 2009, I stumbled on a review of Philipp Meyer's *American Rust* in the *New York Times,* and later *Times* reviews pointed me to Angela Flournoy's *The Turner House* and Matt Bell's *Scrapper.* A family member encouraged me to watch HBO's *The Wire.* In 2013, a new online publication, *Belt Magazine,* began to publish personal narratives and commentaries, and its editors began to produce a series of anthologies focused on Rust Belt cities. In 2015 and 2016, deindustrialization came to the stage, with new plays by African-American writers Dominique Morisseau and Lynn Nottage. Over the past decade, as I have been reading and writing about deindustrialization literature, the genre has been taking shape before my eyes.

As my collecting story suggests, deindustrialization literature includes writing and video production in a variety of forms. By defining the genre around theme and time, rather than form, I hope to emphasize the critical cultural conversation that circulates among literary and media texts of different kinds. A short documentary film, such as Derrick "D" Jones's *631,* works not only as an example of its form but also as a node in a broader exploration of how class, race, space, and memory work together. To separate that text from a novel like Flournoy's *The Turner House,* which like *631* focuses on one African-American family's relationship with their abandoned home, would erase an important connection. The filmmaker and the writer share a common interest, and their texts complement each other. Flournoy's narrative, set in Detroit, in turn links with Ken Meisel's poems about that city, not only through geography but also through both writers' interest in tensions around class and race. These linkages lie at the heart of *The Half-Life of Deindustrialization*, and they suggest the richness of the genre in all its formal and perspectival diversity. No doubt, much could be said about how deindustrialization literature uses these varied forms, and I hope that future scholars will consider how specific forms construct the half-life. At the same time, I hope, my thematic and temporal framework suggests the broader cultural significance of deindustrialization.

Along with all of the standard literary genres, writers are also exploring the long-term effects of economic restructuring through memoir, digital journalism, television series, and documentary films. Drawing a boundary between what is and what is not "literature" has never been simple, of course, and the writers and video producers who contribute to deindustrialization literature blur that tenuous boundary even further by mixing "artistic" and "documentary" techniques. For example, poet Mark Nowak constructs his work from news reports, oral history interviews, photographs, and other sources, while Jones uses similar sources to construct a reflective film about family, community, and place. I have included work in a range of forms in this study because they function as a coherent body of work. Across these varied forms, these texts make visible the experiences, perspectives, and ideas that are emerging in the half-life of deindustrialization.

Like working-class literature more broadly, deindustrialization literature is not white writing. Even more important, not only does the genre include works by Latinx and African-American writers, but it also engages directly with experiences of and ideas about the often-tense intersections of class and race, from multiple perspectives. Similarly, despite the stereotype of the industrial worker as a burly white man, deindustrialization literature includes both works by women writers and texts that explore how economic restructuring, including the loss of factory jobs, affects women as workers and as members of families and communities. That said, because the economic and social displacement of deindustrialization had a particularly powerful effect on white men, their experiences dominate the genre. Their struggles can generate discomfort for readers and critics accustomed to thinking of white men as a privileged social group, but they also remind us that class complicates the social advantages of whiteness and maleness. Difference is always present in deindustrialization literature, but so, too, is the struggle of white men to adapt to the loss of a social position to which many felt entitled. At the same time, some aspects of difference and inequality are less visible in this genre. Very few of these texts address sexual identities, and the experiences of recent immigrants also receive only brief attention. This may change over time, however. Most of the contributions of African-American writers to deindustrialization literature have appeared since 2010, while white writers began to explore the significance of economic restructuring in the 1980s.

Just as deindustrialization literature is not white writing, it is also not—or not only—Rust Belt writing. Although most American deindustrialization literature has been produced and set in the Rust Belt, and while these texts often emphasize ideas about place, the genre is not regionally bounded.[4] *The Half-Life of Deindustrialization* includes narratives set in Baltimore and New England as well as in Michigan, Ohio, and Pennsylvania. No doubt, the Rust Belt has been the primary focus of contemporary analysis and representations of deindustrialization, and the half-life has played out in these communities in especially clear and significant ways. But the economic, social, and cultural effects of the half-life extend far beyond this region. Economic restructuring is a global phenomenon, and communities around the world have been affected, in varying ways, by the movement of industrial capital and production. Writers from many regions and countries have addressed the social costs of and cultural responses to deindustrialization, globalization, and neoliberalism, and deindustrialization literature potentially encompasses all of this work. Put simply, the unifying element is theme, not place.

That said, deindustrialization literature almost always focuses on specific places—cities and towns but also specific neighborhoods or workplaces, staking a claim to local identities and particular communal histories. In grounding its representations in the local, deindustrialization literature only rarely acknowledges directly the larger economic and political forces shaping these places and their economic and social struggles. Instead, deindustrialization literature emphasizes the personal lived effects of neoliberalism and global capitalism—often with only minimal reference to ideology or policy. We can, no doubt, identify the exploitations and tensions of global capitalism within even the most personal of stories, but these stories, poems, and media pieces remind us that the political is not only personal but also grounded and enacted in place.

Literature offers two important contributions to our understanding of the half-life of deindustrialization. First and most simply, these texts are themselves products of the half-life. Literature is a form of representation, and we can read it as we do maps, interviews, photographs, or buildings as qualitative evidence of how deindustrialization and its aftermath have affected people and how they have made sense of that experience. None of these cultural texts provides transparent, unmediated evidence of reality, of course, and while literary texts may offer the most overtly invented versions of reality, they are no less valuable or "true" than other kinds of sources. The characters and plot details may be fabricated, but the insight that emerges through stories is real. Like oral histories, in which, as Alessandro Portelli has argued, people do not just tell us what they did "but what they wanted to do, what they believed they were doing, and what they now think they did," imaginative literature offers insight into how people interpret and feel about their experiences and their social worlds (1991, 67). Like the stories we tell in the context of everyday conversation or in an interview, literary narratives represent experience and perception in coherent and meaningful ways. Just as with any other cultural representation, the writers and filmmakers who create deindustrialization literature draw on the language, ideas, and narrative patterns that were available in their cultural context. Their representations reflect those patterns, even as they add new interpretations and fresh perspectives. Put simply, deindustrialization literature at once emerges from and contributes to the cultural context of the half-life.

But, of course, literature also differs from other forms of evidence, not only because it is more obviously constructed but also because of its artistic aims and functions.[5] An interview subject gives a selective and interpretive account of their experience, but literary writers and media producers take this further. They select and interpret but also actively revise and polish their narratives, and they draw not only on cultural context but also on communicative and artistic strategies. Although anyone telling a story could use different points of view, flashbacks, sensory details, or metaphor, literary writers use these and other tools in ways that reflect awareness of how they work both on the artistic object itself and on audiences. Literature uses these techniques to construct nuanced representations of characters and settings, and in the process it also creates experiences and influences the perceptions of audiences. While we cannot definitively identify the author's intentions, nor is that the goal of literary analysis, when we read literature, we nonetheless assume that the text is designed not only to communicate the author's ideas but also to complicate the reader's experience by generating emotional and intellectual responses. By offering what critic Tzvetan Todorov describes as a "denser" version of "daily life," literature "expands our universe, prompts us to see other ways to conceive and organize it" (17). Literature's capacity for varied and multiple readings can create ambiguity, and this is part of why we turn to it. For cultural geographer Angharad Saunders, this is the value of literature: it offers "not definitive truths, but interrogation of the reasonableness of alternatives" (441). Citing Milan Kundera, Saunders suggests that literature reflects "the spirit of complexity, for it reveals only to confuse, it asserts only to question, it conjectures only to contradict" (440). For literary scholars, the "confusion" and multiplicity that literary narratives offer is part of what makes them so powerful. As scholars and readers, we look to literature to disrupt and expand our understanding.

These qualities enable literary narratives to offer especially rich insight into subjectivity, which is itself multifaceted and shifting. If we want to understand how people experience and make sense of the half-life of deindustrialization, we need to look beyond what has happened and even beyond the stories people tell about their experiences. We need to look at their thought processes and their emotional responses, aspects of human life that lie at the heart of literature. While literary texts do not offer a transparent view into the human mind, their imagined characters, situations, and plots, like the images and evocative language of poetry, offer a representation and interpretation of consciousness and emotion. In offering individual stories, deindustrialization literature makes the global economic and political shifts of the past few decades specific and personal, yet this seemingly narrow perspective also allows us to understand in a more intimate way how people respond to these changes. What do they seek, and what do they find, in newer forms of work? How do they understand their own social positions and life paths in the context of displacement and uncertainty? How do they interact with the material conditions of the deteriorating cities and neighborhoods in which they live? And how do they make sense of the tensions between industrial history, the memory of loss and decline, and competing narratives of hope and despair about the future? Exploring these questions through the personal and social lenses provided by literary narratives can help us understand the cultural effects of the half-life of deindustrialization.

The Half-Life of Deindustrialization examines each of these questions in turn. Threading through these issues is the central theme of deindustrialization literature and of the half-life more broadly: the relationship between the past and the present. Across the genre, writers and characters engage in varied ways with the past. While some of these texts idealize the past, most use the past critically, as a narrative and conceptual resource for highlighting the cultural and psychological tensions of the half-life. These narratives share an understanding that the past cannot be simply brushed aside, that people make sense of their lives in the present through what they have experienced, what they remember, and what they believe about the past. In order for the characters in these narratives to move forward, they must, in various ways, engage with the past. They must reconcile themselves to the loss of jobs and adapt to new conditions of labor as well as new social roles and relations that disrupt their sense of self and community. They must also navigate the landscape of deindustrialization, finding insight but also new ways of seeing the deteriorating built environment and abandoned, remembered spaces that make the past visible and material in daily life. In many cases and in varied ways, both writers and characters find ways to make use of the past, to identify and deploy its resources. They move through the liminal social and psychological space of the half-life, recognizing the power of the past but also their own agency—and the limits of their agency—in defining how the past will shape the future.

We begin, as most working-class literature does, in the workplace. Many scholars, including literary critics, see industrial labor not as merely central but as the defining feature of working-class life. As Paul Lauter writes, the physicality of "labor, including all its pleasures and dangers," is "virtually inescapable in working-class writing" (70). Zandy similarly locates work as the primary experience that shapes the perspective of working-class writing. In deindustrialization literature, work remains central, but the focus is often on the loss of work and on how work has changed. These narratives reveal two related pairs of dualities, about the nature of work itself and about how people remember the work of the past. Whether describing the decline of industrial work or newer forms of labor, deindustrialization literature highlights the way work can be both productive and problematic. It can offer opportunities for workers to build relationships, both intimate friendships and the solidarity that can overcome differences to enable worker agency. The conditions of work, such as automation and management control, can also undermine people's sense of agency and purpose, while some work experiences provide opportunities for pride and satisfaction. In a related tension, narratives about work reveal how the memory of industrial labor can serve as a contrast with contemporary labor, enabling a productive, critical nostalgia, but it can also remind workers that the inequities and injuries of the past, visible and hidden, can resurface in the present, producing what Avery Gordon calls "social haunting," which may inspire continued resistance. As work changes, these narratives suggest, neither people's desire to find meaning in their labor nor the fundamental conflicts of class disappear. As we will see in chapter 1, through poems by Jim Daniels, short stories by Lolita Hernandez, several contemporary novels, and the television series *The Wire*, the memory of industrial labor can serve as a resource for understanding and addressing the conditions of work under economic restructuring, but it can also remind us of what has been lost—not only jobs but also worker agency and solidarity.

Work may be the starting place for working-class writing, but, as Lauter tells us, working-class literature is as much about the lives of working people as it is about the work itself (70). This is true for deindustrialization as well: the displacements of deindustrialization play out in workers' sense of themselves and their relationships. Chapter 2 examines the construction of working-class identities under the continuing influence of deindustrialization. The loss of industrial jobs called into question the dominant image of the American working class: the white, male industrial worker. Although deindustrialization clearly affected workers regardless of gender, race, ethnicity, or sexuality, white working-class men seem to have been especially troubled by their displacement. As we see in Philipp Meyer's *American Rust*, younger men often struggle to redefine working-class masculinity and adulthood in the absence of industrial labor. While some of these narratives treat whiteness almost as a given, other texts raise questions about how race, gender, and class work together but also come into conflict, reminding readers that economic change shifts not only structural conditions but also identities and relationships. In several texts, such as Eminem's *8 Mile*, Dominique Morisseau's *Skeleton Crew*, and Lynn Nottage's *Sweat*, conflicts over class play out in terms of race and gender as individuals stake claims to social positions and strategies for survival. At the same time, in response to neoliberalism and the contingent work structures it justifies, some working-class characters reimagine their identities and question traditional working-class values of belonging and community. Across these narratives, the past shapes how people construct their identities and threads through their relationships. Younger white men remember the apparent stability and clarity of their fathers' lives and mourn the loss of economic and social certainty, while African-American workers, male and female, recall their struggles to gain access to good jobs and union membership. Yet identity is also deeply personal in these narratives, often less a matter of belonging to a well-defined group than a reflection of personal connections, especially family ties. Working-class identity was never singular or fixed, but in the half-life of deindustrialization it appears to be at once rooted in the past and more contingent than ever.

Working-class identities are also shaped by material conditions, not only in the conditions of labor but also of physical space. Along with the loss of and changes in jobs, the deterioration of the built environment is a defining feature of the half-life of deindustrialization. In cities and towns across the Rust Belt and elsewhere, people live amid boarded-up storefronts, abandoned factories, crumbling houses, and empty spaces that still bring to mind the childhood friend who once lived in a now de-molished house or the massive mill that used to fill what is now an empty field. Indeed, the deindustrialized landscape offers the most visible, tan-gible evidence of the half-life, and deindustrialization literature uses the landscape and ideas about place to establish mood, develop characters, and comment on social patterns. In fiction by Matt Bell, Ellen Slezak, Bonnie Jo Campbell, Michael Zadoorian, and Angela Flournoy and in poems by Ken Meisel and Mark Nowak, we see how the industrial and deindustrial past remain physically intact but also present in memory. We also see how both the physical remains and what people remember about a place shape actions and perceptions in the present. Certainly, deindustrialized landscapes have gained significant and sometimes prob-lematic attention through photography and film centered on industrial ruination, which often focus on depopulated scenes. Deindustrialization literature reveals the human presence within the ruins, and in the pro-cess it provides insight into the liminal but also localized experience of living in the half-life. Although a few of these texts acknowledge that the landscapes they describe reflect regional and even global patterns, as I argue in chapter 3, in most cases the focus on landscape anchors dein-dustrialization in place. Deteriorating structures and seemingly empty lots may be common features in all deindustrialized locales, but, for peo-ple living in these places, these remnants of the past are almost always defined in terms of local and even personal specificity.

While a sense of loss runs through much of deindustrialization, the multiform writing of "Rust Belt chic" redefines the struggles of eco-nomic decline and the memory of the industrial past as resources for personal and community revitalization. In blogs, online magazines, and anthologies, Rust Belt writers celebrate the resilience of deindustrial-ized cities. In the process, these younger, mostly white, college-educated writers—some working in professional jobs, some working as journalists, and many struggling as part of the precarious "creative class"—reclaim working-class culture. In many ways, they are reinventing working-class identity, much as third-generation white ethnic communities reinvented Irishness or Italianness in the 1970s, and like these ethnicities, their version of working-class culture is selective, idealized, and optional. While we may question their sometimes idealized representations of belonging, perseverance, and the economic potential of the material remains and social memories of the past, Rust Belt chic nonetheless reminds us that the half-life matters not only for those who were displaced or for those in the next generation who still struggle to find their place in the restructured economy, including the educated, professional children and grandchildren of industrial workers.

Indeed, while the optimism of Rust Belt chic can seem unwarranted given the continuing struggles of deindustrialized communities, these narratives emphasize a significant underlying theme of deindustrialization literature: survival. The common story about deindustrialization focuses on loss, failure, and struggle. When local economies shrink, populations decline, cities and towns struggle to maintain services and infrastructure, and social networks are strained and too often disintegrate. Yet these communities and the people who live in them persevere. For all the difficulties of living amid the half-life of deindustrialization, this literature also offers stories of persistence and adaptation. While they make visible the challenges of living with the uncertainty and limitations of the postindustrial economy, these texts also suggest that American culture, not only the working class, continues to be influenced by the losses and difficulties of deindustrialization.

When John Russo and I wrote in 2002 that Youngstown's story is America's story, we didn't know how prescient we were. As the most dramatic element of economic restructuring, deindustrialization marked the beginning of what would become a long, slow deterioration in American expectations about opportunity and prosperity. Many workers across all industries and social classes in the first part of the twenty-first century have learned the lesson that took so many industrial workers by surprise in the 1970s and 1980s: we are all, as Bruce Springsteen put it, expendable. Too many have found themselves shuttling among multiple part-time jobs, working as independent contractors, losing benefits and job security. The nationwide foreclosure crisis, widespread underemployment, and stagnant wages of the Great Recession continued long after its official end, and the economic and social conditions we associate with deindustrialization have become the norm for many Americans, and many—not only the working class—struggle to reconcile the memory of a more stable past with the reality of an increasingly uncertain future. This struggle has political and social consequences, as we saw in the 2016 election, as people responded to populist messages focused on economic inequality and opportunity from across the political spectrum. Deindustrialization literature reminds us how powerful the continuing wounds of economic displacement can be. Instead of "getting over" the past, we must recognize how it persists in the half-life of deindustrialization.

ONE

Dual Visions

Work and Memory in the Half-Life

In "Last Car," Detroit fiction writer and former autoworker Lolita Hernandez traces the journey of a cobalt blue Cadillac Fleetwood Brougham along the assembly line. It is December 18, 1987, "the final glorious moments of car assembly at Cadillac Motor Company, Clark Street, Detroit" (116). As the frame connects with the chassis, the gas tank is added and then signed by the workers, and the body is finally dropped to complete the vehicle; a crowd gathers. Workers from every part of the line converge with office staff and reporters, cheering but also sad. They wear black armbands, and the "general foreman of final assembly produced a tight smile to mask the noticeable furrow of sadness across his eyebrows." A worker dressed as Santa Claus carries a placard reading "ALL I WANT FOR CHRISTMAS IS MY JOB" (125). The scene ends with the crowd chanting together, "Na na naa naaaa. Hey-hey-hey . . . gooood-bye" (126). It is a week before Christmas, and within just a few weeks, by the Feast of the Epiphany, Hernandez tells us, "there would be little left in final assembly to recall the activity of the last day or any day or year preceding" (125).

As we follow the Brougham down the line, Hernandez rehearses the qualities that make autowork meaningful. Her description of how a car comes together reflects the pleasure workers take in their detailed insider knowledge of the automaking process. Descriptions of workers' interactions with each other emphasize that the line is not just a series of individuals but a community. Details about the car itself—its "diamond twinkles wherever the light hit, simulated convertible top, and light blue leather interior" (116)—suggest that workers have good reason to feel pride about the tangible, valuable, beautiful object they are constructing, and the recognition of this event from fellow workers and the media makes clear that this work and its ending matter. "Last Car" is as much about the social values of autowork as it is about the loss of that work. As Hernandez writes in the introduction to her 2004 collection *Autopsy of an Engine and Other Stories from the Cadillac Plant,* in which this story appears, these workers are losing more than a paycheck.

This is the scene, the transformative moment, that often comes to mind when we think about deindustrialization. The standard narrative of deindustrialization is one of loss and displacement, focused on workers who had relied upon industrial jobs to support their families, to define their identities, and to shape their communities. Yet, as Hernandez suggests by positioning this story in the middle of her book, while the last car matters, it is not the whole story of either industrial work or deindustrialization. "Last Car" appears about two-thirds of the way through the volume, after a cluster of stories that describe workers' interactions on the line, preparations for an impending strike, the challenges women face in a historically male-dominated industry, and workers moving to new jobs as part of the plant shutdown. After this story, a few others consider what happens after the closing. As this structure reminds us, deindustrialization refers not to a single moment or event but to a long, slow process.

That a worker-writer, crafting stories as her plant was slowly shutting down, would view industrial labor as meaningful should not surprise us. What is most interesting about Hernandez's writing is the way it reflects two central themes of contemporary working-class writing about work. First, writing about industrial work emphasizes the dualities of such labor, which is at once problematic and productive, a source of hardship and a good living, humiliation and pride, alienation and solidarity. Deindustrialization literature only rarely romanticizes blue-collar work, and even the narratives that offer mostly positive views of industrial workplaces acknowledge the contradictions and hardships that accompany whatever social benefits work accords. This dualistic representation of work also appears in stories about the service sector jobs that have replaced industrial jobs for so many working-class people in the United States, though many of these more recent stories also critique the way economic restructuring affected the experience of work. While the changes traced in these narratives reflect the conditions of contemporary global capitalism, including the movement of production in search of cheaper labor and less regulation, expanding automation, and the shift from manu-facturing to service work, these stories very rarely address economic or political forces writ large. Rather, deindustrialization literature focuses on what these changes mean for workers, especially how they continue to seek meaning and connections in work despite its hardships. At the same time, deindustrialization literature shows that balancing the dualities of work has become more challenging over time. These narratives remind us that changing labor conditions come with multiple costs—economic but also social and psychological.

The duality of work intersects with a second duality, about how con-temporary working-class writers and their characters think about the past. Memory is an essential narrative tool in deindustrialization literature, which writers use to explain characters' motivations and which charac-ters often seem unable to set aside. In these stories, displaced workers as well as their children and grandchildren draw on the memory of indus-trial labor as they respond to economic restructuring, yet that memory is itself dualistic. It involves both nostalgia and haunting, a longing for what has been lost and a reckoning with past injuries. Remembering the best qualities and effects of industrial labor can be productive and criti-cal, in part because it provides a clear contrast that clarifies the problems of the present. Remembering the hardships and struggles of the past can also foster critical understanding of present conditions. Within deindus-trialization literature, we see both perspectives at work, sometimes within a single text. Both versions of the past can seem simple, even simplistic, yet as Tim Strangleman and Avery Gordon have argued, these ways of thinking can generate critical and complex insights and inspire action.

As Strangleman has noted, many writers and scholars have examined the work of the present by comparing it with earlier forms of work, often suggesting the loss of some "golden age" of labor (2007). While such looking backward has sometimes been dismissed as romanticizing or ide-alizing, deindustrialization literature makes clear that remembering the work of the past as "good work" is not simple nostalgia or evidence of false consciousness. Neither workers nor writers are wrong to remember industrial work as valuable despite its problems, and as Strangleman has argued, we should be wary about dismissing nostalgia out of hand. Cit-ing Fred Davis's notion of "*third order* or *interpretive* nostalgia," Strangle-man suggests that "all nostalgic reflection questions memory in a critical way" (2013, 28). In a sense, we can read deindustrialization literature as enacting interpretive nostalgia. Writers in this genre treat the past and its memory as tools for excavating the critical potential of a working-class culture that emerged during the industry heyday but persists in and is adapting to the half-life. That work is remembered as dualistic and conflicted, and that writers and their characters often wrestle with their memories of work, demonstrates this critical potential. These narratives also illustrate the potential that Strangleman identifies for a more "radical or oppositional" version of nostalgia in which "knowledge of the past makes a dialectic intervention in debates about the present" (28). In deindustrialization literature, writers use memories of industrial work to emphasize what has been lost not for the sake of remembering but to clarify the challenges of the present.

The resistant potential of the past lies not only in the contrasts revealed through positive memories but also in the way conflicts and injuries resurface. As Gordon argues in *Ghostly Matters: Haunting and the Sociological Imagination*, when the social violence of the past remains unresolved, it can resurface in the present. Such haunting, she writes, "is one way in which abusive systems of power make themselves known and their impacts felt in everyday life, especially when they are supposedly over and done with" (xvi). Equally important, Gordon argues, haunting differs from troubled memories or trauma because it inspires action: the "disturbed feelings" that emerge with social haunting "cannot be put away," and this generates a sense that "something else, something different from before, seems like it must be done" (xvi). Gordon develops her argument by looking at fiction that is haunted by slavery (Toni Morrison's *Beloved*) and by the *desaparecidos* of Argentina in the 1970s and 1980s (Luisa Valenzuela's *Como en la Guerra*), both of which reflect systems of power that were overtly abusive and violent. While less specific—and more pervasive—than either of these cases, capitalism is also an "abusive system of power," which is reflected not only in the exploitation of workers but also in the power of the owning class to make decisions that disrupt workers' lives and destroy their communities. Of course, the social violence of capitalism is not time bound. Workers remain exploited and alienated, and the conflicts of labor exist in both the past and the present. Deindustrialization literature makes the continuing injuries of capitalism visible through characters who are haunted by the memory of the long history of economic exploitation and struggle.

Deindustrialization literature illustrates the productive potential of nostalgia and haunting that Strangleman and Gordon identify, yet it also suggests the limits of the past as a resource for responding to contemporary economic and social problems. While comparing a better past with a troubled present or recalling earlier injustices and struggles often illuminates the problematic conditions of work in the present, few of the characters in these narratives are able to draw upon the past to frame effective resistance. Memory may provide insight and inspiration, but it cannot overcome the structural and ideological power of global capitalism and neoliberalism. Yet while these narratives suggest the limits of memory, they do not critique workers for their engagement with the past. Rather, these stories show how it is embedded in working-class consciousness. Further, in showing how memory enables a critique of contemporary conditions of labor and the obstacles working-class people face in moving toward resistance, deindustrialization literature generates a critical awareness and political urgency, what Gordon describes as a sense of "something to be done" (183), for its readers.

This chapter examines the dualities of contemporary writing about work and the memory of work. I begin with several texts that articulate the dualistic nature of work itself and that show how those dualities persist across time and different kinds of labor. In poems and fiction about both industrial and service settings, work is represented as unpleasant and exploitative but also as a source of meaning and community. Workers take pleasure in doing their jobs well, even when they recognize that doing good work brings them little benefit and contradicts their interests. Deindustrialization literature explores these dualities and reveals both continuities and shifts as the structures and practices of work change. Jim Daniels's Digger poems articulate the complex mix of satisfaction and struggle of the industrial workplace through the eyes of a Detroit autoworker, and we see similar tensions in contemporary writing about service work, including Timothy Sheard's mystery novels featuring hospital janitor and amateur detective Lenny Moss and Stewart O'Nan's portrait of a chain restaurant manager, *Last Night at the Lobster*. As these texts show, the specific conditions of labor may change, but workers continue to seek meaning and value in work even as they recognize its problems.

Deindustrialization literature also examines how people use the past as a resource for making sense of contemporary work. A number of these narratives draw on both nostalgia and haunting while also still reflecting the dualities of labor. In her collection of stories about the closing of the Cadillac plant, Hernandez captures the way work can be remembered as both socially productive and conflicted, reflecting the critical potential that Strangleman suggests nostalgia can provide. Other narratives represent more conflicted memories of the past, and in some cases these are embodied not in the resurfacing of social violence, as Gordon describes haunting, but in specific ghosts. In Tawni O'Dell's *Coal Run*, a troubled man must wrestle with the specter of his long-dead miner father, whose ideas about the value of work provide both inspiration and challenge. The ghosts of the past become more concrete in Grady Hendrix's *Horrorstör*, which combines the visual and verbal style of an IKEA catalog with the conventions of a horror film. As workers at a chain furniture store are literally haunted by the ghosts of the nineteenth-century prison on which their store was built, the narrative suggests problematic similarities between the corporate rhetoric of the contemporary workplace and an extreme and abusive version of the Protestant work ethic.

While all of these texts use the past as a resource for critiquing the conditions of the present, deindustrialization literature also raises questions about whether either nostalgia or haunting can generate effective resistance. The past can provide a useful contrast through which writers highlight the problems of the contemporary workplace, but while this can clarify the challenges contemporary workers face, the memory of the past may not enable them to overcome the social and political realities of the workplace. As we see in Dean Bakopoulos's *Please Don't Come Back from the Moon* and David Simon's HBO series *The Wire*, the past is useful rhetorically, but it has limits strategically. Contrary to theoretical claims that nostalgia and haunting can be not only critical but also politically productive, deindustrialization literature offers few examples of workers translating critical cultural memory into collective agency. Stories about the decline and loss of industrial labor and about working-class people adapting to the service labor that now dominates the economy make clear not only the contradictory costs and benefits of work itself but also the way people continue to interpret work through the lens of the past. As workers struggle to find meaning in jobs that offer only limited opportunities to make connections, to feel that their work matters, or to have any sense of agency on the job, their efforts are shaped by the past but also constrained by the present.

While deindustrialization literature sometimes seems nostalgic for an era when unionized blue-collar jobs enabled working-class people to achieve stable, comfortable lives and feel good about themselves and their work, it also reveals how economic restructuring has disrupted the duality of work. In these narratives, the relatively stable, tangible, and communal experience of industrial labor provides a contrast that highlights the contingency, fragmentation, and isolation of contemporary work. Viewing the present through the lens of the past, whether framed as nostalgia or as haunting, makes clear both how deeply the contradictions of labor are embedded in capitalism and how persistently workers seek sources of meaning and value in their work. In these dualities, we can trace the continuities and subtle cultural shifts that reflect the power of deindustrialization in its half-life.

The Dualities of Labor

As in most working-class literature, work is a central concern in deindustrialization literature, which addresses both the decline and the loss of industrial jobs and the conditions of labor in the service jobs that have, for so many working-class people, replaced manufacturing and mining. In writing about old and new work alike, writers emphasize both the exploitation, exhaustion, and drudgery of work and its social and psychological benefits. Industrial labor, especially, can give workers a sense of pride in the act of working and the material goods produced, though we see a similar kind of pride among workers who provide services. Work can also foster important relationships and, at least potentially, provide a site for developing agency and solidarity. Working-class literature has noted these dualities in the past, of course, but deindustrialization literature suggests that the expectation that work will provide social benefits along with income persists within working-class culture, even though contemporary forms of work are less likely to provide those benefits. Through its attention to the dualities of work, deindustrialization literature resists "simple nostalgia" about industrial labor, and it counters the claims of those who have argued that deindustrialization would benefit workers by moving them to "better" jobs.[1] Instead, these narratives insist that work cannot simply be dismissed as hard and exploitative or celebrated as a source of pride and solidarity.

To understand the tensions inherent in the dualities of work and the way contemporary working conditions disrupt the balance between productive and problematic aspects of work, we begin in an industrial setting, specifically in the Sterling Axle plant where Jim Daniels's character Digger works for many years. Daniels traces Digger's working life across a series of poems that appear in clusters within his books, beginning with *Places/Everyone* in 1985 and continuing through the 2007 volume *In Line for the Exterminator*. During the decades when he was writing the Digger poems, Daniels witnessed plant and mill closings, both in Detroit, where he grew up and where members of his family worked in the auto industry (as he also did, briefly), and in Pittsburgh, where he settled during the 1980s when the steel mills ringing that city were shutting down.[2] As the Digger poems remind us, the economic restructuring that led to job loss for many workers also caused a significant decline in the quality of work in plants that remained open. Automation reduced the number of workers on the shop floor, and economic pressure depressed wages, cut benefits, and threatened pensions. During the same period, an industry that had once been a source of regional and national pride struggled to survive and at times became an object of derision. The poems rarely address these tensions overtly, but we can see their effects, through Digger's eyes, especially when we read the poems chronologically, from his first day on the job until after he retires. In Daniels's last set of Digger poems, published in 2007, his character is looking back on a career that would no longer be possible and an industry that values its workers less than ever.

With a very few early exceptions, the Digger poems are written in second person, which invites the reader to imagine being Digger, facing the challenges, disappointments, and occasional small triumphs of his day-to-day life. Through Digger's voice, which is at once critical, self-mocking, a little defensive, and somewhat sad, Daniels creates a character who seemingly cannot help but observe and recognize the dualities of working life. Digger describes the specific material conditions of his world—the buttons on the machine he operates, the clock in his kitchen, the feeling of being hung over, the deterioration of his neighborhood. Through concrete detail and matter-of-fact language, Daniels reveals both the disappointments of Digger's life and his resigned acceptance of the way things are. In "Digger's Melted Ice," for example, he thinks about the ordinary, repetitive task of work: "your machine / how you push two buttons and the press / comes down. Always the same, / so simple you can disappear." These lines move subtly from concrete description into brief, indirect, but powerful commentary. The simplicity of the language and the ironic, self-effacing voice of this poem, typical of many in the series, invite us to empathize with Digger, not to view him as an object of pity or distant observation.

The dualities of work shape these poems from the beginning. In several poems from *Punching Out*, set early in Digger's life in the auto plant, Daniels shows how a new worker learns to navigate the social landscape on the shop floor—to view the supervisor as the enemy and to view his tough and initially threatening colleagues both warily and as allies. When, on his first day, Digger's welding gun stops working and he asks the supervisor for help, two older workers school him about not hurrying to get the job done: "*If you don't know / how to break your machine / then you shouldn't be runnin' it.*" He learns quickly and later lets his machine jam. When the boss tells him to try to fix it, he replies, "*Not my job*." One of his more experienced colleagues agrees: "*need an electrician*."

> Electrician shows up
> but he just wants to jive
> with Nita, the fox at the next press.
> Santino gets on his case
> which is his job
> and the electrician
> fixes the machine
> which is *his* job
> and I go back to my idiot buttons.
> Which is *my* job.

This small-scale resistance reflects dualities of power and knowledge. Digger has learned quickly the central conflict between workers and supervisors, but he has also learned to exercise the limited power he holds—power that resides, at least in part, in the union contract that defines what is and is not "his job." But the poem also highlights a tension between expertise—knowing how to break his machine—and the seemingly simplistic task of pushing "idiot buttons." As Digger learns the mechanical and social rules of the job, the poem reveals how work combines pride and humiliation, conflict and solidarity, limited control but also resistance.

The duality of work remains a core theme as Digger at once resists and embraces his identity as an autoworker. In the 1985 poem "Digger Goes on Vacation," work has become an inescapable part of Digger's consciousness. He sits on the beach, unable to leave the factory behind: "your foot / in the sand outlines the part / you weld onto axles." The image, like the job, seems to be indelible: "no matter / how many times you kick the sand / it still looks like something." When, at the end of the poem, he takes pleasure in telling a bartender that he's an astronaut, we are reminded of Digger's ambivalence about how his job defines him. Almost a decade later, in "Digger, the Birthday Boy" from the 1993 volume *M-80*, the forty-year-old Digger has accepted his identity as an autoworker. At first, he saw the job as temporary: "*Two years tops. Enough money / to get ahead a little / till I figure out what I / really want to do*." After working at the plant for twenty years, he no longer imagines doing something else: "When someone calls you a lifer now / you do not object." In another vacation poem, also in *M-80*, Digger and his family again go to Florida, all wearing items that mark them as from Detroit: a Tiger's cap, a Stroh's towel, T-shirts from "Sterling Plant, Home of the Axle." For Digger, this is a source of pride, a way of proclaiming their identity: "You want everyone to know: *a Detroit family—we do real work*." But again, a tension emerges between pride and resignation as Digger thinks about the inevitable return to the work that shapes his life. At the end of the poem, on the way home, he gets a flat tire. As he rolls the repaired tire along the highway back toward the car, he feels powerless, like "a doll somebody's playing with": "*Some doll,* / you think, and roll right past the car / and down the road. In twenty-four hours / you'll be back on the job." The structure of the poem, moving from pride to resentment, from arriving on vacation marked by signs of work to doing a version of auto-work while on the road back home, underscores the conflicted ways that work shapes Digger's life.

Although the Digger poems do not address plant closings directly, they nonetheless reflect changes in the industry, as always, from the worker's perspective. In "Digger, Power, Speed," the autoworker talks with his "brother the engineer" about the brother's new Ford Escort, which Digger dismisses as a "*little fourbanger,*" not the kind of car a real man would drive: "*they'd've laughed you off the street / for driving one of these suckers / back in '66.*" But times have changed, the brother points out, "*and these little cars / are saving your job.*" Digger knows his brother is right; his small car represents the industry's answer to global competition. They're building "*Toys. Wimpmobiles,*" Digger thinks, and he knows this doesn't bode well for him: "there's not enough room, / not anywhere." The poem highlights Digger's investment in his job but also a conflicted sense of both claustrophobia and displacement, that there is no place for him in a changing economy. The threat becomes real in the 2002 poem "Digger on the Nature Trail," from the chapbook *Digger's Blues,*[3] when Digger's job is taken over by a robot and he is laid off. At home, watching the "slow lazy hours circling" on the kitchen clock, he hears the voice of his dead grandfather, the family's first autoworker, telling him to "quit feeling sorry / for yourself. *Get on with it.*" But when he thinks about service industry jobs, the kind of working-class jobs that someone like him, "a guy who didn't read," could get in the new economy, Digger feels dizzy: "you're suddenly aware of the world spinning." With industrial labor at risk and the prospect of service work taking its place, Digger's world loses its stability. This uncertainty threads through another poem from *Digger's Blues,* "Digger Laps at the Bowl." Here Digger is again on vacation but staying home, contemplating his future: "A buyout's coming // and you'll have to take it or lose out / by retiring later." Digger has difficulty imagining life without work, viewing the week off as "practice, / imagining the clock's endless circle." At the same time, when he thinks about what he would miss, he focuses not so much on the work itself but on moments when work stops or when workers claim power in some way: "the breaks, the lunches, / the Fridays, the overtime, the cheating // minutes, the small satisfying thefts." As he contemplates losing his job, Digger's mixed feelings remind us that even exploited, boring work has value for workers as a site of identification, connection, and resistance.

The loss of work becomes a central focus in the last set of poems, from *In Line for the Exterminator* in 2007, which focus on Digger's retirement. In "Digger Turns in His ID," we follow the character through his last day at work. He resists sentimentality, reminding himself that he will be replaced immediately, "a body always needed at your machine." Amid the stream of workers, moving in and out of the plant, he won't be missed: "not even / your ghost will stand here." Digger's presence at work matters to him and to the few people in his department, but it makes little difference in the larger economy of the plant. Despite a final "factory high five" as the other workers line up to "clink their lunch buckets against yours," Digger understands that the end of the job also means the loss of workplace connections. He and the others go to the bar for a celebratory drink, but Digger leaves early, wanting to get out "while everyone's still sincere." His last day also marks a disruption in identity. He has long ago accepted being "a lifer," but now he has become "A lifer released," a release that suggests freedom from work but also a loss of value that Digger resists. He's released "—but not / for good behavior. Another body / used up?" Finally, Digger gets in the car, not at all sure where he's headed: "The map is empty once more. / Empty, but not disintegrating." Despite his uncertainty about what comes next, Digger is stoic: "That's right. Climb in. / Deep breath, / and start 'er up." In these very short, direct sentences, we can hear Digger's determination to accept his fate, but they also suggest the emotional significance of the end of work. Daniels concludes with a few poems showing Digger's sense of displacement even as he insists on staying in his now deteriorating neighborhood. As he walks the dog at night and observes how the neighborhood is crumbling around him, Digger seems like a benign and somewhat befuddled ghost.

Reading the Digger poems in sequence, across the multiple volumes and more than two decades of their publication, offers readers a worker's view of a changing industry but also insight into why work matters. The poems trace the dualities of work, including between work and home, the two central locations of Digger's life. Few of these poems focus on labor itself. Instead, the significance of the work becomes most visible when it is stopped, for vacation, during a layoff, or when he retires. Through poems that reflect on the everyday life, often outside of the plant, of a lifelong autoworker, Daniels explores the pull between attachment and resistance to work, but he also suggests that, regardless of its dualities, work shapes everyday life and identity.

This understanding of work as both productive and problematic can be seen across deindustrialization literature, though narratives that focus on service reveal how the workplace practices of restructured labor exacerbate the contradictions inherent in the duality of work. The dualities appear sharper and more contested in writing about service work, especially when these narratives consider the intrusions of corporate management, as we see in Timothy Sheard's Lenny Moss mysteries and Stewart O'Nan's *Last Night at the Lobster*. Sheard emphasizes the contrast between exploitative conditions and worker agency, and his novels offer a rather idealized vision of the potential for solidarity. O'Nan takes the opposite approach, showing the dualities of work as intricately interconnected and thus even more problematic. In his novella, contemporary service workers seem caught between their desire to find meaning and connection in the workplace and the impersonal manipulations of a large corporation. In the contrast between Sheard's idealism and O'Nan's resignation, we see how the service labor that has come to dominate working-class life offers workers fewer opportunities for social benefits to balance the exploitation and struggles of work.

Sheard writes about health care from his own experience as a nurse, though his hero, Lenny Moss, is a janitor and union steward who solves both mysteries and labor problems by drawing on a network of dedicated colleagues who work together to defend those with the least power. In the seven novels in the Lenny Moss series, Sheard uses health care's least recognized workers—hospital janitors, security guards, and food service workers—to highlight the inequities and challenges of an increasingly corporatized industry and to make a case for solidarity, unions, and the intelligence of workers. The sixth book in the series, *A Bitter Pill* (2013), directly addresses the assaults on worker dignity and independence as a new corporate owner tries to decertify the hospital workers' union. The new management also exerts excessive control over nurses' labor (through digital monitors that track their every move, for example) while also assigning them more patients. These story lines dramatize the effects—on workers as well as patients—of contemporary anti-union and monitoring practices that have become increasingly common. In contrast to the profit-centered and unethical hospital management, Sheard presents the workers as almost uniformly good—skilled, kind, clever, committed to serving their patients well, and loyal to each other. In *A Bitter Pill*, workers' long-standing friendships and interdependence on the job, as well as their belief in the social value of their work, are tested but ultimately triumph over the corporation's actions, which focus on efficiency and control rather than patient care. By working together and by deploying their insider knowledge of how the hospital functions, the workers not only solve a murder and prove that the corporation is responsible for the decertification effort; they also demonstrate the value of the union and expand membership to include the nurses.

By showing the new hospital administrator as almost purely evil and the workers as almost unbelievably united and powerful, the novel embeds the dualities of labor in the conflict between workers and management. Workers represent the positive, productive aspects of work, and management represents the problems. In this contrast, Sheard also suggests that worker solidarity can be more powerful and significant than the exploitations that are inherent to capitalism. Unlike Digger, Sheard's workers feel no ambivalence about their jobs. Indeed, the novel suggests that working in health care provides an especially strong sense of purpose and meaning. By downplaying any internal tensions workers might feel about their jobs and locating the difficulties of work almost entirely with corporate management, *A Bitter Pill* simplifies the dualities of labor. Yet despite this simplification, Sheard makes clear that contemporary service work involves both social benefits and conflicts, suggesting that the fundamental duality of labor persists across multiple kinds of work.

O'Nan presents the dualities of contemporary service work as more complex and conflicted in his 2007 novella, *Last Night at the Lobster*. Like Daniels, O'Nan focuses on a single character, tracing the contradictory relationships—with a corporate employer, fellow workers, and the job itself—of Manny DeLeon, the manager of a suburban Red Lobster, on the restaurant's last night. After many years as manager, Manny thinks of the restaurant as his own, and he feels betrayed by the corporation's decision to close it. His view of his job reflects a central duality that directly contrasts with Sheard's representation of contemporary corporate-run service labor. Where Sheard draws a clear distinction between the interests of health-care workers and those of the hospital's corporate owners, O'Nan suggests that Manny cannot discern his own interests clearly. Despite feeling betrayed by the corporation's judgment that his restaurant is not sufficiently profitable, Manny remains committed to keeping it open and running smoothly, despite being short staffed, during a heavy snowstorm. Even as he worries that the corporation will "send spies to check on inventory, especially the lobsters and liquor," Manny views the last night as a "test of loyalty"—both his staff's loyalty to him and his to the corporation (13). Throughout the short narrative, O'Nan shows that Manny recognizes the distrust and manipulations of the corporation's practices, yet he cannot muster the anger or skepticism to stop trying to do his job right. As he prepares plates to deliver to a table, Manny thinks that "This could be the last meal they serve, and like everything today, he wants it to be perfect" (110).

Manny also feels a conflicted loyalty to his staff, who do not share his loyalty to the company and who have mixed feelings about him. Manny recognizes that the disdain some have toward the job reflects the company's treatment of them, but he knows that it also reflects resentment toward him. He has been forced to select just a few workers to move with him to an Olive Garden down the road. While being forced to make that choice highlights the tensions in Manny's relationships with his staff, it also emphasizes the discomfort and limited power of his role as manager: "Two months ago Manny had forty-four people working for him, twenty of them full-time. Tonight when he locks the doors, all but five will lose their jobs, and one of those five—unfairly, he thinks, since he was their leader—will be himself" (3). Even as he resents the company's lack of loyalty to its workers, Manny feels betrayed and conflicted about his relationships with his staff, especially a failed romance with one of the waitresses. As in Sheard's novel, relationships among workers are as important as the conflicts between workers and management, but O'Nan offers little hope for solidarity or even significant connections. Instead, he suggests that in the contemporary corporate-managed workplace, workers' desire to find meaning and connection on the job might not help them.

Indeed, O'Nan makes clear that the pleasure and pride Manny takes in his work provide only partial compensation for the conflicts he experiences in his interactions with the corporation and the other workers. He recognizes that his adherence to company rules and his commitment to his job yield only minimal benefits, yet he remains loyal to the company, or at least willing to put its interests above his own. After locking up at the end of the day, he considers stealing the big plastic marlin that hangs on the wall as a memento of his years running the restaurant but worries that he would get caught. Instead, he heads home to bed, so he can "make it in early tomorrow" for a final inventory (146). As Nathaniel Rich notes in a review of the book, O'Nan conveys the "powerful dignity" in "Manny's proud desire to do hard, productive work and contribute something of value to the people with whom he lives and toils," but the novel also reveals the contradictions in Manny's commitment to the company and his team. By highlighting Manny's concern for his workers, his desire to identify with the job, and his conflicted loyalty to the company, the novella presents the dualities of labor as problematically muddled. Unlike Sheard's characters, Manny cannot disconnect his commitment to doing good work from the manipulations and mistreatment of the corporation.

In stories about industrial work and service work alike, we see how all kinds of jobs can provide opportunities for interpersonal connection, pleasure, pride, and worker agency, even as they also involve exploitation, control, and struggle. Does this duality lie in the nature of work itself, across all sectors and ages? Or does it reflect what Strangleman suggests is an "industrial residual structure of feeling," in which people draw upon "previous patterns of understanding their circumstances in facing new challenges" (2017, 477)? Perhaps both. Writing about work has often addressed the dualities of labor, of course, yet the loss of industrial jobs and the conditions of contemporary work also exacerbate the tension between the productive and problematic aspects of work. As we will see, deindustrialization literature often articulates the contested nature of work through another set of dualities—between past and present but also between ways of imagining the past.

Remembering Work: The Duality of Nostalgia and Haunting

In deindustrialization literature, the industrial labor of the past often represents "good work" that offered clear and reliable social and psychological benefits. When the conditions of work change, when workers worry about losing their jobs, and when plants actually close, nostalgia for the work of the past is heightened. Yet within this nostalgia, the dualities remain, so that people remember factories and mines as sites of material and social productivity but also as sites of hardship and conflict. We can read this as a "reflective nostalgia," to use the term coined by Svetlana Boym, who argues that remembering the past can "open up . . . potentialities." Reflective nostalgia "reveals that longing and critical thinking are not opposed to one another" (2001, 49–50). Deindustrialization literature shows the productive potential of nostalgia through characters who use memory to make sense of what has been lost but also to understand the emerging future. Nostalgia for the work of the past reflects not only attachment, to the job and to work-based social networks, but also anxiety about how things are changing. In these narratives, memories of the positive aspects of hard and often unpleasant jobs reinforce workers' sense of agency and value. At the same time, writers use the past to critique restructured labor, using comparison to emphasize the problems of contemporary working conditions. In deindustrialization literature, we see how remembering and articulating the benefits of industrial labor can highlight the significance of what has been lost while also clarifying the challenges of emerging forms of labor.

In her stories of the Cadillac plant, Lolita Hernandez engages in reflective nostalgia that articulates an affective and critical understanding of what she and her coworkers lost when that plant closed. She captures the physical nature of the work itself, the human interactions and connections among workers—men and women, mostly black and Latinx—and the combination of sorrow, pride, and uncertainty that workers feel as they watch their plant first change and then be dismantled. Hernandez makes an unusual contribution to deindustrialization literature, not only as a Latina writer but also as one of very few authors whose writing emerges from her own experience of economic displacement. For her, deindustrialization is personal, since she wrote most of the stories in the volume while she herself experienced the contraction and then closing of the Cadillac plant. She has described writing the book as "a grieving process" ("Lolita Hernandez") and the book itself as "my *adiós*," though she also insists that she wants to resist "tired nostalgia" (18). Instead, she uses the memory of the labor to explain how it was not the "weekly paycheck" that brought her and her colleagues to work every day for all those years. The Cadillac workers were "fabricating more than painted hunks of steel that could go honk honk honk in that rich melodic Cadillac way and then hog up the highways, humming away like we used to on the lines." They were also, she writes, creating a family (19). Her stories describe the grime, noise, repetition, and relentlessness of working on the line, but they also show workers singing and laughing together. Hernandez writes about workers who do not want to get up to go to work, women who accept harassment as part of the job, and union members who are preparing for a strike. Throughout these stories, we see a tension between worker solidarity and individual experience, pride, and frustration. In her reflective nostalgia, Hernandez offers an idealized vision of work and workplace relationships, but her characters also recognize the contradictions and tensions of the job. Their awareness of and appreciation for the dualities of their work are heightened by the experience of loss.

The memory of their shared experience of work is a source of connection and meaning for Hernandez's workers. This becomes especially visible in "Thanks to Abbie Wilson," a powerful elegy both to the physicality of work and to workplace relationships. Abbie worked on the motor line, helping to build "those big cast-iron 472 engines" (100), but her line has shut down, and she has been reassigned as a janitor, cleaning offices upstairs in the same building. On lunch breaks, she returns to her old floor, which is now empty. At first, Abbie mentally fills in the empty space, remembering what equipment and workers occupied which parts of the floor. After a while, though, she begins acting out the physical movements of her job:

> It began as a simple recall exercise for Abbie. How did I used to do that job? She went through the motions, slowly at first, pretending to lift an oil pan from a pretend rack. She installed pretend rubber gaskets on each end of the pretend pan and swung the pan onto a pretend engine. Then she reached for another pan, another set of rubber gaskets. She flipped the pan on another engine. Some things never leave you, she said out loud. It's like riding a bike. (106)

The remembered physical actions are simple and repetitive, internalized, embodied, and, for Abbie, also symbolic. Reenacting work that she valued functions as a kind of healing ritual that reminds Abbie of her competence but also of the way her work was part of a larger productive project.

Hernandez emphasizes the social significance of remembered work by constructing Abbie's actions as a performance that is valuable for other displaced workers, who begin coming to watch her reenactment. Her actions activate and embody their memories. One coworker is described as feeling "as if he were part of whatever she was doing. Soon he began hearing a noise, a buzzing. Then a whirring. Then braap braap. Then he heard the buzzing, the whirring, the braaping all at once as if in concert" (109). The description of the sound of the work, like the initial scene where Abbie recalls the movements of her job, suggests that the experience of working on the line had become, for these workers, deeply familiar but also meaningful. Neither the movements nor the sounds seem inherently pleasurable, but the workers feel drawn to them. Unlike Digger, for whom the repetitive familiarity of pressing the same two buttons over and over creates a sense that he is disappearing into the work, Abbie and her colleagues find a stronger sense of self in remembering the physical conditions of the job. By combining the very practical motions of attaching gaskets to pans or the noisy concert of machinery with the workers' attachment to the memory of the job, and by setting the story on the now-empty shop floor, Hernandez shows how the duality of labor as both unpleasant and personally meaningful is heightened by loss. Abbie's performance is evocative, for her colleagues and for readers, because it occupies the literal and imaginative space of loss.

The motion of putting imaginary gaskets on imaginary pans functions as a kind of physical synecdoche, standing in for the social experience of the job. As her coworkers watch, Hernandez tells us, their individual and collective past is activated, made visible, and embodied. They feel "amazed and happy because they all looked so young, energetic, and hopping in ways they hadn't for years." They recall their informal worker-to-worker economy, "when Peanut Man hawked hot roasteds all through the shift, when Sweet Sadie sold her blouses and jewelry, when Red took liquor orders for lunch." They think fondly about celebrating holidays together: "Thanksgiving was one long banquet of tamales and greens, and Dancing John, dressed up as Santa Claus, drove his jitney on the last day of work before Christmas break singing ho, ho, ho we'll soon be out the doh." Equally important, they remember conflict, how they were "at their best when struggles with the bosses and each other were at their hottest" (110). By linking the memory of repetitive physical labor with the social network produced on the line, Hernandez emphasizes worker agency, both the individual strength and vitality that workers remember of their younger selves and the satisfaction and pride of standing together, in day-to-day life but also against the bosses.

Readers might question the pleasure Abbie and her colleagues take in remembering the repetitive labor of the factory line, but Hernandez does not represent this as a simple nostalgia. In remembering their work together, the workers engage in an internalized version of the kind of storytelling that Alessandro Portelli describes as common in oral histories, in which people remember not just what they did "but what they wanted to do, what they believed they were doing, what they now think they did" (1981, 100). In Hernandez's stories, labor that was repetitious, noisy, and sometimes dangerous is also remembered as a site of resistance and the construction of self, social networks, and agency. In the memories that Abbie's performances of physical and emotional labor generate, the story suggests that loss can lead workers to appreciate but also to better understand what they gained from work in addition to a paycheck.

While some characters in deindustrialization narratives remember their own work, in other texts, industrial labor is remembered as the work of the previous generation or even an earlier century. This reflects the temporal distance between the era when both American industry and labor unions were strong and the decades of economic restructuring when most of these narratives were written, but it also shows that the industrial past still serves as a touchstone for working-class people in the twenty-first century. Many of the writers in this genre, like most of their characters, grew up during or after the shutdowns, and while both writers and characters have inherited the memory of industrial labor, they view that history through the lens of economic decline and restructuring. Because of this, the memory of industrial work serves to highlight the uncertainty and contradictions of the deindustrialized economy and the restructured workplace. In some narratives, the comparison clarifies the social benefits that were lost as well as the uncertainty of working life in the present, while in others, the comparison identifies similarities, especially the persistence of conflict between workers and owners. This comparative awareness complicates memory, clarifying but also disturbing our understanding of the present. In Gordon's concept of social haunting, disturbance is evidence that unresolved conflicts of the past have resurfaced. Haunting, she writes, is "the domain of turmoil and trouble, that moment (of however long duration) when things are not in their assigned places, when the cracks and rigging are exposed" (xvi). We see this in two narratives in which the past emerges in the form of specific ghosts who haunt present-day characters in very different ways. In Tawni O'Dell's *Coal Run*, a son is haunted by the ghost of his father as well as his own troubled past, and this memory goads him to change his behavior and to embrace the value of a job he resists. Grady Hendrix offers a different version of haunting in *Horrorstör*, as contemporary retail workers recognize that the ideology and practices that shape their work bear an uncomfortable resemblance to the experiences of the zombies who now haunt their big-box store. As these examples suggest, the work of the past haunts writing about work in the present, but in complex and varied ways.

Set in a western Pennsylvania coal town, *Coal Run* weaves together a narrative of industrial struggle and decline, which affects the whole community in which the story is set, with the psychological drama of one man trying to reconcile his own past and to construct a more settled, connected life in the present. The novel follows Ivan Zoschenko, a former professional football player who now works half-heartedly as a sheriff's deputy in his hometown, where the coal industry is nearing the end of a long decline. After several years of avoiding his family and his hometown, Ivan has returned to resolve his guilt over an incident from high school, when he had used his strength and social power to date rape an especially vulnerable girl, Crystal. When she got pregnant, Ivan refused to marry her. She married another classmate, Reese, who later beat her into a coma. When he learns that Reese is being released from prison, Ivan returns to Coal Run, believing that killing Reese will compensate for his own mistreatment of Crystal.

As Ivan struggles with his own history of social violence, O'Dell shows how he is haunted by the idealized memory of his father, Rado, who was killed in a 1967 mine disaster along with ninety-six other local men when Ivan was in kindergarten. More than two decades later, Ivan's promising professional football career has been halted by his own accident at the same site. During a late-night visit to the abandoned mine, a large piece of industrial machinery falls on him, a strained coincidence that highlights the continuing influence of Rado's work on Ivan's life. It is not simply that Ivan feels drawn to the mine or haunted by his memories of his father; the material remains of his father's labor and of the accident that killed him put Ivan at risk.

The twin hauntings at the heart of this novel contribute to Ivan's sense that he is not a good enough man. In part because he was so young when Rado died, Ivan has idealized his father, imagining him as an unattainable role model and silent judge. He has heard many stories, from his mother and family friends, describing Rado as tough, virtuous, and hard working but also wise about the value of labor. Even in the 1960s, Rado believed that the demise of the coal industry was "inevitable," but he was concerned not about potential economic effects but rather about the loss of "spirit" and "a poverty of purpose" that men would feel without productive labor (31). "No man," he said, "can protect himself against uselessness" (32), and useless is exactly how Ivan feels. He has never done truly productive labor. Although playing football involves the kind of masculine toughness Ivan associates with his father, he knows that Rado wouldn't have wanted him to be a football player: "in his eyes professional athletes—even though they made a lot of money—were no different from factory workers or miners." They were all just "*sovok*," physical laborers (156). Full of self-loathing about his treatment of Crystal and his failure to find purposeful work, Ivan has spent several years in Florida, battling depression and addiction, and he has cut himself off from his family and his community. Isolated and defensive, he wonders whether he would have been "a better person" if his father had lived (138). While Ivan's story focuses more on his relationships than on his work, his responses are shaped by his desire to live up to his father's ideals about work as a source of purpose.

Like the workers in Hernandez's stories who recognize what they will miss about their jobs in part because they are losing them, Ivan begins to reconcile with his father's ghost through encounters that reflect his community's losses—both the mine disaster and the continuing decline of the mining industry. O'Dell describes him as haunted by a sense of failure, feeling that he has "let everyone down" (295), but as his family and the community struggle with the injuries of work and its loss, Ivan finds opportunities to help. Some of this involves the emotional labor of repairing relationships. After being out of touch during his years in Florida, he reconciles with his mother and sister. He spends time with Crystal and accidentally meets their son, whom she had given up for adoption. Although he resists the connection at first, he also becomes a father figure for his two young nephews. Equally important, Ivan finds a sense of purpose in his work as a sheriff's deputy. He had taken the job grudgingly, sure that the sheriff had hired him only because he "love[s] Penn State football" (346). Early on, he drinks and takes pills while on the job, and he struggles with his temper. Over time, however, Ivan finds that the job allows him to combine the toughness he associates with his father with the strength and aggression he developed as a football player for a positive purpose: to protect others. For example, he intervenes several times to stop domestic violence that, O'Dell suggests, has its roots in job loss and economic difficulties. Ivan overcomes his sense of uselessness through both relationships and work, taking on a protective, caretaking role in both parts of his life. Building personal relationships eases his guilt and anger, and stopping abuse gives him a sense of purpose. Haunted by his father and his own failures, he feels compelled to protect his family and members of the community. As Gordon argues, haunting can prompt action. Although Ivan's haunting is, in many ways, explicitly personal, tied to his father and to his own behavior, it also occurs in the context of industrial decline and the community's memory of the mine accident. Equally important, O'Dell suggests, Ivan can only translate his personal struggles with the past into productive social labor by engaging with the community.

For Gordon, social haunting occurs when "the people who are meant to be invisible show up without any sign of leaving" (xvi), and while she may not intend this literally, her description would apply well to the zombies who appear in Grady Hendrix's comic novel *Horrorstör*. The novel parodies both zombie movies and contemporary retail culture, and its ghosts are not memories but physical presences, in the figures of zombie prisoners and their master, Josiah Worth, warden of the Cuyahoga Panopticon, the nineteenth-century prison on which Orsk, a fictional big-box furniture store, has been built. In a humorous play on the style of an IKEA catalog, early chapters are accompanied by line drawings of cheap furniture and overblown descriptions, such as the promise that a storage bin will "Let your imagination—and your friendships—roam" (24). By the last part of the novel, though, the faux catalog illustrations promote torture devices, including a treadmill desk with shackles, a device whose "rustic handle mounted on resistance gears" invites users to "embrace the simplicity of eternal repetition" (168), and a waterboarding machine (204). The narrative centers on the parallel conflicts between present-day workers and management and between the workers and the zombies, especially Worth, whose attempts to discipline the resistant retail clerks—whom the company refers to as "partners"—highlight the coercion in contemporary corporate management practices.

The parallel is introduced in the opening line of the novel, which calls to mind the title of one of the most famous zombie films of all time, George Romero's *Dawn of the Dead*: "It was dawn, and the zombies were stumbling through the parking lot, streaming toward the massive beige box at the far end" (9).[4] The zombies in this opening reference are Orsk workers, though, not the undead prisoners who will soon haunt them. During the first part of the novel, Hendrix pokes fun at the rhetoric of corporate retail management, noting the "Bright and Shining Path" that guides shoppers through the store and the company's goals of "distribut[ing] joy" (19) and "teach[ing] customers how elegant and efficient their lives can be if they're fully furnished with Orsk" (18). He also draws attention to the conflicts embedded in the company's rhetoric about work, offering a cynical version of the dualities of labor in the way management discourse masks exploitation by appealing to workers' desire to find meaning and connection at work. The deputy store manager, Basil, reminds the protagonist, Amy, of "the importance of human capital in Orsk culture," and he talks "at length" about "the value of teamwork, about store pride, about the Four A's (Approachable and Agreeable Attitude)" (37–38). In the break room, a sign reminds workers that "The hard work makes Orsk a family, and the hard work is free" (39), a phrase that readers will likely recognize as a loose translation of the infamous "Arbeit Macht Frei" sign at the entrance to Auschwitz, the Nazi death camp. Basil encourages Amy to commit herself more fully to the job, to view it as "a calling" (41) that "has a purpose beyond making money" (42). He tries to talk her out of transferring to the Youngstown store by suggesting that she has potential to become a "Shop Responsible," but she rejects that idea, noting that such a "promotion" would bring more responsibility, more blame, and more meetings, all for "a whopping seventy-five cents more per hour" (40). Even before they encounter the zombies who haunt the store, Amy and her colleagues must contend with a corporate culture that tries to extract loyalty and effort but offers minimal rewards. Hendrix also emphasizes the limits of the job through Amy's situation. She had started college, hoping that education would help her get a better job, but she cannot afford tuition. While Orsk pays her twelve dollars an hour and provides some benefits, she struggles every month to cover her bills.

In this opening section, as Hendrix establishes the problematic conditions of contemporary retail labor, the ghosts of the past appear only in the form of small disruptions—a stinky mess that mysteriously appears on a sofa overnight, odd graffiti in the women's restroom—that are not yet tied to the history of the site or ideas about work. Soon enough, though, the novel connects the contemporary with the ghostly, as a small group of workers begin to encounter Worth and his prisoner zombies. They first meet Worth in a séance held in the showroom in the middle of the night, as two of the clerks try to prove that the store is haunted. The warden speaks through Carl, a homeless man who has been living in the store. He explains how he "prescribed the toil that purified" the souls of the "penitents" whose labor produced profits for the investors in the prison (121). In a twisted variation of the dualistic nature of work, Worth prescribes labor as "the moral treatment that will mend your degraded minds" (123). As we learn over the next few chapters, Worth designed the prison around this ideology, but instead of healing the prisoners, he worked them to death or "lunacy." One page of the novel shows what appears to be a ledger in which Worth recorded the sentences of several prisoners, including one who has been assigned to hours on a treadmill and another to ten thousand turns of a crank each day (195). Worth's notations on this handwritten sheet look very much like Basil's notes on an earlier page, evaluating Amy and the other partners. Like the prisoners, each employee is listed with a number and a name, but rather than listing the length of their sentence and their offense, the Orsk ledger states how long each has worked at the store and in what departments (95). The two illustrations highlight parallels between Worth's ideas about the moral value of work and the company's rhetoric. The connection between the two goes beyond their rhetoric about the moral value of work, however. *Horrorstör* also highlights discourses that combine false claims about opportunity with judgment of working-class people. The prisoners' "crimes" are minor infractions of the social rules of middle-class self-control: "consorting with low women and public inebriation" or "threatening behavior" (195). Amy's only "crime" is being young and having few options, but she, too, is trapped and abused by a system that offers manipulative claims about the meaning of work and empty promises about self-improvement. The difference between Basil's insistence that Amy should embrace work as a source of "purpose beyond making money" and Worth's mantra that "toil is the great grinding stone to make keen the blade of your spirit" (200) is a matter of degree and semantics, not of substance or intent.

The real threat of these ideas, Hendrix suggests, lies in internalization, when workers blame themselves instead of the system for their difficulties. When the zombies, on Worth's orders, shrink-wrap Amy to a *Hügga* office chair, and after Worth diagnoses her as "restless" and involved in "pointless activity," she begins to reconsider her situation, reflecting that "for all the fighting, all the struggle, all the scrimping, and saving, and double shifts" of recent years, she has made no headway. She never has enough money to buy gas and food, and she is always in debt. Rather than recognizing the external causes of her difficulties, however, Amy tells herself that she deserves this. She has been running from what "she'd been born to do: wear a uniform and work a register . . . to answer phones in call centers, to carry bags to customers' cars, to punch a clock, to measure her life in smoke breaks. To think otherwise was insane" (145–46). While the extravagant language and twisted logic of Worth's analysis makes him as comedic as he is threatening, Amy's acceptance of her fate is more troubling because it reveals how the social violence of capitalism operates. In punishing Amy, Worth uses seemingly innocuous elements of her workplace—an office chair, one of the products she sells; and shrink-wrap, a tool that she uses on the job every day—to torture her. Worse, after initial resistance, Amy embraces first the literal trap of the chair and then the economic trap of low-wage service work.

In its use of zombies, *Horrorstör* makes haunting a central, visible, even visceral trope in its exploration of the contemporary workplace. Gordon describes haunting as "the domain of turmoil and trouble, that moment . . . when things are not in their assigned places, when the cracks and rigging are exposed, . . . when disturbed feelings cannot be put away." Worth and his penitents disrupt the big-box retail workplace, and Amy's experiences of being pursued and punished by Worth bring "disturbed feelings" to the surface. According to Gordon, social haunting creates a situation in which people feel compelled to take action, to do "something different from before" (xvi), but Hendrix suggests that contemporary workers' power to do things differently is limited. Although Amy ultimately persuades the zombies to turn on Worth, they then attack her, and while she escapes, several of her colleagues do not. At the end of the novel, after months of recovery from her night battling zombies, Amy returns to the site, which has been taken over by another chain store, to try to rescue them. At the entrance, she meets Basil, who quit Orsk but, like Amy, has gotten a job at the new store to continue fighting the zombies. No doubt, Amy and Basil have changed their views of the store, returning to save their colleagues, yet they are also back where they began, working for a corporate retail chain. Equally important, their new focus does not challenge corporate culture or capitalism. Instead, they intend to do battle with the zombies, who are also victims of the system. This may reflect the demands of parody, yet *Horrorstör*'s critiques are sufficiently sharp and powerful to generate, for readers if not for its characters, a sense that something must be done, even if that something remains unclear.

As these narratives suggest, the past plays multiple and contested roles in deindustrialization literature. While writers like Hernandez focus on what workers lose when plants close, for others the past serves to clarify contrasts and continuities between industrial and service work. Significantly, the dualities of labor thread through both nostalgia and haunting, though the more troubled past that we see in the haunted texts reminds us of the contradictions involved. In *Coal Run*, the ghost of Rado Zoschenko highlights the importance but also the challenge of viewing work as a source of purpose. In *Horrorstör*, haunting makes clear how capitalism, in all its forms, exploits workers' desire to find meaning and agency. This is the most significant duality of labor: the contradiction between labor as a source of value for owners and a source of meaning for workers. Deindustrialization literature locates and explores that tension through the duality of past and present.

Whether workers are haunted by the past or remember it nostalgically, deindustrialization literature treats the memory of past work as a resource for understanding the present, for both characters and readers. But while the ideals of the past can inspire workers in the present, as we see in Hernandez and O'Dell, and more critical representations of past work serve to articulate problems in contemporary work, as we see in *Horrorstör*, deindustrialization literature treats memory with some ambivalence. It can be a source of expectation, inspiration, and critique, and writers often use the past to remind readers how work and its social benefits can enable workers to stand up to exploitation, or at least better understand their struggles. Yet these narratives also sometimes question the value of the past as a source of agency. Rather than providing models for resistance to problematic changes in work, memories of earlier forms of work and labor activism can instead highlight the limitations that workers face in the present. Economic restructuring fragmented and destabilized employment, undermining worker agency by disrupting workplace relationships and making work itself more contingent, a point reinforced by workers' memories of widespread layoffs when plants and mines closed. At the same time, neoliberalism generated corporate and governmental practices that directly undermined unions. These interconnected developments contributed to the decline in union membership but also to limits—sometimes perceived and sometimes quite real—in workers' ability to intervene in workplace policy and to resist exploitation. A few deindustrialization narratives use the memory of past work to examine these challenges to worker agency. A long story in Dean Bakopoulos's novel-in-stories, *Please Don't Come Back from the Moon*, uses a powerful moment of labor history to highlight the lack of power felt by contemporary retail workers, for whom activism and solidarity seem beyond their reach. The past of great labor victories is too far removed from their experience to offer anything more than a fantasy. While the past that workers long for in David Simon's HBO television series *The Wire* is their own, it, too, seems out of reach, and their memories of good work cannot counter the social and economic changes that undermine their work lives in the present. These narratives suggest that looking to the past may be useful for understanding present conditions, but it may not be sufficient to foster worker solidarity or to challenge the power of neoliberal capitalism.

Please Don't Come Back from the Moon follows Mike Smolij from an uncertain adolescence into a still somewhat tenuous adulthood. Across the course of the novel, Mike moves from high school and a summer job as a lifeguard through his twenties, as he attends college part-time and works in a mall bookstore and finally begins a career as a radio news reporter. "Knights of Labor," a long story in the middle of the novel, focuses on the period when Mike and several of his friends are working at a local mall. Comparisons between industrial and service work thread through the story, starting with Mike's description of the labor of three generations of Detroit families: "Our grandfathers used to work the afternoon shift at Ford Rouge and Dodge Main," and "Our fathers walked into factories and warehouses and fluorescent-lit buildings." The contrast between the familiar names of specific sites and the more anonymous buildings where the next generation worked suggests that industrial work had begun to lose coherence long before factories and warehouses began to lay off large numbers of workers. Mike and his friends work at Book Nook, Top Banana Smoothies, Ingenuity Unlimited, and American Pants—stores with names that sound clichéd and generic. Anyone who has spent time at a suburban shopping mall can imagine these stores, which, despite their names, are every bit as anonymous as the unnamed "fluorescent-lit buildings" where the fathers worked (146–47). The difference is further demarcated by what each generation eats for lunch. The grandfathers ate homemade cabbage rolls, traditional food that, we can imagine, was often prepared by immigrant wives and mothers. The fathers carried sack lunches of bologna sandwiches and Fritos, processed food though still packed at home. Mike and his friends eat "chili dogs and cheddar beef sandwiches and Taco El Grandes" from the food court (146). No one makes lunch for them, so they eat fast food and sneak shakes spiked with vodka from a friend who works at the smoothie stand. As Mike notes, drinking and smoking pot on the job "made the days go by with ease. It made $6.50 an hour seem almost worth it" (148). Working at the mall, which was built on the site of the park where they played as children, makes the young men in the novel seem stuck in adolescence, doing jobs and eating food fit for teenagers. But while they view their jobs as temporary, they are adults, and they are not earning spending money. They rely on these jobs to make a living and, in some cases, to support families.

Bakopoulos expands on these contrasts but also emphasizes the contradictions of the retail workers' position by turning to labor history. The story revolves around a plan for a clerks' strike on Black Friday, an idea initiated by Mike's cousin Nick. Inspired by labor history courses he has audited at the University of Michigan, Nick reaches out to the other workers, building relationships that lay the groundwork for a strike. As he and Mike walk through the mall one day, Nick identifies the problems various workers are facing: paying college tuition, providing for children, covering family medical bills, and getting by after an ex-husband "lost all of their savings in one weekend in Atlantic City" (160). While he is troubled by other workers' stories, Nick also looks to the past for inspiration. When the workers gather at a bar near the mall, he tells stories about the 1937 sit-down strike in Flint, and he promises his friends that they, too, can gain power through collectivity. As he tells them, "Solidarity is the most powerful weapon against power and wealth" (166). As Mike watches Nick encourage his friends to connect with "every mall employee who could be trusted" to develop support for the strike, he sees that his cousin's campaign was not "quixotic." The other workers are excited. They would be "willing to follow [Nick] anywhere" (168). The relationships Nick has forged and his inspiring stories of past examples of worker agency change the way the clerks view themselves and their jobs. Nick encourages his friends to "take pride in your work, or at least in the fact that you get up for work every day" (166). He had, Mike comments, "found a way, if only for a brief time, to make working at the mall seem interesting and full of meaning" (181).

The key to the story, however, lies in the interjection—"if only for a brief time." Nick's stories of past labor activism generate excitement but not enough determination or solidarity to sustain a strike. The structure of their work and their anxieties about the economy undermine their agency. While they don't like their jobs and want to earn more money, the clerks are more engaged with Nick's enthusiasm than with a shared sense of injustice. Their resentment focuses on personal rather than social or structural concerns, in part because they lack a clearly defined entity from which to demand change. They work for many different and seemingly amorphous corporations, and the only visible representatives of corporate power at the mall are the often-petty store managers. Unlike the Flint autoworkers, who were members of a fledgling but identifiable union battling a specific company, the retail clerks imagine a general strike over the conditions of retail labor, without any connection to a union or, as Nick later notes, any legal protection. The workers also feel vulnerable. Several of those who are supporting families on retail wages tell Nick they can't risk losing their jobs. Nick ultimately calls the strike off for the same reason: his girlfriend is pregnant, and he needs the health benefits from his job. He also worries that he could be fired and unable to find a new job if he is known as a union leader.

As other workers back out, Nick himself questions the idea of solidarity. As he tells Mike, "It would have been you and me out there all alone—a couple of stupid fucks against the world" (189). In the end, Mike, his girlfriend, and a few others show up with picket signs, but without Nick's dynamic leadership, "nobody wanted to go out on a limb" (196). The agency they felt when gathered in the bar has clearly disappeared, a change that Nick embodies in his posture when he finally shows up. He walks quickly past the few strikers, with his shoulders hunched up protectively, a posture described as similar to his father's (197). While the link is subtle, the image reminds us that the retail clerks are the sons and daughters of men who were displaced as the auto industry downsized and who have since disappeared, part of an imaginative framing that highlights the long-term influence of deindustrialization. As Mike explains in the opening story, the fathers "went to the moon," one by one, during the era when "the factories seemed to vaporize." While some walked or drove away, others simply vanished. "Many of them were out of work" (6), Mike comments, and the setting—a working-class Detroit suburb in the late 1980s—suggests the erasure of a generation of men displaced as plants closed and downsized. They leave behind a generation of sons who seem permanently lost.[5] Bakopoulos presents economic restructuring as a problem of masculinity, linking the lack of good jobs with the absence of fatherly role models. Mike and his friends cannot follow their fathers' paths, not only because the fathers are gone but also because the culture of work that shaped their fathers' lives has disappeared. Neither the immediate past of the previous generation nor the earlier history of labor activism provides a usable model to help these young men. Despite their shared problems of low wages, humiliation, boredom, and resentment, and despite an inspiring narrative about the power of solidarity, they see themselves as too vulnerable to take action or push for change.[6] Their economic position is too precarious for them to risk resistance, and they have neither the solidarity that Hernandez describes in the Cadillac plant nor the sense of purpose that Rado Zoschenko found in mining or that his son found in police work.

Where Nick and Mike look back to the work and activism of earlier generations, in *The Wire*, workers' own memories shape their perspectives, providing inspiration but only limited resources for resistance.[7] The show's creator, producer, and head writer, David Simon, has described the series as "a meditation on the death of work and the American working class" ("Totally Wired"), which the series suggests extends beyond the industrial sector and the loss of jobs to the decline in the quality of work. The series links the declining number of jobs on the docks of Baltimore harbor and at the local newspaper with the frustration of workers in the police department, public schools and government, and neighborhood drug trade. Across these industries, workers in *The Wire* draw upon shared memories of "good work" to reinforce social networks and articulate the values associated with their jobs. As in other deindustrialized narratives, the series shows how workers view the present through the lens of the past, but while this highlights the problems of contemporary work, it provides only a limited basis for resistance.

Workers in *The Wire* struggle to preserve and defend good work, which they almost always define in terms of the work of the past. In some cases, as with the dockworkers, they simply want to protect jobs. Longshoremen's union president Frank Sobotka does everything he can, including participating in human trafficking and smuggling, to "return the port to a former glory that he himself remembers" (Carroll 264). The police officers, however, complain that good work has been undermined by poor management. They evoke the quality of "natural police" or "real police" work, which they see as once central to their profession but now threatened by management's interest in personal advancement or good public relations. Similarly, in season 5, veteran journalist and city editor Gus Haynes wants to preserve high-quality reporting, which is being undermined by the economic challenges of his industry and by managers who do not share his commitment to serious journalism. While nostalgia for good work reflects what critic Hamilton Carroll identifies as the series' "prolonged examination of the transformations of white masculinist privilege" (264), the pattern also appears among the African American drug dealers, especially in seasons 4 and 5 as older dealers lament the way a younger dealer, Marlo, violates the unwritten rules and hierarchies of their industry. In all of these story lines, *The Wire* connects the loss of jobs associated with deindustrialization with changes in work tied to economic restructuring, and the costs involved in both losses are articulated through references to the good work of the past.

The memory of good work serves several functions in the series. Perhaps most significant, it helps to create and maintain social networks that provide personal satisfaction and connections but also to enable workers to do their jobs safely and effectively. Across several industries, we see how newcomers learn their jobs from experienced workers, who draw on memory and tradition to pass along not only skills but also shared values and identities. Experienced detectives instruct younger officers in the elements of "real police" work: serious, sometimes creative, investigative labor that focuses on getting to the root of the problem rather than on producing the splashy headlines and evening news shots—"drugs on the table," as the police commissioner puts it—they're now pressured to provide. We see a similar process as two young reporters learn the practices of "good journalism" from Haynes and later help him gather evidence that one of their peers, Scott Templeton, has fabricated a story. This process not only helps novices learn the practices of the job, but it also encourages them to take on a shared work-based identity. We also see shared identity being produced among the members of the longshoremen's union when they gather at the bar to reminisce about the "good old days" when they had steady work.[8]

While *The Wire* shows the value of shared memory, it also emphasizes the duality of the past by showing that memory has limited value as a resource for resistance. Workers in *The Wire* are not powerless victims, and they respond in varied ways to the social, political, and economic changes around them. Some—like Haynes and Detective Jimmy McNulty, who functions as the primary protagonist in the series—focus on doing good work regardless of pressure from their bosses. Haynes does this largely by adhering to traditional journalistic ethics, while McNulty regularly circumvents police department rules and deploys creative, sometimes even illegal strategies in his pursuit of the drug dealers. Others, as we see in Sobotka's lobbying to have Baltimore harbor dredged to reinvigorate its shipping industry, try—and fail—to defend and maintain good work by influencing the system to return it to old ways of operating. Haynes, the detectives, and the longshoremen all reminisce about how the system once valued them, but they cannot imagine, much less take action to create, a different future. The contrast between the memory of good work and the contemporary reality is highlighted in a conversation between Sobotka and his son. Ziggy describes his memory of the good old days: "I remember you, Uncle Walt, Uncle Jerry, Peepop, always talking shit. . . . I remember when youse all went down to picket them scabs down at the piers." Frank's response—"So tell me Mr. Back-in-the-day, what the fuck are we doing down here with the wharf rats in the middle of the night?"—references their specific history, but it also encompasses the larger economic shifts that have shaped it. Frank and Ziggy know that the past will not come back, and they find little consolation in remembering the past, much less insight about how to respond. Similar scenes appear in relation to other types of work over the course of the series, as characters recall good work but struggle to imagine how to intervene in its decline.

The limitation of the past as a source for resistance is highlighted by the success of characters who reject the traditional ideals. The upstart dealer Marlo gains power and territory by refusing to follow the advice of Prop Joe, one of the older leaders in the Baltimore drug trade. Instead of respecting long-established territorial divisions that assigned each of the gangs a particular area, Marlo uses violence—killing dozens of low- and mid-level dealers in other operations—to expand his own territory. Similarly, Templeton's violation of the practices of good journalism wins him a Pulitzer Prize. Both Marlo and Templeton succeed by making their own rules, unlike McNulty, who has mixed success and gets punished for his efforts, or Haynes, who is demoted. Despite their success, Marlo and Templeton are presented as problems, not heroes, because they pursue their own interests instead of respecting either community or tradition. In contrast, McNulty is cast as a troubled hero who has limited power to resist changes that undermine good work, but he remains committed to his ideals. He continues to do his job as well as he can, even as self-serving leaders push for approaches that yield good public relations rather than real change.

In showing the past as the basis for worker socialization and identity, *The Wire* highlights the social productivity of good work, including workers' continuing desire to find meaning and connection through labor, even as the conditions of work undermine its social benefits. However, in revealing the limits of shared memory in resisting economic change, the series makes visible the power and intractability of neoliberalism and global capitalism. This ambivalence about the past reflects what Strangleman describes as an "unease in contemporary culture" (2013, 33). As with all cultural memory, *The Wire* approaches the past from the perspective of the present, and in particular, it reminds us that an investment in the past may reflect anxieties about the present. Characters cling to the past when the conditions of the present become more problematic—when dockworkers lose shifts, when police officers feel pressured to produce results quickly rather than take the time for careful investigation, or when editors press for dramatic stories that will sell papers. Yet as these conflicts suggest, the focus of the series' critique is not workers' nostalgia. Indeed, even as the series reveals the limitations of memory, it invites viewers to identify with McNulty, Haynes, Sobotka, and others who are invested in the past. While they only rarely prevail, the problem lies not with memory but in the power of the force they are up against: what Simon calls the "Olympian god of capitalism" (Pearson).

The Half-Life of Labor's Dualities

Deindustrialization literature emerges out of and exists within the liminal space between industrial and postindustrial economies. Downsizing and shutdowns displaced hundreds of thousands of workers in the last decades of the twentieth century, but the loss of manufacturing jobs did not mean the end of work. Instead, many in the working class moved into service occupations, so that, by 2015, the largest occupations in the United States were retail, food service, office support, and nursing ("Employment"). This shift was accompanied by business practices that increased control over workers, kept wages low, reduced benefits, and disrupted work schedules, changes that increased productivity while undermining the stability of workers' lives. But, of course, these realities tell us only part of the story of how work has changed. Through narratives that trace how workers' experiences of contemporary capitalism are shaped by the memory of industrial labor and its loss, deindustrialization literature helps us see how working-class people have responded to these shifts.

What it reveals is that people make sense of the contemporary service workplace by drawing on the memory of industrial labor and its loss. While a few of these narratives focus on factory and mine closings, most consider the way deindustrialization continues to ripple through working-class people's lives, disrupting work and its dualities long after the shutdowns. They remind us that the shift from an industrial to a postindustrial economy is neither immediate nor neatly defined. In some narratives, like *Coal Run* and *The Wire*, industrial and non-industrial economies coexist in the same time and place. But even in texts set entirely in postindustrial workplaces, like *Last Night at the Lobster* or *Please Don't Come Back from the Moon*, industrial labor remains present in the way workers think about their jobs. While the past is often defined as better than the present, the contrast does not serve primarily to emphasize what has been lost. Rather, these narratives highlight workers' persistent desire to find dignity and meaning in work and reveal the obstacles that desire encounters in the contemporary workplace.

Whether workers feel nostalgia for the productive aspects of labor, wrestle with ghosts who represent ideal or exploitative models of past work, or encounter the limitations of history and memory as sources for resistance, nearly all of the characters in these narratives struggle to make sense of economic and social changes that, as Simon reminds us, reflect powerful ideologies and policies. A central problem facing the contemporary working class is whether the "webs of significance" they are constructing will foster a sense of belonging and "shared dispositions" that, as Ira Katznelson argues, make collective action possible (22). Contemporary writing about work reminds us of workers' resilience but also of the difficulties of creating working-class solidarity and activism, even in the face of growing inequality. As stagnant wages, cuts in benefits, and the increasing contingency of work of all kinds shift more and more people into the working class, deindustrialization literature suggests that class consciousness itself is becoming harder to grasp. Working-class culture, like work, is becoming contingent and precarious.

TWO

Reconstructing Working-Class Identities

At a party sometime in the early 2000s, a woman I had just met expressed surprise when she heard that I was the codirector of the Center for Working-Class Studies. "Does the working class even exist anymore?" she asked. I was stunned at first. We were in Youngstown, Ohio, after all, where, decades into deindustrialization, thousands of local people still made cars, specialty metals, and steel tubing in factories that could be seen from local highways and were regularly discussed in local news. But I knew what she meant: the working class, as most Americans had long imagined it, did seem to have disappeared. Autoworkers and steelworkers still do old-fashioned blue-collar jobs, but many more people now work in hospitals, call centers, restaurants, and retail stores. The manual-laboring, union-protected working class has definitely shrunk, and that is especially visible in places like Youngstown. The working class of the twenty-first century looks more and more like the middle class. They wear clean shirts and khakis, and they provide services rather than material goods. Many earn college degrees but continue working at big-box stores, at restaurant chains, or as aides in nursing homes both during and after their years of higher education. Despite all this, the phrase "working class" still brings to mind a white man wearing a hard hat, heavy-duty gloves, steel-toed boots, and grimy jeans. A Google Image search for "working-class people" yields mostly images of white men, including many historic photos. "Working-class people," according to such a search, are white male coal miners and construction workers, not Latina cashiers, African American janitors, or Filipina home health-care aides.

Of course, the working class has never been singular or homogeneous. While historians have analyzed the formation of "the" working class and scholars from several disciplines have offered summaries of the qualities or elements of "working-class culture," even those who address the working class as a unit recognize its inherent and multiple diversities. When scholars examine "working-class identity," they do not present it as a single, fixed, unified identity. Instead, they trace the way differences of race, gender, ethnicity, and sexuality shape how working-class people see the world and define themselves. Despite scholarly attention to the diversity of the working class and to the changing nature of working-class jobs, the old image resists updating. The media, especially, it seems, during election years, typically treats the white working class as if it were a coherent group, too often defined solely by level of education and described as racist, socially conservative, and susceptible to manipulation. This is true despite coverage of movements like the "Fight for $15" that involve whites and workers of color, many of them immigrants. In the American popular imagination, the working class remains well defined and explicitly industrial, and working-class identity, like good industrial jobs, seems stuck in the past.

The persistence of the traditional image of the industrial worker reflects the cultural influence of the half-life of deindustrialization. American culture is still adapting to the changes wrought by economic restructuring, and our images have not caught up with the material and structural conditions of working-class people's lives. But this is not just a matter of public perception. This old-fashioned version of working-class identity also haunts working-class people as they make sense of their own experiences and relationships. People who defined themselves through industrial labor and the relative economic and social stability it provided have had to reimagine their identities, and that challenge carries over to their children, who struggle to construct adult lives in an economy that no longer provides access to traditional markers of adulthood, such as stable employment or a living wage. Their perceptions of themselves and the social worlds in which they live are filtered through the traditional image of the working class. Some share their parents' sense of loss and betrayal, and in a constrained economic landscape, many have learned to expect little for themselves and of others. Some find alternative sources of identity in relationships; in violence; or in overcoming family drama, addiction, and other forms of trauma. If a well-defined and readily accessible working-class identity ever existed— and some would argue that it never really did—such clarity now seems out of reach. In the liminal period of the half-life of deindustrialization, working-class identities, like working-class labor, have become increasingly contingent and uncertain.

"Identity" is a slippery term, like "class" and "culture." It can refer to the set of traits that make an individual unique, but it has also been used as shorthand for distinct social groups. It involves both external perceptions, how one is seen by others, and the internal sense of how one understands oneself. It is at once performative and experiential, social and emotional. And it is always, for every individual and every group, multifaceted, complex, and under construction. No one has just one identity, nor does any aspect of a person's identity operate in isolation from others. Even within well-defined groups, individuals vary in myriad ways. Class identities are always shaped by and lived through race, gender, sexuality, and other less contested social and personal categories, such as age or place. All of this may seem obvious, but to understand contemporary narratives about working-class identity, we must recognize not only that "the working class" is not a fixed and bounded entity but that identity itself is not stable. Put simply, the contingency of contemporary working-class identity reflects two liminalities: one inherent in identity itself and the other reflective of the half-life of deindustrialization.

Identity has always been a problematic concept in working-class studies. When discussion focuses on individual identities, it can seem to ignore the structural and material bases of class as well as the political dimensions of class conflicts. When identity focuses on the working class as a group, it can seem to erase not only individual agency but also difference and intersectionality, presenting "the working class" as homogeneous. Despite these challenges, a focus on identity provides opportunities to tease out the multiple dimensions of social class, and an analysis of how working-class people navigate identity connects the personal with the political and economic. It also allows us to treat working-class people as actors whose agency reflects multiple dimensions—class as well as gender, individual experience along with group affiliations. The social and economic positions of working-class people may be determined by the exploitative conditions of capitalism and, increasingly, by the damaging ideologies of neoliberalism, but they are not helpless in the face of those conditions. As labor historian Herbert Gutman famously argued, what matters is not (or not only) what was done to a people but what they did with what was done to them.[1] While resistance and collective action are, of course, part of what the working class did in response to capitalism, so, too, is everyday life, including the construction of working-class identity. Indeed, working-class identity may be a necessary prerequisite to class activism. In addition, if we ignore identity, we may see working-class culture as a reflection of false consciousness, a judgment that treats working-class people as fools whose lives are best interpreted by scholars, not by themselves.

Scholars have generated a significant body of research about how working-class people have responded to economic restructuring, including how they are reshaping their identities. Using both statistical analyses and ethnographic approaches, they have analyzed social patterns and, in some cases, attended to the voices of working-class people. The work of researchers such as Lois Weis, Linda McDowell, Valerie Walkerdine and Luis Jimenez, and others provides valuable insight into the way changes in work and the long-term economic struggles of deindustrialized communities have affected working-class identities.[2] While social scientists analyze these shifts as social patterns, literary narratives imagine the process of negotiating identity. Indeed, these narratives suggest that identity is constructed through stories. The psychological concept of "narrative identity" suggests that people define their identities in part by translating experiences into stories, an iterative and interactive process through which "personal experiences are . . . edited, reinterpreted, retold, and subjected to a range of social and discursive influences" (McAdams and McLean 235). Because telling the story plays a central role in the process, identity narratives integrate the performance of identity, including the way people are seen by others and their awareness and construction of this external identity, with internal self-narration, the stories they tell themselves about who they are and how they came to be that way. Both performance and interior monologue are embedded in social contexts, of course, but they also allow us to see, in very intimate ways, how people negotiate identity in the destabilized context of deindustrialization.

The identity narratives of deindustrialization literature emphasize two sets of tensions that working-class people often navigate in constructing their identities. First, these stories illustrate the always present and often conflicted interaction among different aspects of identity. Class at once shapes and is lived through gender and race, especially, and the economic and social displacements of deindustrialization heighten the tensions among these elements of identity. Those tensions play out in narratives about white working-class masculinity, such as Philipp Meyer's *American Rust*, but also in stories focused on African American workers, such as Dominique Morisseau's *Skeleton Crew* and Stewart O'Nan's *Everyday People*. Eminem's film *8 Mile* and Lynn Nottage's play *Sweat* remind us that people navigate multiple affiliations and multifaceted identities through interaction with others, but, under economic pressure, connections based on class or gender can fracture along racial lines. As these narratives show, in part because class identities are rooted in work and because access to and power within employment has often been divided along raced and gendered lines, deindustrialization exacerbates those tensions.

Economic restructuring and neoliberal ideology further complicate working-class identities, however, by bringing in a second point of tension: between individualism and belonging. Although psychologist Barbara Jensen has identified these values as representing a clear distinction between middle-class and working-class culture, sociologist Jennifer Silva suggests that, in response to economic insecurity, younger working-class people increasingly embrace individualism. Lacking the "sources of dignity and meaning" that shaped their parents and grandparents, notably the "daily toil of the shop floor, the making of a home and family," they construct their identities though "emotional self-management and willful psychic transformation" (2013, 10). Deindustrialization literature reflects this shift in characters who develop their sense of self by navigating personal challenges and embracing an ethic of self-reliance, yet these narratives suggest that connection and belonging remain powerful elements in working-class culture. While working-class literature has often been read as illustrating the way class identities are embedded in social networks, and proletarian literature (and some later texts) actively promotes solidarity, deindustrialization literature views the relationship between the individual and the community as less certain. In *Sweat*, solidarity seems fragile, while in *8 Mile*, the working-class protagonist determines that he must take individual responsibility for his future instead of relying on his connections with others. For the narrator of Christie Hodgen's *Elegies for the Brokenhearted*, becoming an adult involves both rejecting and reconciling with family and community. She must, like Silva's informants, overcome family traumas, but her life choices and her sense of self rest not only in resilience but also in relationships.

While these fictional narratives emerge and function differently from the identity narratives that psychologists have studied, like the stories we tell to and about ourselves, they interpret experience within social and discursive contexts. They make visible what working-class people have done with what deindustrialization did to them. In the process, they reveal not only the lived and felt experience of individuals navigating the uncertain, shifting realities of economic change but also the way working-class culture more broadly is adapting and how that adaptation draws on older patterns. Much as we saw in literary representations of work, in these identity narratives the past is at once a reminder of loss and a source of inspiration.

"Losing the Narratives of Their Lives"

In 2015, the National Academy of Sciences released a study by Anne Case and Angus Deaton documenting significant increases over time in death rates of middle-aged white working-class people. Early in 2016, a similar analysis by reporters for the *New York Times*, focused on younger people, showed a similar pattern: whites between the ages of twenty-five and thirty-four died by drug overdose five times more often in 2014 than they had in 1990, while death rates among African Americans had fallen during the same period.[3] Both reports identified drug abuse and suicide as the primary drivers of the increase, and they suggested a common cause for the trend: economic insecurity. As Deaton told one interviewer, working-class whites had "lost the narratives of their lives" (quoted in Belluz). In op-eds in the *New York Times*, Ross Douthat and Paul Krugman echoed Deaton's comment. Douthat suggested that economic changes left white working-class people with "a feeling that what you were supposed to have has been denied you." Krugman wrote that white working-class people had been "raised to believe in the American Dream, and are coping badly with its failure to come true." While Silva's study suggests that "coping badly" may be too simplistic a description of the way younger working-class people are responding to the uncertainty and contingency of the neoliberal economy, these studies provide persuasive evidence that the sense of displacement and betrayal that many workers felt when they lost industrial jobs in the 1970s and 1980s continues to haunt their children and even their grandchildren.

As the research on death rates suggests, that loss has been especially difficult for white working-class men, the group that was most closely associated with industrial labor, both in the social imagination and in their own identification. That identification, reflected in the traditional image of the working-class person as a white male industrial worker, has a complicated and contested history. Although white native-born women were some of the first factory workers in the United States, by the late nineteenth century most industrial workers were white men, many of them immigrants from western and northern Europe. By the early twentieth century, with the influx of African Americans and eastern and southern European immigrants to industrial cities, the children and grandchildren of the earlier immigrants used race, ethnicity, and gender to defend their right to jobs. They pushed for laws that would "protect" women by limiting their hours and the kinds of work they could do. They supported anti-immigration policies and excluded immigrants and African Americans from unions of skilled workers. Women and workers of color had to fight both companies and unions to gain access to better jobs, and when, starting in the 1960s, Equal Employment Opportunity laws enforced more diverse hiring policies, many white men resisted, often taking their anger at what they saw as a threat to "their" jobs out on their new coworkers. As plants began to move to Mexico and Asia later in the twentieth century, many workers blamed their counterparts in other countries for taking "American" jobs. Because white working-class men often viewed industrial jobs as their property, they saw the loss of those jobs as a betrayal, one sometimes framed in terms of race, gender, and nationality.[4]

While we can critique white men's sense of ownership of industrial labor, both its basis and its consequences are as real as they are problematic. Among those consequences is the disruption of white working-class masculinity. Industrial work provided economic and social resources that defined and supported a working-class ideal of manhood: a decent wage that helped secure men's position as head of the household, arduous and sometimes risky activity, appreciation for physical strength, pride in producing the materials and goods that defined American economic dominance and prosperity, and shared experiences that created masculine networks not only at work but also in neighborhood settings—bars, union halls, football fields—where workers' relationships extended into social life. Blue-collar work helped to create working-class communities and cement white men's roles as producers and providers within those communities. As Walkerdine and Jimenez have suggested, those patterns became the embodiment of masculinity, "sediment[ed] over time to be simply what one needed to do," passed down "from father to son, . . . central to community survival" (94). Their phrase "what one needed to do" reminds us that industrial labor was an economic but also a social necessity for working-class men. It defined their role within the family, and the physical challenges and dangers of the job became part of the cultural mythology of working-class masculinity. As providers and manual laborers, white working-class men were seen, and often viewed themselves, as capable, dedicated, and important. Deindustrialization did not simply put many men out of work; it undermined the resources that they and their sons relied upon to define their identities.[5]

Narratives about younger working-class white men often focus on the challenges of constructing adult masculinity in the absence of those social resources. For many white working-class boys growing up before the mid-1970s, the path into adulthood was clear: follow your father into the factory or mine and construct a life much like his. For the children of deindustrialization, neither their fathers' jobs nor their models of masculinity are available, and as these narratives suggest, that leaves younger men not only lacking economic opportunity but also without a clear sense of how to be a man. These characters have difficulty imagining or enacting a path to adult masculinity, and their uncertainty reflects low expectations of themselves and of the world around them. In many cases, they seem to have internalized the economic losses and constraints of deindustrialization, translating social conditions into a lack of self-efficacy. We see this in the two protagonists of Philipp Meyer's *American Rust*. Billy Poe and Isaac English, recent high school graduates in a declining western Pennsylvania steel town, struggle even to envision, much less to achieve, stable lives as adult men. The novel positions the two characters' limitations as emerging from but also as responses to the economic and social legacies of deindustrialization. In addition, Meyer's use of internal monologue emphasizes the two characters' interpretations of their experiences in relation to social forces. In the way Poe and Isaac tell their stories, we see how they define their identities through gender and class. Whiteness is assumed and only briefly attended to, but masculinity and class positionality must be demonstrated.

The opening scene sets in motion a plot that will bring to the surface the underlying problems that have shaped but also undermined the two men's expectations. Early in the novel, Poe and Isaac go into an abandoned mill to stay warm while they wait for the train that Isaac plans to jump on, like an old-fashioned hobo, to escape their western Pennsylvania hometown of Buell. Isaac has stolen $4,000 from his father and is intent on running run away to California to pursue his dream of becoming an astrophysicist. One of the smartest students in their high school, Isaac was Poe's math tutor. In contrast to Isaac's specific if unrealistic vision for his life, Poe cannot imagine any future for himself. Having given up the football scholarship that would have taken him away from Buell, he lives with his mother in a trailer outside of town, and he has just lost his job at a local hardware store. We first see him sitting outside the trailer, "looking like he intended to cut firewood, . . . his glory days already past, a dozen empty beer cans at his feet" (5–6). When the boys take shelter in the abandoned mill, they are attacked by three men who claim it is "their spot" (13). One of the men grabs Poe, the former football player who regularly gets in fights in local bars and is both larger and tougher than his friend, holds a knife to Poe's neck, and puts a hand down his pants. Isaac rescues his friend by throwing a large rock at the men, killing one of them and setting the novel's key story lines in action.

From the beginning, the protagonists' perspectives, presented in alternating chapters (along with chapters told through the eyes of Poe's mother, Isaac's sister and father, and the local police chief), demonstrate how deindustrialization has constrained not only their economic opportunities but also their social conditions and their personal agency. We see this most clearly as Poe reflects on his experiences. In his internal identity narrative, he repeatedly moves between hope and resignation, making plans for how he could improve his situation but at the same time accepting the limitations of his life. Some of his ruminations focus on his personal choices and habits, such as when he returns to the trailer after the opening scene and berates himself both for failing to cut firewood for his mother and for not standing up to the men in the abandoned mill: "you are a shit a genuine shit who cannot even keep your own mother warm, a fucking chickenshit punk can't even keep his hours at a goddamn hardware store. . . . Getting cockhandled by those bums and pissing your pants" (20–21). For Poe, these failures reflect different elements of what he thinks it means to be a man: he is neither a reliable provider nor an adequate fighter.

Yet he is also conscious of the economic decline of Buell and of the broader contemporary scene, and his low expectations reflect his awareness of the limited options of his context as well as his personal failures. He sees signs of recovery in Buell, but he also knows that it would never again be prosperous: "it had been a wealthy place once, or not wealthy but doing well, all those steelworkers making thirty dollars an hour," but "No one blinked at taking a minimum-wage job now." He tries to accept this, to focus on "the good parts" rather than dwell on loss. Minimum-wage jobs are, after all, the only economic option that his generation knows (97). His skill as a football player provided him with unusual opportunities, but he has turned down both a college scholarship and several job offers, including some that involve managing waste rather than producing tangible goods. He dismisses installing plastic seals on landfills as "working with other people's trash," while dismantling closed mills and factories requires too much travel. Poe also recognizes that such work would end one day, and he is troubled by the idea of helping to erase America's industrial history: "there would be no record, nothing left standing, to show that anything had ever been built in America" (289). Although these observations make clear that Poe understands the broader economic challenges that are shaping his life, he nonetheless condemns himself for not taking action to improve his situation. His running internal monologue reveals that he sees himself as at once powerless and responsible for his own problems.

Meyer reinforces this contradiction by tracing the economic struggles of Poe's parents and by highlighting the contrast but also the similarities between his hard-living father and his settled-living mother. In her 1976 book *Worlds of Pain: Life in the Working Class Family*, Lillian Rubin described the settled-living working class as people who struggle to achieve and maintain stability and respectability despite economic hardship, while hard-living people "gave up the fight, and, more often than not, escaped their pain in drinking, violence, or desertion" (30). Rubin notes that these categories represent "extremes" and that families and even individuals may display characteristics of both. Poe's father, Virgil, moved from settled living to hard living after being laid off from a series of industrial jobs. At the time of the events in the novel, he has deserted the family and lives on disability after a workplace accident caused by his own negligence. He spends his time drinking, hunting, and picking up women. In Poe's eyes, his father "had a talent for making things go his way," though he was also a "lazy bastard" (113). Poe worries that he is similarly prone to "trying to game it" (112), and his record of losing jobs and getting into bar fights suggests that he could easily follow his father into a hard-living pattern. His settled-living mother, Grace, also exerts a strong influence on Poe. She works hard as a seamstress in a small factory, despite increasing problems with arthritis. While she is acutely conscious of the way she's being exploited, earning "Brownsville wages" even though the wedding dresses she makes sell for about the cost of the annual mortgage on the trailer where she and Poe live, she will not take action to improve her situation. Like her son, Grace constantly imagines alternative paths but repeatedly passes up opportunities. She rejects the possibility of service work, because the only options are part-time jobs in fast-food or big-box stores. Making dresses provides more dignity, she thinks, than "coming home soaked in rancid grease, getting bossed around by teenagers for five-fifteen an hour" (41). When Bud Harris, her lover and the local police chief, offers to help her get a government job, she can't bring herself to accept his help: "Not when it was handed to you like that, you couldn't take it" (190). She volunteers at a women's shelter and dreams of getting a college degree and becoming a counselor, but she never gets beyond fantasizing. Instead, she tells herself, she should simply "Choose to be happy" (43), though she doesn't accomplish that either. Between his awareness of the economic constraints of deindustrialization and Grace's model of settled (and settling) working-class adulthood, Poe feels stuck. When he imagines his own future, he rejects what seems possible—both his father's hard-living model and the unsatisfying jobs on offer—and he cannot bring himself to take action toward options that he believes are beyond his capabilities, like going to college. While Poe worries about being like his father, he has learned from Grace to resist accepting help from others and to doubt his own capabilities.

These contradictions play out in the contrast between Poe's external performance of toughness and his internal narrative of inertia and self-doubt. Without productive labor, he channels the physicality of masculinity, which won him acclaim on the football field, into non-work-related behaviors, like getting into fights, enacting a pattern identified by geographer Anoop Nayak as common among young white working-class men in deindustrialized communities. Because his reputation in town has shifted from football star to bully, he is seen as the most likely suspect in the murder of the man in the mill, and while he awaits trial, he accepts prison as an almost inevitable conclusion to his story: "this place had been waiting for him. There were those who had capabilities and those who didn't and even in his glory days he had known it, known they would figure it out one day, a bullet he would never dodge" (271). He recognizes that he is in prison not because of "some unfair twist of fate" but because of "his own choices," and he thinks that he should "be a man about it" and "accept the consequences" (288). His resignation echoes his mother's determination to "choose to be happy," but for Poe that acceptance is even more tragic. While he considers telling the police that it was Isaac who killed the man, he decides that "from the natural standpoint he was where he was supposed to be, he belonged here and Isaac didn't" (288). His lack of expectations and his reliance on physical strength, violence, and bravado as his only options for performing masculinity almost get him killed when he becomes involved in a prison fight to prove his toughness. By the end of the novel, he is lying in a hospital bed, having been badly beaten in prison, and Meyer offers no sense of hope or resolution for him. At that point, Poe embodies the limitations of white working-class masculinity. Without appropriate work or opportunities, and lacking both vision and the self-efficacy to pursue a more productive version of adulthood, he is immobilized psychologically as well as physically. He accepts his situation as "natural" and inevitable, as part of his identity. Poe's story illustrates a contradiction inherent in contemporary working-class identity: even though his life chances are clearly constrained by the conditions of deindustrialization, he interprets those limitations in very personal ways. Meyer's representation of Poe's internal narrative emphasizes the troubled mix of his belief in taking responsibility for himself and a deep sense of inevitable failure and inefficacy.

His friend Isaac faces a different but related set of problems, though with less self-awareness. While Poe's struggle with identity emphasizes low expectations of himself and the economy, Isaac's internal narrative focuses more specifically on family difficulties, represented by his mother's suicide and his father's dependence due to a disabling accident at the steel mill. If Virgil Poe represents the increasing instability of industrial labor in the last decades of the twentieth century, Isaac's father, Henry, represents workers' determination to hold on to whatever stability that work provided, no matter the cost. When his union steel job ended in Buell, he took a job at another mill in Indiana. He spent three years away from his family, living in a boardinghouse and working in a nonunion shop where the conditions reflected the decline of the American steel industry: "most of the other big American mills were the same, the places were all falling apart" (347). In part because of those conditions, Henry was injured on the job. Now paralyzed, he offers a human parallel to the disintegrating, poorly maintained American steel mills, and as such, he embodies the failure of the traditional model of industrial masculinity. He also worries that his dependence on his son is holding Isaac back. Near the end of the novel, Henry contemplates suicide because he believes he is "dragging" his family down with him: "it was time to do what was best for others" (350). Of course, doing what was best for his family, being the good provider, is what had sent him to the Indiana mill a few years earlier. Henry represents both the traditional model of working-class masculinity and the destruction of that model, and he serves as a problematic example of manhood for Isaac.

Like his father and his friend, Isaac is immobilized, even though he spends much of the novel on the road, presumably pursuing his dream. Where Poe rejects realistic options and harbors only modest fantasies, Isaac has big dreams but no realistic sense of how to pursue them. Having stolen $4,000 from his father, he doesn't buy a plane or bus ticket to California but instead follows a romantic notion of life on the road, hopping railcars and hitchhiking. He has no idea how to do this, a point emphasized by his interior monologue, in which he refers to himself as "the kid":

Traveling properly on foot, the kid is now beyond the places he knows anyone. His material comforts falling away, no place will be foreign. The world is his home. He teaches these lessons and sends them through the ether for others to soak through their skins. A child speaks his first words, a mother conceives a daughter. An old man in India and his deathbed realization—that's the kid. (103)

It is as if Isaac has prepared for his journey by reading *The Grapes of Wrath* or *On the Road* rather than by studying maps or developing his survival skills. His ideas about what will happen when he gets to California are equally unrealistic: "A year to get residency and apply to school: astrophysics. Lawrence Livermore. Keck Observatory and the Very Large Array." Even he recognizes that he doesn't know what he's doing: "Listen to yourself—does any of that still make sense?" (4). For all the specificity of his fantasy, he cannot figure out how to achieve it, nor can he survive on the road. He spends a freezing night in a railcar, and he is later beaten up and then robbed. After shoplifting food and clothing from a Walmart, he realizes the futility of his journey. When he thinks, "There was nowhere he was going" (308), the structure of the sentence emphasizes the passivity embedded in his journey. As he reflects on his family's traumas and on the fight at the abandoned mill, he contemplates two ways of thinking about manhood: "Love honor morals. Someone to protect," but also the need to survive, to "Strip away what's decent. Hang on to your knife. Keep on until you're stopped" (315). He seems to be testing out personal mottoes, looking for a stable idea to guide and justify his actions, but he cannot commit fully to either. He ultimately returns to Buell to confess to the murder, but the police chief stops him, explaining that the two witnesses have died (the chief has killed them out of loyalty to Grace), and Poe is about to be released. Isaac has embraced the responsible version of masculinity, only to find that he no longer needs to do what is right.

In the end, both Isaac and Poe are positioned ambiguously. Neither has made significant progress toward adult masculinity, and their lives are still constrained by personal and socioeconomic conditions. The limited nature of their agency is reinforced by the vague resolution of the novel. Each boy's effort to protect the other by claiming responsibility for the murder is rendered meaningless by Harris, who kills the only witnesses to protect Poe, and Meyer offers barely a hint of what will become of Poe and Isaac. At the hospital, a nurse tells Poe that he is "going back somewhere," but not to the prison where he was injured (364), and Meyer offers no further clarification. We last see Isaac standing on the side of the river, watching "a pair of terns headed for open water," thinking that "soon that would be him, gone" (361). He has told Harris that he might go live with his sister, but Meyer leaves both boys' futures unclear, a narrative strategy that reflects the novel's underlying concern with the constraints of the half-life. That Poe's and Isaac's narratives cannot be resolved reflects the challenges of navigating adulthood for younger white men whose circumstances have offered few good models of masculinity and even fewer options.

American Rust represents a common pattern in deindustrialization literature. As we saw in chapter 1, economic changes influence not only the experience of work but also the way men see themselves, a shift that is often emphasized through generational comparisons. Yet while deindustrialization literature often examines contemporary challenges to white working-class masculinity, few of these texts even acknowledge race as an element of identity or social structure. Most of the white working-class men in these novels do not even seem to recognize that they are white. Instead, whiteness is assumed as part of working-class identity, and deindustrialization is represented as having destabilized masculinity, which is itself defined as central to working-class identity. This emphasis on white masculinity is problematic, not only for the perspectives it erases but also because it contributes to the misrepresentation of "the working class" as white, male, and engaged in industrial labor. At the same time, these narratives reflect the very real and significant sense of loss that many white working-class men feel about the economic changes that have occurred since the 1970s. Their sense of betrayal is evidence of their racial and gender privilege, yet as novels like *American Rust* suggest, white working-class men have been genuinely injured, economically and socially but also psychologically, by deindustrialization. These narratives thus provide an insightful complement to reports of rising rates of addiction and mortality. They reveal what it feels like to have "lost the narrative of their lives."

Working Race

In its focus on white working-class men, deindustrialization literature sometimes ignores or downplays the relationship between class and race. For example, in *American Rust*, Isaac does not overtly acknowledge his class or his race, and we saw a similar erasure of race in Dean Bakopoulos's story of a young white working-class man in *Please Don't Come Back from the Moon*, discussed in chapter 1. Yet race does matter in contemporary working-class narratives of the half-life, as Meyer acknowledges in an undeveloped plotline in *American Rust*. In the chapters presented from the perspective of Isaac's sister, Lee, we learn that, for this family, neither class position nor whiteness are givens. Their mother came from a middle-class Mexican family, and she had a master's degree in music composition. Lee won a scholarship to Yale, married a wealthy classmate, and is now in law school. In his desire to leave home to pursue an education, Isaac imagines following a similarly middle-class path through education to professional work, but his mother's suicide and his sister's departure have left him in the traditionally feminine role of caretaker for his father, a position that also traps him in the working class. At the same time, the two women also represent the complication of race, although Meyer only barely touches on this theme. Although Isaac and Lee had inherited their mother's "Mexican coloring," their father encouraged them to identify as white. Lee reflects that Henry would not have approved of her identifying herself as Latina in her college and law school applications, and she herself had hesitated, knowing that, in their family, class mattered more than race: "She could look [Latina] if she wanted, . . . but she was the daughter of a steelworker, it was a union family." The family identity, defined by Henry, suggests that being a "union family," being working class, requires them also to be white. For Lee, aligned with her mother and now married to a wealthy white man, that distinction is complicated. While she believes that her good grades and high test scores would have gotten her into college without claiming minority status, "she wished she could know for sure" (77). In locating this part of the story entirely in Lee's sections, Meyer suggests that identity is negotiated individually, within social contexts, so that Lee and Isaac think about race differently, and their perceptions reflect tensions among class, gender, and race. While both siblings navigate along the borders of these categories, Lee moves toward her mother's positionality, becoming a middle-class woman in part by making use of a largely submerged racial identity, while Isaac never questions his whiteness. Isaac also feels compelled to take on the feminized role of caregiver, keeping him out of school and at home even as he fantasizes about pursuing a more middle-class path. Although Meyer devotes very limited attention to the role of race in the novel, unlike most narratives about white working-class masculinity, *American Rust* at least acknowledges that the class identities are at the same time raced and gendered.

Yet some deindustrialization literature does engage actively with race, even as it echoes the notion that economic change creates particular challenges for men. In her 2016 play, *Skeleton Crew*, Dominique Morisseau considers the intersections of gender, class, and race through Reggie, a recently promoted supervisor in a Detroit stamping plant. The new role tests Reggie's class and race affiliations, and it highlights the precariousness of black masculinity. Stewart O'Nan focuses his 2001 novel, *Everyday People*, on a working-class black neighborhood in Pittsburgh in the mid-1990s. Social and economic constraints, including racism, economic decline, and conflicting ideas about solidarity and responsibility, create challenges that emerge in O'Nan's portraits of eleven characters, especially three working-class black men. Marshall Mathers (aka Eminem) problematizes the intersection of class and race in his 2001 film, *8 Mile*. The film's protagonist, widely read as a fictionalized version of Mathers himself, embraces a "white trash" identity that at once connects and contrasts with working-class African American culture. In *8 Mile*, the economic struggles associated with deindustrialization highlight tensions within the intersection of class, race, and gender, tensions that can be seen most clearly when characters interact across differences. Those tensions lie at the heart of Lynn Nottage's 2015 play, *Sweat*. By following the interactions among a diverse but closely connected group of steelworkers as they react to demands for concessions and a subsequent lockout, the play reveals how the threatened loss of jobs and wages disrupts affiliations built around class and gender commonalities. Together, these narratives remind us that we cannot extricate class from race or gender, but they also show how deindustrialization exacerbates the already complicated nagivation of difference in working-class identities.

Morisseau's *Skeleton Crew* completes a three-play cycle about black lives in Detroit, following *Paradise Blue*, set in 1949, and *Detroit '67*. Set in 2008, *Skeleton Crew* focuses on the interactions among four African American workers at a Detroit auto plant that they fear is about to shut down. Across the four characters, Morisseau traces the way working-class identities involve not only economic and social status but also gender, sexuality, and race. The play draws attention to the challenges and gains of black autoworkers, as Faye, the oldest of the workers, recalls struggles over access to good jobs, union membership, and workplace rights. It also emphasizes the economic and social problems of Detroit, with references to crime rates, gambling addiction (in a city that, like other deindustrialized communities, built casinos in an effort to revitalize the local economy), and the limited alternatives available to displaced workers. Morisseau draws our attention as well to the way gender and sexuality shape workers' identities. A young woman worker, Shanita, is about to become a single mother, while Faye's son has broken off his relationship with her because his pastor "done convinced him a lesbian grandmamma wasn't the best influence or some shit" (70). Significantly, it is the play's two female characters who most clearly embrace industrial labor as central to their identities, especially Shanita, who defines herself through her work: "Workin' in this industry is what I do. Uncertainty is always there. But it's the work I'm made of. . . . Being a skilled trades worker . . . that's something I can stand on. Everybody can't say that. Everybody can't do what I do. I belong here" (41). The two men in the play, however, aspire to more independence and status. Reggie has moved from the line into a supervisor's job, while Dez wants to open his own repair shop. Yet they also struggle with other people's negative assumptions about them because of their race and gender. When Reggie threatens to search Dez's locker because the company suspects he has been stealing from the plant, Dez resists, noting how Reggie and his bosses assume that, as a younger black man, "I'm up to no good. Like I ain't got a righteous bone in my body. Won't matter why I do what I do or what my intentions are. Won't matter what plans I got or what I'm trying to build. You got your mind made up that I'm shit and you just waiting for proof" (57). While Reggie denies this, he later finds himself in a similar position, being defined by his supervisors by their assumptions about African American masculinity.

With its focus on the precariousness of black working-class masculinity, Reggie's story provides the fullest insight into the challenges of intersectionality. As a supervisor, Reggie can be a good provider, buying a house in a nice neighborhood and starting a college fund for his children. Taking responsibility for others is central to his definition of masculinity. At the same time, he recognizes that the economic security on which this manhood relies is tenuous. Although his job seems more secure and is clearly better paid than Dez's, he recognizes in the younger man's sometimes defensive behavior a familiar anxiety that is rooted in economic insecurity. Reggie knows what it feels like to "Walk around with your manhood on the line cuz you never know who's gonna try to take it from you. Cuz you never know when you're gonna be the next one out there, desperate and needin' to feed your family by any means necessary" (71–72). Reggie also recognizes that becoming a supervisor isolates him, positioning him on the other side of an "invisible line" (72) that separates him from the others. It isn't just that he is now part of management; his identity is at risk in ways that theirs are not. His class affiliation, masculinity, and race come into conflict when his boss instructs him to push Faye to retire before she can earn her full thirty-year pension. Reggie responds by "attacking" the boss, though as he quickly explains, "I ain't touch him at all. Just got swole on him for a sec. But I came close enough. I would've. And he know it." The moment terrifies Reggie, because he understands that, in showing his anger, he has enacted the stereotype of the threatening black man: "I see him lookin' at me—stiff. Like I scared the shit outta him. Like he was under attack. Like I'm that nigga" (86). In that moment, Reggie realizes the precariousness of his positionality. He strives to be both the self-controlled supervisor who can provide a stable middle-class life for his family and the committed, loyal working-class black man who stands up for his colleagues and resists the exploitative actions of the company. By revealing Reggie's awareness of his position and by suggesting similarities between Reggie and Dez, Morisseau reminds us that, in a racist society, black working-class masculinity is always contested, but it becomes even more difficult with the added stresses created by the threatened plant closing.

Everyday People similarly examines the way economic decline heightens tensions in black working-class masculinity. In the novel, O'Nan, a white novelist who grew up in Pittsburgh in the 1960s and 1970s, imagines life in the working-class African American neighborhood of East Liberty in the late 1990s.[6] The novel takes us into the lives and perspectives of eleven men and women, all but one of them black. Like other authors, O'Nan emphasizes changes across generations. Here, the older characters work in a local Nabisco factory (which has closed by the end of the novel), a bank, and a call center. While they are not necessarily satisfied with their jobs, they persevere. Although the older generation hopes that their children will secure stable jobs and good lives, the younger men instead turn to the alternative economy of drug dealing and find a basis for identity and belonging in a local gang. The novel presents this pattern as evidence of how economic change reinforces racial inequities, but the internal monologues of three black men of different ages also show how, like Poe, even when people recognize the ways their lives are shaped by social realities, the challenge of navigating adulthood can also feel like a personal rather than a social or economic struggle.

Before turning to his characters' narratives, O'Nan draws our attention to structural racism and the decline of working-class African American neighborhoods. The novel opens and closes with the image of a busway that has been built to connect a mostly white, middle-class township on the edge of Pittsburgh to downtown, an infrastructure project that supports economic opportunity, but only for some. For African Americans who ride the bus, even those dressed in nice suits and headed to good jobs, the busway emphasizes class and race divisions, so that, even in 1998, they still feel that they are "back in the back of the bus" (1). The busway cuts off the black business district from the rest of the city, and it makes it harder for ambulances or fire trucks to get to the African American neighborhood. It also functions allegorically, reflecting the structural racism that obstructs neighborhood residents' access to jobs and services. The neighborhood's economic decline is also evident in stores that have closed, deteriorating houses, and the opening statement about the need for a new community center. By framing the novel with the busway, *Everyday People* links racial division with economic decline and offers a fictional account of the patterns articulated in William Julius Wilson's landmark 1996 study, *When Work Disappears: The World of the New Urban Poor*. East Liberty is not, or not yet, struggling with the levels of joblessness that, Wilson argues, "trigger . . . neighborhood problems that undermine social organization," but O'Nan identifies what seem to be the first steps in that direction: increases in "crime, gang violence, and drug trafficking to family breakups and problems in the organization of family life" (Wilson 21). As Wilson suggests, and as O'Nan shows in this novel, these "neighborhood problems" represent "cultural responses to constraints and limited opportunities" (Wilson xviii), not moral, personal, or communal failures, though the characters do not always recognize this. The novel shows how individual stories are embedded in and shaped by history, economic challenges, and social conditions and tensions, but it also shows how individuals critique and resist those social forces.

O'Nan's representation of black working-class masculinity has much in common with narratives that focus on white men. In the stories of a middle-aged father, his twenty-something son, and a teenage neighbor, we see how constructing working-class black masculinity requires characters to reconcile conflicting desires that are embodied in the contrast between traditional patterns and gang life. As with *American Rust*, this novel devotes more attention to characters' thought processes than to the actions they take, a narrative strategy that emphasizes how their choices reflect their desires and their responses to limited circumstances. For example, we follow LJ, a teenage gang member whose older brother has recently been killed, as he drives around Pittsburgh in a stolen Caprice. As he drives, LJ thinks about his relationship with his older brother, who was killed by a member of a rival gang, but also his desire for a better life, though he has conflicting visions of what that might entail. He first imagines a middle-class, suburban version of his family's life, "a big house in Shaler where his mother would be vacuuming the living room, his father at work downtown in the PPG Tower, his office with a view of Station Square," and his brother going to college or working at a job that LJ can't quite conjure up (139). A few pages later, his fantasy life returns to the streets of East Liberty, where he imagines executing the gang leader who ordered his brother's death, drawing attention to himself and "earn[ing] back the respect they'd taken from him" (143). As he cycles through these contrasting fantasies, he continues driving, enjoying the sense of freedom and control it provides, even as he realizes that he will "eventually . . . have to turn around and go home" (143). The chapter emphasizes the contrast between LJ's dreams and his limited reality, which is articulated most explicitly when he fears he is about to be pulled over by the police and feels that he is "boxed in" with "nowhere to go" (151). LJ's internal narrative reflects the conditions in which he lives, and the desires that motivate him suggest the logic of his attraction to gang activity. He acknowledges, at least briefly, that "he couldn't go on living this way," but he feels trapped: "what was he supposed to do?" (146). Although the specific circumstances differ significantly, LJ's perspective is similar in many ways to Isaac's. Both young men can readily imagine alternative lives for themselves, but neither is prepared to act on his desires, and both are, in different ways, "boxed in," with few alternatives.

LJ's neighbor, Eugene, wrestles with similar challenges and desires. While he had earlier found connection and respect in the gang, after a stint in prison he spends most of the novel trying to adhere to a more staid and traditional path. Eugene's internal narrative emphasizes the limited options he believes are available to him. He constantly reminds himself of advice from his prison counselor and vows to guide LJ into a better path, yet while Eugene focuses his attention on working, attending church, and helping others, those choices are neither easy nor simple. His emotional ties to the gang and the sense of purpose provided by its ongoing cycle of revenge still draw Eugene in. Although he reflects that he doesn't "feel tight with any of the fellas now," he almost immediately notes that "he had their backs if any serious, for-real funk went down" (92). When LJ is killed, Eugene tames his anger and recommits to his effort to mentor younger boys. This is not an easy choice, as O'Nan makes clear, especially since Eugene has little reason to believe that his efforts will make a difference. His efforts made almost no difference for LJ, and no one shows up for the mentoring sessions he schedules at the church. O'Nan reinforces this sense of futility at the end of the novel, when he describes a neighborhood mural alongside the busway that depicts people who have died. The narrator suggests that the mostly white people riding the bus past the mural every day might recognize a few of the famous black faces, but although "for a split second they might see what you see, the dreams of a people that will not be denied," they might not notice "the three new faces one day" and would not ask "Who is Fats? Who is Smooth? Who is Eugene?" (295). This closing image reconnects Eugene with members of his gang and suggests that he ultimately failed in his effort to construct a more settled version of working-class masculinity.

Yet O'Nan also problematizes the settled model of working-class masculinity through chapters that focus on Eugene's father, Harold, a closeted gay man torn between his desire to be with his lover, Andre, and his sense of responsibility to his sons. While this internal conflict complicates Harold's construction of black working-class masculinity, it is defined as a tension between individual desire and commitment to others, not as a conflict over sexuality per se. Harold does not seem worried about what people would think if they knew he was gay, nor does he feel shame or discomfort about his sexuality. For him, the conflict is about the relational meaning of masculinity. Andre challenges Harold to "be a man" and tell his wife about their relationship, but for Harold, being a good man means taking responsibility for others, a model he learned from his steelworker father. Without making a direct comparison, and without direct reference to his sexuality, Harold's narrative suggests that he feels himself to be less manly than his father. When his father came home from the steel mill, Harold could see the evidence of the physical challenges of his labor: he was "exhausted," "his hands and face swollen from the heat, as if he'd been beaten" (79). Harold's work at the Nabisco plant is more passive: he "mulls over" his relationship with Andre while "rows of crackers vibrated by, the noise of the conveyor just a pinprick of sound inside his earphones, the steady buzzing of a gnat" (70). When Harold recalls small, everyday gestures of love from his father—sharing the newspaper, teaching him about constellations, offering bits of advice (80)—he feels inadequate as a father. He thinks about "All those years he was working, putting money in the bank," but he sees his sons struggling, and he feels that somehow they had "gotten away from him" (74). He wants to be "a better man" (76), which for him means finding whatever dignity and honor "that might be salvaged, if he could just keep his eye on what was important" (211). For all three of these men, belonging and responsibility to others, conceived in varied ways, lie at the heart of working-class masculinity, yet they all also struggle with how best to enact their identities.

Through these three narratives, O'Nan explores the individual, internal identity narratives of working-class black men in ways that highlight conflicts between personal desires and social conditions. Like Meyer, he also shows how the limited circumstances of economic decline are embedded in social networks and patterns. *Everyday People* also does not have a single protagonist. While the book includes multiple chapters focused on Harold and Eugene, most of its characters, including LJ, take center stage for only one chapter. At the same time, no individual chapter focuses entirely on a single character. We learn about Harold and LJ by reading about how Eugene sees them, just as we learn about Eugene from chapters presented through the eyes of his family and LJ. This structure emphasizes the way identity involves both how people define themselves and how they are seen by others. It also makes clear that the constraints that shape these characters' choices involve not only economic or psychological forces but also the needs and expectations of others. Constructing identity requires both an internal navigation of the relationship between class, race, gender, and sexuality and an external negotiation between the individual and those with whom he is connected. As O'Nan suggests, contemporary black working-class men must renegotiate their internal and external relationships in circumstances that are constrained both economically and socially.

Eminem's film *8 Mile* articulates the limitations and conflicts of identity negotiation, focusing on the contested relationship between class and race. No doubt, *8 Mile* is a problematic text, critiqued as a commercial and rhetorical effort at self-validation by Eminem and as a troubled representation of the way race and class intersect.[7] Despite these concerns, the film situates its protagonist's identity narrative in the context of social conditions and networks that are shaped by economic insecurity and deindustrialization. The film's title references the geographical border between Detroit and its suburbs, a border that marks a racial divide and, to a lesser extent, a class divide as well. These divisions were deepened when auto companies moved plants to the suburbs, deindustrializing the city long before the industry began to shrink.[8] For the film's young white protagonist, Rabbit, 8 Mile Road thus represents multiple tensions: over class and race but also between the industrial past and a present in which industrial work is not only less available but also less desirable. In unionized plants in the 1990s, when the film is set, younger

workers like Rabbit were often paid less than more senior employees because the older workers had negotiated tiered contracts to protect their
wages and benefits. In part because of this, the millennial generation was
beginning to reject the idea of long-term stable employment, and some
younger working-class people began to dream instead of creative success
and entrepreneurial independence. The city of Detroit, especially, which
had lost so many industrial jobs starting in the 1960s, became a center
for the development of techno and rap music, genres that responded to
declining economic and social conditions but also offered alternative
opportunities for success—at least for a few.[9] In that context, the stakes
involved in rap battles like the ones that open and close the film were
high, because creative labor seemed to offer a more promising and more
satisfying path out of poverty than working in an auto plant. Such battles
involved not simply who had the best rhymes but who had "the right
to rap" and what qualities would allow a rapper to break through and
win the dreamed-of record deal. At the same time, given hip-hop's deep
association with African American cultural history, especially the experience of urban youth in deindustrialized cities, pursuing the new ideal of
creative success also requires Rabbit to navigate tensions between race
and class as sources of conflict and connection. As in *Everyday People*, *8
Mile* emphasizes the relational and conflicted nature of identity.

The film follows Jimmy "Rabbit" Smith Jr. as he moves from an em-
barrassing defeat in an initial rap battle, in which he is so uncomfortable
and frightened on stage that he cannot speak, to a final, triumphant re-
match in which he in turn silences his rival, Papa Doc. To find his voice
and gain respect in the hip-hop world, Rabbit must lay claim to his own
raced and classed identity. He wins when he embraces his identity as a
white working-class man, which he does in his final rap: "I'm a piece of
white trash, I say it proudly!" But accepting his own identity is not sufficient; he must also persuade others to recognize his authenticity. He
does this by comparing his willingness to embrace a marginalized and,
in this context, suspect identity with the class passing enacted by Papa
Doc, whom Rabbit outs as middle-class and suburban. Critics have read
the film as part of a broader effort by Eminem, across his career, to stake
a claim to working-class whiteness as a class-based otherness that, as Russell White argues, exists on the edge of the color line, a position in which
"white trash" identity is different but also "as near to black ethnicity and
its negative connotations as white ethnicity gets" (72). Rabbit's story and
his raps make working-class whiteness visible but also argue for its valid-
ity as a marginalized identity. To define his identity in a productive way,

Rabbit must work through his own experiences of class, race, and gender and claim the power to define how others see him as a working-class white man.[10] While Eminem has been criticized for engaging in what White describes as a contemporary version of blackface minstrelsy, he also "articulate[s] the effects of post-industrialization on working-class masculinity—both black and white—in the United States and, judging by his global popularity, elsewhere as well" (74). Read alongside other narratives about younger white working-class men struggling to construct manhood in the absence of the kind of labor that legitimized working-class masculinity, and especially given the way most of those narratives erase or elide race and emphasize gender, *8 Mile* offers a useful reminder that race can be neither avoided nor, for white working-class men, negotiated easily.

While critics focus primarily on *8 Mile*'s representation of the contested relationship between race and class, the film also points to tensions within working-class culture by tracing Rabbit's relationship with his mother and his experiences at work. Rabbit feels trapped by but also rejects his mother's hard-living model of working-class life. Single, poor, and unemployed, she is more interested in the immediate pleasures of drinking and sex than in raising her children. She is also ineffectual, pinning her hopes for economic stability on a much younger boyfriend and weekly bingo games. Not only does the film critique the mother's behavior and lifestyle, highlighting Rabbit's anger and frustration (which, critics note, echoes Eminem's critiques of his real-life mother), it also shows how Rabbit pursues a more settled version of working-class identity, one that the film at once critiques and embraces. Early in the film, we learn that Rabbit has lost his job at a pizza parlor, but he has replaced this low-wage service sector position with a new job in the auto industry. Although the film does not specify whether Rabbit's job at Detroit Stamping is a nonunion or a lower-tier union position, it does present industrial work with some ambivalence. During a lunch break rap scene, the workers complain about their pay and working conditions, and Rabbit teases a coworker for having been at the plant for many years. Several of Rabbit's friends from the hip-hop crew poke fun at him for working at the plant, referring to it as a job for "losers." Their disdain for industrial work reflects both their rejection of older working-class models of long-term, repetitive, standardized labor and their dreams of making it big through music or modeling, creative careers that they imagine will make them rich and famous. Rabbit neither wants nor, given current working conditions and wages, could have the kind of settled-living working-class identity that was available to autoworkers in the mid-twentieth century, but while he also dreams of a career as a rapper, he recognizes that his friends' fantasies about success in the music business, like their promises to help him break into the industry, are unlikely to come true.

Rabbit thus rejects both his mother's hard-living working-class model and his friends' fantasies of commercial success. Instead, he decides that his best chance of personal fulfillment and success as an artist rests on earning enough money to take care of himself, both in day-to-day living arrangements and as an artist. When Rabbit first begins working at the plant, he ducks responsibility for arriving late or making errors, and he resents but also sloughs off his supervisor's complaints. Yet Rabbit wants several things that require him to earn more money—his own apartment, a better car, and enough money to pay for studio time to make his own demo. These desires motivate him to become a more reliable worker—to take on a more settled-living attitude—in order to be eligible for extra shifts and added income. Near the end of the film, Rabbit accepts an overtime shift on the evening of the big rap battle, choosing autowork over hip-hop, but when he changes his mind a coworker agrees to cover so Rabbit can compete in the battle. He relies on the social network of the workplace to make it possible for him to keep his job but also to redeem himself in the hip-hop world. After he wins, when Rabbit rejects his friends' invitation to go out to celebrate and instead returns to the plant, he pursues a dual path. He chooses to be a responsible worker, not for its own value but to earn the possibility of escaping his working-class position on his own, through his art. While reviewer Roy Grundmann rightly suggests that Rabbit is, at that moment, choosing individualism and whiteness over the connections with his mostly black friends, he is also following a more traditional industrial working-class path. In this way, Rabbit not only navigates 8 Mile as a racial border; he also navigates a class border. By tracing Rabbit's negotiation of both class and race through the hip-hop community as well as in the trailer park and the auto plant, *8 Mile* locates its exploration of white working-class masculinity within emerging tensions in working-class culture between the older model of industrial labor and an emerging but far from certain ideal of entrepreneurial creative self-expression.[11]

In tracing Rabbit's construction of a "white trash" identity that directly challenges African American claims to marginality, *8 Mile* approaches identity as both relational and contested. Lynn Nottage similarly considers how working-class identity involves navigating allegiances and conflicts in her 2015 play, *Sweat*, which won the 2017 Pulitzer Prize for

Drama.[12] While *8 Mile* has a single protagonist and thus focuses clearly on white working-class identity within a multiracial context, Nottage uses a diverse circle of characters to show how economic struggles can heighten the already complicated intersection of class, race, and gender. Set primarily in a workers' bar in Reading, Pennsylvania, in 2000 and 2008, the play follows a group of friends as they respond to demands for concessions at the steel mill where they work. The group includes three clusters of characters—men and women; black, white, and Latinx—across two generations, with multiple and sometimes conflicting allegiances. Three middle-aged women—Jessie, Tracey, and Cynthia, two white, one black—started at the mill around the same time, nearly thirty years earlier, and their close friendship was formed as they helped each other survive in a factory that wasn't especially welcoming to women. Two men of the same generation, one white, one black, have already been displaced, one by injury and another by a lockout at a different factory. Stan, who was injured at the mill, now manages the bar, while Brucie walks the picket line and battles a growing addiction to drugs that is undermining his marriage to Cynthia. The younger generation includes three men: Tracey's son, Jason, and Cynthia's son, Chris, who both work at the steel mill, and Oscar, a Columbian American busboy at the bar. As in *Everyday People*, the multiple characters allow Nottage to represent varied perspectives, highlighting different histories with industrial labor and showing how economic challenges disrupt workers' relationships with each other.

At the heart of the play lies a complicated set of we/they relationships, reflecting the way people define their identities on the basis of multiple differences. The three women bonded around commonalities of class and gender, in part because in the mill, their gender made them all minorities, even though two of the three are white. However, they bring into their friendship different histories of class and race. Tracey sees herself as having inherited a working-class identity from her steelworker father and her German immigrant woodworker grandfather. As she explains to Oscar one night, her family literally helped to build Reading, and she remembers the pride she felt as a child when her grandfather would point out his decorative woodwork on buildings downtown. For her, industrial labor is a family tradition, and her son, Jason, represents the third generation to work at the steel mill. Stan echoes this sense of family investment in industrial labor, recalling how his grandfather and father both worked at the mill and helped to build the union. Cynthia has a different history, and her memories emphasize how African American workers had to fight for jobs and union membership: "When I started at the plant it felt like I was invited into an exclusive club. Not many of us folks worked there. Not us" (99). Brucie reinforces the more recent arrival of black workers in the factories when he recalls how his father "picked his last bale of cotton" in 1952 before coming north and landing a job at a hosiery plant (46). The racially differentiated working-class histories of these characters lay the groundwork for divisions that will emerge later, when Cynthia wins a promotion to supervisor and when Oscar crosses the picket line after the steelworkers are locked out.

For Cynthia, the promotion represents both an opportunity to improve her own life and a next step up the ladder for her family. She had wanted to be a supervisor "Ever since I stepped into the plant, and saw how the white hats left work in clothes as clean as when they walked in. They seemed untouched. No one in my family has ever made it beyond the floor" (98). But that individual advancement feels like a betrayal to Tracey. She applied for the promotion half-heartedly, but when it is awarded to Cynthia, she insists that the company "wanted a minority" because "They get tax breaks or something" (63). When Cynthia confronts Tracey, the lines of affiliation and difference shift from race to class as Tracey complains that Cynthia seems to be "getting pretty chummy with 'them'" and barely acknowledges Tracey on the plant floor (76). Their almost thirty-year friendship cannot withstand the disruption of loyalty along class lines, which Tracey articulates in terms of differences of both class and race. The fracturing of this relationship, which is primarily about shifting class allegiances, is also rooted in and emerges through racial difference.

Conflicts around class and race intensify when the company begins pushing for concessions from the union. Cynthia finds that she doesn't have the power to fight on behalf of her friends, and although she predicts that the company will use the workers' refusal to accept a wage cut to break the union, her friends resent what they perceive as her taking management's side. Yet Cynthia also feels exploited by management, and when the managers force her to stand at the door of the mill at the beginning of the lockout, telling her friends "they weren't welcome," she speculates that this is why they gave her the job (99). The lockout reinforces a growing division between Cynthia and the others, and as with Tracey's response to Cynthia's promotion, class conflicts get reframed in racial terms. Despite their anger with the steel company, the union members focus their anger most directly at the immigrant and Latinx American workers who cross the picket line. When Jason and Chris come to the bar after a stint on the picket line, they weigh their options: accept concessions, give up and find some other kind of work, or try to keep the scabs out. Here, too, different histories shape characters' perspectives. Chris, like his mother, Cynthia, hopes to improve his situation, in his case by going to college to train to be a teacher. While he is frustrated by the lockout, he is also resigned to the situation, in part because he sees how a long lockout has affected his father. Perhaps because he has heard his parents' stories about the exclusion of and discrimination toward black workers, he sees the immigrants who are replacing the union workers at the mill as a "bunch of pathetic hungry guys" (125). Jason, who like his mother sees the steel mill job as a kind of inheritance, has a harder time accepting that he may never get his job back, and he focuses his anger on the scabs. When he learns that Oscar is leaving the bar to take a nonunion job in the mill, Jason attacks him, and Tracey urges him on from the sidelines. She invokes her many years of working in the mill, which Jason echoes: "We got history here. Us! Me, you, him, her! What the fuck does he have, huh? A green card that gives him the right to shit on everything we worked for?" (129). As his statement suggests, white workers, especially, view the Latinx workers not only as an economic threat but also as a threat to their social identities. "We" are long-time industrial workers, the people who built this place, while "they" are interlopers, intent on stealing "our" jobs. The altercation reveals how differences and loyalties around class and race are heightened in the context of economic restructuring.

Yet Nottage also makes visible the perspective of the "others." Early on, Brucie tells a story that highlights the repetition of racial battles over ownership of work. He describes how a white union member blamed him and other black workers for taking their jobs: "I was at the union office signing up for some bullshit training and this white cat, late 50's, whatever, gets in my face, talking about how we took his job. . . . About us coming here and ruining everything. Like I'm fresh off the boat or some shit" (46). We hear a similar awareness of exclusion from Oscar, who recalls how his father struggled for access to jobs and union membership: "he swept up the floor in a factory like Olstead's," but "those fuckas wouldn't even give him a union card. But he wanted a job in the steel factory, it was the American way, so he swept fucking floors thinking 'one day they'll let me in'" (116). Oscar views the lockout as an opportunity to get what his father was denied and to earn more money. Like African American workers who were brought into factories as strikebreakers in the late nineteenth century, he is willing to cross the picket line to gain access to better work. His story emphasizes the parallels between the labor histories of black and Latinx workers, even as his willingness to work without a union contract sets him apart from Brucie and Chris, whose family gained access to both jobs and union membership a few decades earlier. By making Oscar's perspective visible and by identifying potential, if unfulfilled, sources of solidarity among the nonwhite workers, *Sweat* suggests the contingency and contestations of multicultural working-class identities.

Nottage describes race as "part of the subtext" of the play, which, she insists, is primarily about class (quoted in Foster). By acknowledging both the white workers' backstory of family history, pride, and solidarity and the experiences of black and Latinx workers facing discrimination on the job, the play reveals the irresolvability of conflicts within the working class and between classes as well as the consequences of those conflicts. In several sections of the play set in 2008, we learn that Chris and Jason have both gone to prison for the bar fight, which ended with Stan being hit on the head with a baseball bat, and that the steel mill ultimately closed, displacing everyone. Like Brucie in 2000, in 2008 Tracey is unemployed and addicted to opioids, while Cynthia has lost her house because she could not keep up with the mortgage. She now works several part-time jobs to scrape by. Jason has come home from prison with white supremacist tattoos on his face and even more anger than he had before, while Chris has found religion. The only person whose position has stabilized is Oscar, who now manages the bar, where he looks after Stan, who was left with severe cognitive and physical disabilities. When Oscar explains, in the closing line of the play, that he takes care of Stan because "that's how it oughta be" (141), we are reminded of the ideal of solidarity as well as the difficulty of achieving it. As Oscar, Stan, Jason, and Chris stand together onstage, the stage direction describes them as "uneasy," waiting uncertainly for "the next moment in a fractured togetherness" (141). In this image, Nottage suggests a continuing but problematic commonality for working-class people in the aftermath of deindustrialization. The characters are together, but they are clearly a long way from solidarity.

At the same time, the 2008 sections make clear that the workers are up against a larger set of obstacles than they understand, obstacles that do not differentiate along racial lines. As Nottage has explained in interviews, *Sweat* was inspired by her concerns over the way economic restructuring undermined the stability of American workers and made insecurity a central, shared working-class experience. She describes how, in a meeting with a group of locked out steelworkers in Reading, she realized

that these were "white, middle-class, blue-collar men—who had traditionally been on the opposite side of the divide from me, this African-
American artist living in Brooklyn, and I thought, for the first time, we're
standing eye to eye. They understood what it meant to be marginalized
by your own culture." Through the play, Nottage says, she hopes to show
that this is

> not just the narrative of steelworkers, it's the narrative of people in
> white-collar jobs, who had this assumption that they had taken all the
> necessary steps to assure their job security, and then one day they
> wake up and everything they know is gone. . . . We live with a level of
> uncertainty in America that we haven't known, at least in my lifetime."
> (quoted in Foster)

Even as *Sweat* explores the allegiances and divisions of multicultural
working-class identities, it also indicts the exploitative business practices
and, by extension, if only obliquely, the neoliberal ideologies that underlie economic restructuring and that serve the interests of corporations
at the expense of workers' lives. For her characters, as Tracey declares at
one point, the threat to their jobs feels personal, but for Nottage deindustrialization is both personal and political.

Together, *Sweat, 8 Mile, Everyday People,* and *Skeleton Crew* offer a
corrective to the whiteness and maleness of so much deindustrialization literature, but they do more than simply bring African American
perspectives to the story. They reveal how deindustrialization disrupts
working-class identities and how that disruption plays out through gender and race. For both white and black men, masculinity emerges from
a mix of work and responsibility to others, the labor performed and the
living provided. Where Reggie's story in *Skeleton Crew* reminds us that
the work black men perform and their responsibilities to others are
complicated by the mix of race and class, *Everyday People* suggests that
these two elements of working-class masculinity can create internal pres-
sures, especially when deindustrialization undermines settled-living options. In *8 Mile*, we see a white working-class man constructing identity
in multiple relations, with African American peers in the hip-hop battles
at work and with his mother in the trailer park but also in relation to
industrial and creative labor. In Rabbit's story, race and class are at once
intertwined and at odds, within each category and between them. *Sweat*'s
narrative of the disruptions and conflicts in working-class identities operates on multiple axes, extending *8 Mile*'s meditation on the fragile and
contested relationship among race, class, and gender by distributing the

story among a diverse cast but also by emphasizing commonalities. As these texts show, deindustrialization's disruption of identity challenges class solidarity even as more and more Americans find themselves in the shared condition of uncertainty.

Trauma and Connection in Working-Class Identities

These narratives emphasize how the always contested intersections of class, race, gender, and sexuality are further complicated by deindustrialization, but contemporary working-class identity narratives also reveal tensions between individual and collective identity. Social categories imply shared experience and perspectives, and as narratives focused on the intersections of class with other categories suggest, identities rooted in social categories are based at least in part on a sense of commonality and affiliation. While shared identities matter for all social groups, the idea of the communal has been especially central in studies of working-class identity and culture, where shared labor and struggle have been seen as the basis for class consciousness and solidarity. Some have suggested that valuing belonging and connection over individual achievement marks a central distinction between working-class and middle-class cultures.[13] Yet in the half-life of deindustrialization, where for many neither work nor community life is stable, consistent, or shared, we see evidence of a growing doubt in, and in some cases active resistance to, class identity and solidarity.

As sociologist Jennifer Silva argues in her ethnographic study of young working-class people, *Coming Up Short: Working-Class Adulthood in an Age of Uncertainty*, some younger working-class people adopt a more individualized and therapeutic sense of self. Lacking access to the traditional elements of adulthood, such as steady employment and economic independence, they base their identities in overcoming their own and their families' traumas, and they "embrace self-sufficiency over solidarity." As Silva suggests, this individualization represents an internalization of "the cultural logic of neoliberalism" that "resonates at the deepest level of self" (2013, 18).[14] Silva's analysis suggests a grim prognosis for the working class, as younger adults "come to see themselves as profoundly isolated" and "unable to imagine or act toward a future that holds little promise" (2013, 147). In many ways, deindustrialization literature illustrates these tendencies, as we see in characters like Poe, who cannot imagine his own future, or Jason and Chris, who struggle to find work and connections at the end of *Sweat*. Yet deindustrialization literature also shows that, even when individuals have difficulty imagining their futures and even when they try to construct individual identities separate from their families and communities, working-class characters not only retain but often actively seek class connections. In other words, while these narratives reflect the therapeutic attitude that Silva identifies, they also suggest that belonging, if not solidarity, remains central to working-class culture, at least as imagined by writers.

Both traumas and connections present challenges for these characters, and both reflect the contested influence of the past on working-class lives. Silva argues that a central theme in contemporary working-class identities is overcoming trauma. Instead of viewing the challenges of their lives in terms of economic or political "obstacles," Silva writes, the people she talked with "crafted deeply *personal* coming of age stories, grounding their adult identity in recovering from their painful pasts" (2013, 10). Such personal struggles drive many narratives in deindustrialization literature. In Tawni O'Dell's series of novels set in declining western Pennsylvania coal towns, for example, characters experience physical and sexual abuse, rape, incest, and shootings, and some respond by abusing alcohol and drugs. In *Coal Run*, not only must Ivan rebuild his family relationships, but he must also forgive himself for committing rape and recover from his addiction to painkillers. O'Dell's earlier novel, *Back Roads*, centers on one family's dysfunctions, including domestic violence, sexual abuse, and incest, which results in two murders, lands a mother in prison, and leaves the novel's twenty-year-old protagonist working two low-wage jobs to support his three younger sisters. In her short story collection *American Salvage*, Bonnie Jo Campbell includes portraits of men and women struggling with their own and their loved ones' methamphetamine addictions along with stories of people responding to economic decline. Two of the characters in *Sweat* battle addiction to painkillers, and one appears to be an alcoholic. Both *Skeleton Crew* and Angela Flournoy's novel *The Turner House*, which we will consider more fully in chapter 3, include characters whose lives are disrupted by addictions to gambling. The catalog of trauma could continue for pages, and as research on the social costs of deindustrialization suggests, much of this trauma has roots in economic displacement and the decline of communities.

Yet few of these fictional works include the kind of redemption narratives that Silva suggests have come to define the identities of many younger working-class people. Instead of constructing identities based on redemption and self-sufficiency, the characters in these literary texts survive and persist despite their traumas, often without resolving them. Those who overcome trauma do so not solely or even primarily through individual resilience but by embracing their social networks. We see this in *Coal Run*, as Ivan's move toward stability rests not only on overcoming addiction and reconciling with his troubled past but also on embracing his connection to the local community, which has its own troubled history going back to the mine accident that killed his father and so many other men. In this and other novels, working-class writers link trauma with class conflict and economic decline, but they also show that individual redemption rests on a return to the communal, or at least the connected, basis of working-class identity.

Christie Hodgen's 2010 novel, *Elegies for the Brokenhearted*, illustrates this especially well. The novel reveals how the kinds of trauma Silva identifies are rooted in and enacted through the conditions of neoliberal capitalism while also embedded in family dramas. Family and community tensions are never entirely separated from the economic context, and while characters find redemption not through class solidarity but through personal relationships, they also recognize how those relationships are shaped by economic conditions. Class, community, and family affiliations remain central, if troubled, and while characters sometimes resist those affiliations, their stories also require reconciliation. Hodgen embeds her characters in the context of economic struggle while also examining how they translate it into personal trauma and persistence.

Hodgen deploys an unusual narrative strategy, revealing Mary Murphy's life story through five elegies in which Mary addresses people who played key roles in her life. As she remembers each of these people, Mary recounts her own story, from a childhood of poverty and instability through a somewhat half-hearted and uncertain education and into a tenuous adulthood. In tracing how Mary views and responds to family traumas and her determination to construct a more stable life for herself and the nephew she ends up raising, *Elegies* imagines the kind of therapeutic narrative that Silva identifies. At the same time, by constructing Mary's story through her relationships with others and by emphasizing her reconciliation with the memory of those relationships, if not with the living people, the novel insists that working-class identity remains rooted in family and community even when those institutions seem broken. In the context of economic and social insecurity, the individual cannot fully separate from others, even if what others offer is disruptive or unreliable. Hodgen suggests that her characters' choices and perceptions are shaped by their circumstances, especially by the economic insecurity of the deindustrialized New England town where most of the novel is set.[15] Mary Murphy's individual narrative is thus particular to her situation but also embedded in a broader context of economic and social constraints.

The novel's conceit of revealing Mary's story through elegies emphasizes the way her identity develops both through and in resistance to her relationships. At the heart of her relational identity is Margaret Murphy Collins Francis Adams Witherspoon, Mary's five-times-married mother. While Margaret is represented as self-absorbed and inconsistent, sometimes devoted to her two daughters and sometimes annoyed by, distracted from, and even neglectful of them, the elegy devoted to her life suggests that her movement in and out of marriage was driven by conflicting desires for excitement and stability, a tension that, in many ways, parallels the hard-living versus settled-living tension we saw in *American Rust* and *8 Mile*. Margaret's first husband, the girls' father, was a "degenerate drunk, missing in action," but he was followed by Michael Collins, "high school history teacher, Knight of Columbus, Old Spice cologne" (104). While that marriage provided "a dull, steady life in a three-bedroom ranch home, in a quiet suburban neighborhood," Margaret was "not at home here." This life, her daughter imagines her thinking, was "the kind of place . . . where people go to die, quietly and alone" (225). She escapes that marriage, and the next few years are marked by impulsive, uneven behavior. She drinks heavily, forgets to pay bills, and moves frequently between jobs and boyfriends. After a brief and troubled third marriage, Margaret swings back toward stability by marrying Walter Adams, an African American mechanic whose life is "impeccably ordered" (231), but when their daughter dies soon after birth, she feels that the life she was trying to create, "the simplicity, the beauty, has died with her" (233). She doesn't find "the ease, the luxury, the excitement" she had imagined (227) until later in her life, when she moves to Atlanta and marries a televangelist. At that point, she feels that she had "been driving all along toward a happy ending. . . . The past twenty years have been a horrible detour, but now all your troubles are gone and you have been delivered" (236). This version of Margaret's life appears only at the end of the novel, providing a reconciliation for Mary after several chapters that first highlight the effects of Margaret's choices on her daughters and then emphasize Mary's rejection of her mother's model.

No doubt, Margaret's internal struggle has taken its toll on her daughters, who seem to have aligned themselves with the two halves of her desires. Hard-living Malinda battles addiction and abandons her child, while Mary becomes more responsible and settled over time. She goes to college, tries to reconnect with Malinda (who disappeared after high school), goes to graduate school, returns to their hometown to teach French at the high school, and raises the son Malinda abandons. As she explains in the elegy to her mother, Mary became responsible in response to her mother's erratic life: "I knew when you came home late you'd need a glass of water and two pills by your bedside. I knew when you were about to quit a job, and started circling the classifieds. With men, I knew when you were working up to leaving, and started preparing for another move" (238). In the end, it is also Mary, not Malinda, who travels to Atlanta to visit their mother as she is dying. At that point, not only has she overcome the traumas of her youth, but she is also ready to empathize with Margaret.

As in the other elegies that make up the novel, Mary's recounting of her mother's story serves two functions. It provides a frame through which to advance her story while also exploring why people make choices that seem irrational and self-destructive. In the process, Hodgen connects personal and social traumas, the particularities of individuals' lives and the social context of deindustrialization. The pattern first emerges in the opening elegy for Mary's uncle Mike, the kind of lovable loser that, Mary says, "Every family had":

> the slouch, the drunk, the bum, the forever-newly-employed (garbage-man, fry cook, orderly, delivery truck driver) and the forever-newly-unemployed (*I didn't need that shit*, you'd say), the chain-smoking fuckup with the muscle car . . . the bachelor uncle with the bloodshot eyes and five-day beard come late to holiday dinners, rumpled shirt and jeans, breath like gasoline. (1–2)

Mike's elegy describes the mix of instability and love that shaped Mary's youth, highlighting the way Mike and Margaret both live precariously, moving between jobs, drinking too much, prone to inappropriate love affairs and only minimal parenting. Like Margaret, Mike clearly loves the two girls, yet they also spend many evenings with him in bars, doing homework and making dinners "out of tiny bowls of pretzels and cheese puffs, little plastic spears stacked with orange slices and waxy red cherries" (16). Like Margaret's husbands, Mike plays a fatherly role but proves a temporary presence. After taking eight-year-old Mary with him to New York to join the crowds mourning after the shooting of John Lennon, Mike moves to the city and loses touch with his family. A year later, he is found dead of an overdose, alone in a Brooklyn hotel room.

If we are tempted to blame Mike for being irresponsible and erratic, the next elegy reminds us that individual choices are made in social contexts. As she remembers how an awkward and not very intelligent high school classmate inadvertently helped her mother connect with Walter Adams, the fourth husband who would become her most stable, long-term parent figure, Mary reflects on the way poverty and community decline shape people's lives. Mary describes her hometown as "a land-locked settlement that had failed long ago." She also explains that those who stayed internalized this failure. When she asks, "what could be said of them except that they were foolish, stubborn, hopelessly stupid?" (83), the judgment seems both external and internal, something that an outsider might ask but also a reflection of the self-doubt and self-blame that often emerge in deindustrialized communities. Those economic and communal traumas also shape the next generation, Mary suggests, describing how, during her youth, after

> generations of decay, the place was falling down, a third of its population jobless and walking the streets, drunks and drug addicts, crippled veterans, raving lunatics. We were poor, our lives filled with the stupid things that poor people did, the brutalities we committed against each other, the violence, the petty victories we claimed over one another, crabs topping each other in a basket instead of trying to climb out of that basket; . . . all that we drank and smoked, the serums we shot into our veins; the hours we spent at grueling, mind-numbing jobs, one day after another, how, in order to survive these jobs, we scraped our minds clean like plates, cleared them of all thought. (83)

The challenges described here apply not only to Elwood LePoer, the subject of this second elegy, and not only to Mary, but to most of the core characters of the novel.

In the next elegy, for Mary's college roommate Carson Washington, Hodgen suggests that these effects can be seen in anyone who grew up poor but that they are exacerbated by race. The first person in her working-class African American family to go to college, Carson has left behind a difficult childhood but a close family, including, it turns out, her own baby, who is being raised as her sister's child. While Mary shares Carson's uncertainty and alienation as a first-generation, working-class student at an elite university, she lacks both Carson's sense of connection to home and family and her roommate's experience with the added difficulty of being "fat and black": "fat and black groceries on credit; fat and black winter coats on layaway; fat and black and the bank calling for the mortgage; fat and black and your father gone missing with his paycheck for days, weeks at a time" (107). Both misfits at the university, the two form a tenuous friendship, though Carson at first seems more resilient, if only because she has a more forceful and stubborn personality. Ultimately, though, she drops out, returns to her small southern town, and is killed in a car crash. Elwood's and Carson's narratives present Mary with two problematic options. Staying in her hometown seems to doom her to the kinds of struggles she outlines when she considers Elwood's life. "In order to turn out any differently," she sees, "one had to leave that place" (84). Yet in Carson and in her sister, Malinda, Mary recognizes that leaving is not sufficient, in part because she cannot escape her history: "something about being poor stayed with a person and managed to trouble that person's new life no matter how far away she traveled" (84). While she begins this passage talking about Elwood, by the end, Mary is referring to herself, recalling her own sense of being out of place among wealthier people, a feeling that defines much of her college experience.

Elwood, Carson, and Malinda exemplify in different ways the limited opportunities and internalized low expectations that Mary attributes to those who grew up in poverty. As Silva writes about the younger working-class people she studied, they have learned "to expect nothing of life as a defensive strategy" (2013, 148). This is true of Mary, too, who, despite being the more careful, responsible daughter, shares the low expectations and uncertainty Hodgen identifies in other characters. Mary leaves for college almost on a whim, after a summer of doubt. Although she cannot bring herself to commit either to escape from home or to stay, at the last minute she boards a train, still questioning her decision and without telling her mother she is leaving. Other actions seem similarly unplanned, suggesting that, even as Mary moves toward a stable adulthood, she is wrestling with the same self-doubt and mixed feelings as her peers. Near the end of her freshman year, having barely passed her classes, she signs on to become a French major because an advisor suggests it, not because the language or culture has a particular attraction for her. As she comments about her college self, "I was nothing if not suggestible" (125). She drifts toward adulthood, applying to graduate school and imagining "teaching high school, living a quiet life in a tiny apartment, probably with several cats" (130). Although Carson's death inspires her, for at least a while, to do "the things I would regret if I never did them" (130), her suggestibility surfaces repeatedly. After college, she goes looking for Malinda, and when their reconnection proves unsatisfying, Mary settles for a while in a Maine tourist town, working in a restaurant, until a friend arranges to have her fired to force her to go to graduate school. There she again feels out of place, living in a dingy apartment, "the kind of place people lived in when there was something wrong with them" (200). While her thesis "developed into a musing on lost connections, on effort and failure" (201), it is a past connection that determines her next move. Her mother's fourth husband, Walter, writes to ask her to return home to teach in the local high school. The city has declined further, as major employers "failed or relocated," and "every third house or business was boarded up, abandoned" (239). The city needs her, Walter writes: "You might find other useful things to do with your life, . . . but you will find nothing more useful than this" (240). So again Mary's path is set not so much by her own desires or intentions but by suggestions from others.

At the same time, even as her path to adulthood seems to be shaped more by accident than by intention, many of the steps along the way are rooted in her past, especially her relationships with people and with her hometown, a pattern that suggests the power of the communal in an otherwise unsettled working-class life. When Mary returns, she discovers that her town is the only place where she feels at home. Although other places have offered "versions of life, which I acknowledged to be superior in all ways to the life I'd known," those possibilities "also struck me as deluded" (240). By returning home, ironically, she fulfills much of her own earlier vision of her life, becoming a teacher and living in a small apartment. She becomes a parent in the same way: when she takes responsibility for Malinda's son when her sister disappears again, she returns to the familial life of an earlier period, sharing weekly Sunday dinners and chess matches with Walter, who keeps reminding her that "Family's important" (259).

This idea that family matters dominates the last part of the novel, as Mary goes to Atlanta to be with Margaret, who is dying of cancer, even though Mary thinks that her family lacked "Whatever instinct it was that brought normal families together" (265). She explains that she felt "too distant" from her mother to reconcile with her, but being with her also consolidates Mary's construction of her adult self. She embraces her role as a mother, recognizing that what binds her to her sister's son is not blood but daily living, "all the mundane things [Margaret] never wanted to be bothered with." She holds her mother's hand as she dies, "because this is what people did when they loved each other." Yet while she tells herself that she doesn't really feel that love, she is surprised to discover how much she misses her mother after her death: "I spent long hours conjuring you, trying to remember everything that had ever happened between us—every gesture, every word, every color and shape and texture and sound and scent" (269). She recalls her mother telling her that "the dead were still with us," and she sees how "Every moment that had ever passed between us was still alive in rooms all around me" (270). Mary's adult selfhood results not only from the interactions she has had with others but also from her acceptance and understanding of their influence.

In tracing the way Mary's life and perceptions have been shaped by those around her, Hodgen offers an important counterpoint to Silva's concept of therapeutic narratives. Like the people in Silva's study, Mary must overcome personal traumas rooted in the economic instability of working-class life after deindustrialization, but unlike Silva's informants, she not only reconciles with her past but also learns that she can be at once self-reliant and connected to others. Where Silva found young people defining themselves through emotional resilience and independence, Hodgen suggests that belonging remains central to the process of constructing adult working-class identities. Like Silva, Hodgen locates the challenges of that process in the context of economic decline while also emphasizing individual experiences and narratives. For Mary, the constraints of a deindustrialized economy both shape and are played out through personal relationships, reminding us that the large-scale processes and effects of capitalism are, for most people, lived much more intimately. Rather than embracing what Silva terms "the culture of self-reliance fostered by neoliberalism" (151), Mary finds redemption by accepting that her life is embedded in working-class families and relationships. This is a personal kind of solidarity that reflects the fragmentation and uncertainty of economic restructuring, yet it does not entirely lose sight of the broader, shared conditions of contemporary capitalism.

Twenty-First Century Working-Class Identities

Deindustrialization literature explores the shifting terrain of working-class identity, providing intimate, internal perspectives on the challenges of constructing adult lives in the twenty-first century. These narratives remind us that identities are often constructed on the foundations of work and social networks, both of which have been disrupted by deindustrialization, including the immediate loss of jobs, as we see in the plays of Morisseau and Nottage, and the long-term socioeconomic declines that shape the narratives of Meyer, O'Nan, Eminem, and Hodgen. That disruption heightens the inherent complexity of identity, making more visible the overlaps and disjunctions among class, race, gender, and sexuality. At the same time, these narratives insist, identities are negotiated at multiple levels, from the intimate interactions between individuals to the social networks in which people operate and also to the broader political and economic context of cities, regions, and the global. In the half-life of deindustrialization, work, relationships, and identities change, bit by bit, over time, as people and communities adjust to a new economic and social order.

Although a singular, well-defined working-class identity has always been a fiction, obscuring both the diversity of working-class experience and the contingency and complexity of identity itself, the economic changes reflected in deindustrialization have troubled those unsettled waters even further. Even forty years into economic restructuring, it may be too soon to project the future of working-class identities. Some remind us that the global conditions of working-class life are becoming more visible in ways that both emphasize and, at times, enable connections across cultural differences.[16] Others, like Silva, suggest that working-class identities are becoming more individualized and separate, as people turn inward, unable to find sources of hope or agency in the contemporary economy. As inequality, migration, and globalization continue to shape people's experiences and consciousness, working-class identities shift in multiple ways, fissuring along fault lines of race, gender, and national identity but also cracking internally as individuals struggle to maintain whatever faith they may have in class, solidarity, and institutions. Working-class identities will continue to involve negotiating both the multiple social categories that shape individual lives and the contested relationship between personal histories and shared experience. Working-class identity was never simple, but in the half-life of deindustrialization, it is becoming more complicated than ever.

THREE

Deindustrialized Landscapes

Living amid the Ruins

Julien Temple's 2010 documentary film *Requiem for Detroit?* opens with grainy footage of a middle-aged white man in a suit, sitting at a desk, inviting us into "the very exciting story of a city and its people." As he goes on to predict that this "will be an adventure that will open new sights and familiar surroundings," his image is superimposed over what have, indeed, become familiar images—the ruins of a deteriorating building seen through a chain-link fence, the interior of a once grand theater, a crumbling house, an abandoned office building. This opening scene contrasts the past and present, highlighting the exaggeration implicit in the self-congratulatory optimism of the past. The filmmakers drive the point home a few minutes later, accompanying a montage of images of Detroit's ravaged landscape with a voiceover intoning lines from Percy Bysshe Shelley's "Ozymandias": "Look on my works, ye Mighty, and despair!"

Requiem for Detroit? is just one of dozens of films, photographic projects, and websites produced and distributed since the mid-1990s featuring what some have dubbed "ruin porn."[1] The photographers and filmmakers who have drawn our attention to the deindustrialized landscape recognize the aesthetic and social power of ruins. Abandoned and deteriorating buildings have a genuine beauty, captured well in the large-scale color photos of Andrew Moore's exhibit and subsequent book (with an essay by Philip Levine), *Detroit Disassembled*, for example, which showcase the often-grand design of industrial and civic spaces as well as the often surprisingly lovely natural elements—mold, greenery, cobwebs—

that demonstrate the resilience of nature. Part of the appeal of ruins is, of course, the way they evoke reflective and critical thinking not only about the past but also about the present and future. Walter Benjamin saw in ruins "'allegories of thinking itself,' a meditation on ambivalence" (quoted in Boym 2011). As Svetlana Boym writes in "Ruinophilia: Appreciation of Ruins," they "tantaliz[e] us with utopian dreams of escaping the irreversibility of time." When we look at ruins, she suggests, we both "[marvel] at grand projects and utopian designs" and "begin to notice weeds and dandelions in the crevices of the stones." This combination of beauty and ambivalence creates a political aesthetic, so that, as Tim Edensor argues, ruins function as "symbols through which ideologically loaded versions of progress, embedded within cultures of consumption and industrial progress, can be critiqued" (15). Equally important, he suggests, even seemingly empty ruins "are haunted by numerous ghosts," enabling "experiences of memory which are contingent, frequently inarticulate, sensual and immune from attempts to codify and record them" (18). This capacity for representing both power and decline, past and present, and the simultaneous absence and presence of human life helps explain the draw of the deindustrialized landscape.

The half-life of deindustrialization affects how people think about work, how they see themselves, and how they navigate relationships with others, but in the devastated landscapes of Detroit and other Rust Belt cities, the half-life becomes tangible and visible. Created over time by disuse, disinvestment, and decay, these landscapes are also among the most evocative evidence of the half-life, because they represent not only loss and decline but also the complex and contested histories that shaped them. Like other works of deindustrialization literature, documentary films about Detroit often make use of the aesthetic appeal of ruins, with pans and montages that reveal the beauty in the deteriorating urban landscape, but they also use these images to frame examinations of larger problems. The films explore the hubris and contradictions of American capitalism, the auto industry's failure to respond appropriately to global competition, the racial conflicts that divided the city's residents, the neglect and poverty that have allowed the grand structures of Detroit to deteriorate so dramatically, and the city's struggles to address its many challenges. At the same time, as Dora Apel argues, representations of the deindustrialized landscape reflect contemporary culture's "anxiety of decline" (5) and a "steady erosion of faith in progress" (100). Enabling multiple uses and readings, the deindustrialized landscape is meaningful as a remnant of the past, as a product of economic change, and as evidence of the contradictions and anxieties of the present.

Yet, as sociologist Alice Mah reminds us, deindustrialized landscapes are not just places to be observed from the outside. Rather, the "forms and processes of industrial ruination are experienced by people," including those who "identify them as home" (9). Although the films sometimes include local residents as commentators, tour guides, or human-interest stories, they are only rarely the center of our attention, nor do we gain insight into their everyday lives. That inside, experiential, everyday perspective does emerge, however, in fictional and poetic narratives that are set in deindustrialized places. In focusing on individuals, relationships, and people's interactions with both the physical environment and each other, these texts make clear that the deindustrialized landscape has meaning not only for cities or as a reflection of economic and political changes but also as an element of subjectivity. By focusing our attention on human interactions with and within the ruins, these narratives trace the interconnections between past and present; between material conditions and memory; and among individual experience, social relations, and political conflicts.

In this chapter, we will consider how writers and filmmakers use the deindustrialized landscape, and we will explore the insights about material conditions and the meaning of place that their narratives suggest are embedded in the landscape. Most writers use setting to construct the fictional world in which their narratives unfold, so that place not only locates the events of a story but also communicates mood, conflicts, and aspects of character. This use of place is even more central in deindustrialization literature. By tracing characters' interactions with the deindustrialized landscape, writers invoke the social history of economic change while also narrowing the focus of contemporary representations of urban decline. In this chapter, we will first consider how writers use the landscape to present an intimate but also contextualized understanding of the day-to-day material reality of working-class people's lives in the half-life. We will also examine how these narratives use the deindustrialized landscape to construct and develop characters, revealing the psychological and social power of deterioration and abandonment. Third, we will examine what Michel de Certeau calls the "palimpsest of place" (109). We will see how landscape becomes place through relationships and associations, which are rooted in social memory and the rich but contested relationship between past and present. Finally, literary representations of deindustrialized places reflect the conflict that geographer Don Mitchell suggests is embedded in the formation of the landscape (6). Like most literary narratives, deindustrialization literature focuses on individuals, often without overt reference to larger social forces, but even some of the most personal of these narratives reveal both immediate and broader social, economic, and political conflicts. While the global politics of capitalism thread through all deindustrialization literature, a few texts draw particular, specific attention to how contemporary social problems play out in the local landscape. They link issues like foreclosure, racism, and corporate disinvestment with narratives about individual interactions, family relationships, and the particularities of place. In the process, they show how most people experience the global, political forces that shape their lives in deeply personal and explicitly local ways.

Before we proceed, I want to say a brief word about terminology. For geographers, landscape and place both refer to ways of understanding a specific locale, but with somewhat different emphases. *Landscape* brings to mind a distant perspective, as in a landscape painting that offers a view of a segment of space, framed by the painter to shape the way a viewer sees it. Geographer John Wylie takes this a step further, defining landscape as "that *with which* we see" (215), suggesting that landscape functions as a lens to shape the way we look at not only space but also social relations. *Place*, on the other hand, refers to the meanings assigned to a locality through relationships, practices, associations, and memory. In his introduction to the concept of place, Tim Cresswell clarifies the distinction by citing a passage from Raymond Williams's novel *Border Country*, in which Matthew Price visits his hometown after being away for a long time. Price realizes that, after he left, his memory of his home took the form of landscape, as a visitor might see it, not from the perspective of the inhabitant, who sees "a place where he works and has his friends" (quoted in Cresswell 17). In this formulation, landscape and place represent two ways of relating to a locale: an individual can either see space as an outsider, as a landscape, or experience it as an insider, as a place. These terms represent more complex concepts than my brief definition captures, but the distinction between Wylie's way of seeing and Cresswell's emphasis on relationships offers a useful articulation of two often overlapping themes that run through deindustrialization literature.

In literary and cultural studies, the distinction between these terms is less sharp, and as we will see, within a text, we may both observe space from some distance and get a sense of how space is infused with meaning. In deindustrialization literature, we encounter a range of representations of the material conditions and social meanings of particular spaces.

Wylie's notion of landscape as "that with which we see" reminds us that the physical manifestations of deindustrialization, as well as the remembered elements of particular spaces, function, for both characters and audiences, as lenses into the half-life of deindustrialization. While these texts draw our attention to views of deindustrialized spaces, we rarely remain as outside observers. Through characters' perspectives as well as through narratives, we are invited to connect the material landscape with the relationships embedded in particular locales and the meanings both writers and characters attach to them. In other words, within these texts, the distinction between landscape and place is often not absolute or clear. As I will show, this ambiguity reflects the multiple meanings and experiences of the material environment of deindustrialization as well as its significance. Everything that happens in deindustrialization literature occurs in a particular setting, and those settings offer both ways of seeing and social frames within which people interact with each other and with the places in which they live.

Fabulous Ruins: The Landscape of Deindustrialization

Critics of visual representations of industrial ruins often note that they tend to be depopulated. Apel argues that this erases the "victims of the city's decline," so that any "discourse about people and the effects of abandonment and decay on their lives" is "displaced" (76). Perhaps more accurately, depopulated images of the crumbling built environment, especially spaces that once would have thrummed with human activity, define deindustrialization and urban decline entirely in terms of loss. Empty landscapes invite viewers to imagine earlier times and people, but they largely ignore the people who live and work amid the ruins. While deindustrialization literature uses the landscape to remind readers and viewers of what was lost when American industry declined, it also offers an intimate look inside the ruins and, in the process, inside the half-life. In part because they imagine how individuals not only see but also interact with the deindustrialized landscape, these narratives put human experience at the center of the ruins. They also make connections between past and present, imagining how people inhabited these spaces in earlier times while also revealing how people live amid the ruins in the present.

The familiar trope of urban explorers leading documentary filmmakers and viewers through abandoned factories or schools invites us to marvel at the scale of decline, but the films only rarely tell us anything about the explorers' experiences or motivations. The emphasis is on observation, by the filmmakers and viewers, rather than on the urban explorers' subjectivity. In contrast, Michael Zadoorian's "Spelunkers," from his 2009 collection, *The Lost Tiki Palaces of Detroit*, foregrounds the perspective of a young urban explorer, a freelance photographer who runs a website called *The Paris of the Midwest Is Crumbling* (169). Like other young artists and adventurers, he regularly breaks into abandoned buildings and takes photographs of what he describes as "fucked-up shit," which he posts with comments and stories about their history.[2] The site is, he tells us, "*uber*-urban, *echt*-industrial, proto-apocalyptic, rustbelt cool, or whatever the underground magazines who worship Detroit are calling us these days" (170). The narrator is intrigued by the evidence of the past that he encounters in the buildings he visits, but he also disdains the idea that the past has become cool. He creates and posts images of decay but also mocks those who find meaning in his images. While, as Walter Benjamin suggests, this ambivalence is embedded in ruins (177–78), the narrator's attachment to the past and his ambivalence about his uses of it reflect the contingency of his own experience as a freelance graphic designer. Although neither the character nor Zadoorian make the connection overtly, we can read the more stable industrial past as representative of a better but unattainable alternative. As geographer Bradley L. Garrett suggests, urban explorers are drawn to the deindustrialized landscape out of "an interest in trying to get back to what we have lost in late capitalism: a sense of place, a sense of community and a sense of self" (86). The narrator imagines the pleasures of social connection as he contemplates an abandoned movie theater: "you can tell that people laughed and cried and applauded here, smiled at each other. They threw popcorn and drank Pepsi and broke their teeth on Jujubes" (179). Without imagining the possibility of returning to earlier days, the narrator laments the loss of the structure and longs not simply to preserve it but to make it meaningful and useful: "It's awful that this would even happen to a building. This should never happen anywhere. But I see something like this and I want to try to find the beauty in it, make some sense of it, give it a reason, *fill* it with something" (179). Without explicitly expressing a desire to return to the past, the statement suggests that, for the narrator, the abandoned building represents both the memory of a better past and his own need, in the present, for purpose and connection.

The old theater not only represents the past, however. It also bears evidence of a different and more recent use in the graffiti on its walls, suggesting the continued social meaning of places that seem to serve no purpose. As the narrator comments, the graffiti suggests that people "wanted to be heard, to offer proof that they existed." While he wonders why people would choose to mark their presence in "a deserted, broken place" (177), his own work functions in the same way, to make himself and his perspective visible. His interactions with the ruins highlight his desire for connection and stability, and they ultimately lead him into a relationship that fulfills those desires. Jenna, a grad student who is studying graffiti as art, sees his website and asks him to take her into one of the abandoned buildings. As they become romantically involved, he begins to construct a more settled life and to let go of his engagement with the past.

Over the course of the story, the narrator spends less and less time exploring Detroit's ruins, but he remains aware of how tensions between past and present shape the city, and Zadoorian makes that visible through the landscape. At the end of the story, the narrator goes on one last expedition, to the top of the Fine Arts Building, which is slated to be torn down soon. In the closing scene, as he looks out over the city from the roof, his observations of the landscape clearly reflect his emerging sense of optimism:

> Before long, I started to relax. First by focusing on the horizon, velvet black and studded with golden light; then on the darkened carcasses of the empty buildings I had explored—all that history soon to be gone. Finally, my eyes settled on the new buildings going up, their shiny exteriors, work sites mercury bright even in the nighttime, the cranes and other leviathans that move earth and girders from one place to another. I saw that the old city was going away. (192)

This ending is ambiguous, because the new buildings—like the narrator's relationship with Jenna and his move toward more professional stability—represent an as-yet-unfulfilled potential even as they erase the past. Elsewhere in the collection, Zadoorian comments cynically about economic development in Detroit, and because "Spelunkers" is one of the last stories in the volume, readers of the whole volume are likely to read this passage with some skepticism. In the broader context of the book, we see how the emerging city is more attractive than the "darkened carcasses" of the abandoned buildings of the past, but its "golden light" also does not seem quite real. The references in this passage to "shiny exteriors" and "mercury bright" work sites remind us that new construction may be a work in progress, like the narrator's situation. The character may feel hopeful about his own and the city's future, but Zadoorian remains attentive to the ambivalence represented by the deindustrialized landscape.

Ambivalence also characterizes Ellen Slezak's "Here in Car City," a story from her 2002 collection, *Last Year's Jesus*, though she focuses even more directly on uncovering the contradictions within the deindustrialized landscape. Set early in the era when Detroit was being redefined as a cool place that could attract artists, entrepreneurs, and tourists because of its mix of cheap real estate and evocative ruins, the story follows CeAnn, a young waitress who turns an old apartment building into the Pensione Detroit, a "European-style hotel for students and travelers" (79). In contrast to Zadoorian's evocative description of the old movie theater, Slezak draws our attention to both what has been abandoned and the continuing presence of working-class people. She describes what surrounds the Pensione: three recently burned-out houses that "needed razing or at least a good board-up service, five lots where the buildings had been abandoned long enough so that grass was growing between the remains of windows and walls, two decrepit frame three-flats that seemed to house about a dozen families each" (80–81). Young, optimistic CeAnn initially sees potential in the abandonment, noting that the quiet reminds her of "northern Michigan, where the lakes and dunes and birch trees created a natural serenity that settled me whenever I visited there," but over time, she comes to understand that the quiet comes not from nature but from "the rotting timber and crumbling brick of abandoned houses" (81).

Slezak addresses the contradiction between the appearance of the landscape and its reality even more directly later in the story, as CeAnn walks through empty lots that seem, at first, to reflect the promise of renewal. She recalls a magazine article that optimistically described how "the land's original growth—squibby trees and flowers and mosses, the forest floor—was actually reclaiming parts of the city that had been long abandoned" (86). But while the empty lots were "host to phlox and violets, and creeping, berry-tipped shrubs and bushes," she finds that the new growth "only covered up empty beer cans, jagged edges of broken liquor bottles, disposable diapers, and other trash. And even under that layer of discard, the remains of long-gone homes— old foundations and rotting two by fours—jutted up amidst the growing brush." The natural cycle CeAnn initially imagines—"from forest floor to modest working-class community, to fraying neighborhood, to abandoned slum, and then back to forest, seemed balanced and hopeful, like something I should be part of"—turns out to be an illusion.

The seemingly natural landscape is "not to be trusted" (89–90). The economic losses of the past are inscribed on this landscape, not only in buildings that represent the city's history of prosperity and decline but also in the trash and rot hidden among the weeds and shrubs. The past is present, lurking beneath the appealing but deceptive surface, even when it cannot be seen.

In her study of visual representations of industrial ruins, Apel suggests that, when images and films treat the return of nature as "redemptive," they also "obscure" and "neutralize" the "political forces of decline" (89) and "naturalize" the role of capital as "the real agents of decline" (100). Slezak resists this erasure, using CeAnn's interactions with the deindustrialized landscape to show that the return of nature is not sufficient to heal the economic wounds of the past and that the social and political effects of deindustrialization complicate efforts to reclaim the city. Among other difficulties, CeAnn encounters problems when she tries to get the city to demolish the remains of the burned-out house next door. Her many phone calls to various city offices yield nothing, and she finally takes the advice of one of her tenants, who says that back in Poland people would tear the house down themselves. CeAnn starts to do this by hand, one brick at a time, but by the end of the story, after her tenant—who turns out to be an alcoholic and a scam artist—has crashed her Monte Carlo into the side of the crumbling house, CeAnn takes a more active approach, ramming the car into the building over and over, until she can simply gather up the broken bricks. That she destroys the abandoned home, a remnant from Detroit's heyday as the automaking center of the United States, again connects past and present, here inverting the relationship so that, instead of building Detroit, the car helps to tear it down. As in Zadoorian's work, the deindustrialized landscape plays an active role in the story, providing context and conflicts that shape CeAnn's experience and lead her to claim whatever power she can, limited though it may be. To move from observing the landscape to acting upon and within it, she must recognize what it hides and what it makes possible.

Matt Bell's 2015 novel, *Scrapper*, tells a more troubled story set in a dystopian future version of a deindustrialized Detroit. The novel opens with a six-page tour of the iconic Packard plant, a written variation of a scene that appears in many of the documentaries. Like the filmmakers, Bell invokes both the industrial heyday of the mid-century and the years of deterioration after the plant closed, but he also insists that readers must see, actively and critically:

See the body of the plant, one hundred years of patriots' history, fifty years an American wreck. . . . See the factory roads left open to an incurious public, see the once-famous sign stuttering in broken glass across the bridge between buildings. . . . See how names were not just markers but promises. . . . See the high discard of the room where engines had been tested prior to installation. . . . See the room where seamstresses wove plush interiors, stitched and fitted without a sewing machine, using only human hands, human skills. . . . See the half-life of every man and machine and place. (1–3)

Bell's description enacts the idea of landscape as a way of seeing that Wylie articulates. He insists that readers must "see" the factory as it once was as well as how it has been ravaged by time and by what Tim Strangleman describes as "the absent presence of workers" (2013, 30). When he references the "human hands, human skills" that once occupied "the room where seamstresses wove plush interiors," Bell makes explicit the kind of labor once performed there as well as the humanity of the women who did that work (3). He acknowledges that the plant's earlier life is part of a "barely imaginable past," but he urges readers to "Imagine anyway" (2). Bell's description emphasizes "the imprint of work and workers in the context of abandonment" that Strangleman suggests is often present in visual images (2013, 30).

Bell also invites readers to imagine moving from observing to interacting with the abandoned factory. He first asks us to "see the unsteady structures of the plant's surface," but he then instructs readers to find "entrances inside the plant where if you knew where to crawl you could get beneath the piled rubble." This shift translates the image of a crumbling building into the imagined experience of exploring it, pointing to layers beneath the surface, to "basements, cellars, long-locked storage" (2). This way of seeing the landscape puts readers in the position of the novel's protagonist, Kelly, who makes a living by breaking into abandoned buildings and stealing scrap metal, a man who struggles to find a place for himself in a city that is itself struggling to survive the loss of industry represented by the ruined plant. Throughout the novel, readers follow Kelly through multiple forays into the abandoned zone of Detroit, where the city has cut off electricity, policing, and other services.[3]

Bell disrupts the deindustrial aesthetic as his narration moves from the huge and lavishly decaying structure of the iconic factory into the more ordinary deterioration of surrounding neighborhoods. As we begin to follow Kelly's everyday life, Bell describes how "the neighborhoods sagged, all the wood falling off brick, most every house uninhabited, the stores a couple of thousand square feet of blank shelves, windows barred against the stealing of the nothing there. Paint scraped off concrete, concrete crumbled, turned to dust beneath the weather" (11–12). Bell's language is often poetic and beautiful, but the story he tells highlights the struggles and contradictions of survival in the worst outcomes of deindustrialization. He goes on to disrupt both the aesthetic beauty of the opening and its appreciative social history of autowork with a narrative that involves violence, abuse, conflict, and anxiety. The primary plot of the novel begins when Kelly rescues an abused young boy who has been chained to a cot in the basement of an abandoned home. While Kelly is rewarded for his actions with a better job and a better apartment, he is ambivalent about the attention he receives, and he becomes obsessed with locating and punishing the perpetrator. His efforts take him deep within the Packard plant, which in these later scenes Bell reimagines as a site of violence and cruelty rather than labor and memory. By recasting the deindustrialized landscape as a dark, dystopian, conflicted space and by imagining a near-future economy in which survival depends on scavenging the remains of that landscape, Bell encourages readers to "see" how economic change is inscribed not only in the physical environment but also in social relations and personal struggles.

As these narratives make clear, the half-life of deindustrialization is embodied in the landscape, but even more important, the landscape functions as more than a backdrop to or even a symbol or representation of the past and what was lost. It is, as Mah tells us, the daily material reality in which many people live. Unlike many of the photographs and films that offer an outsider's look at the deindustrialized landscape, these stories take us inside both the deteriorating structures and, crucially, the perceptions, responses, and struggles of individuals who live and work in them. In the process, these writers not only repopulate landscapes that we often imagine as abandoned but also make a case for the significance of the material conditions of decline. Architects argue that the built environment shapes the way people think, feel, and behave—they provide *affordances*. Structures and physical details afford certain uses and responses. The classic example in writing about architecture and design is the door handle: a knob affords turning, while a flat metal panel invites us to push a door open. Deterioration is not designed in the way new structures are. It is, rather, a product of neglect, time, and sometimes vandalism. But the "unbuilt environment" of the deindustrialized landscape offers its own affordances, shaping and reflecting how characters and readers see economic, social, and personal change. It also provides a basis for critical awareness of the material and social effects of the half-life.

Subjectivity amid the Ruins

As we see in Zadoorian, Slezak, and Bell, the deindustrialized landscape functions in multiple ways—as the material embodiment of the half-life, a symbol of economic and social change, and a space within which people navigate their lives. In deindustrialization literature, landscape provides an especially active and significant resource for framing and developing stories and characters. In many of these texts, plotlines emerge within but are also shaped by the landscape, and characters' subjectivity is made visible through their observations of and their interactions with the physical environment. Wylie's claim that landscape is "that *with which we see*" (217) applies nicely here: landscape functions in these stories as a lens through which readers see characters. But deindustrialization literature also suggests that landscape provides characters with ways of seeing themselves. It is not only that writers construct characters' subjectivity by showing their interactions with the physical environment. Characters change as they look at and interact with the deindustrialized landscape.

In "The Yard Man," from her 2009 collection evocatively titled *American Salvage*, Bonnie Jo Campbell uses the deteriorating industrial landscape of a semirural region of Michigan to reveal tensions of social class and individual subjectivity. The story is set on the site of a defunct construction company, where Jerry lives with his wife and stepchildren in a run-down house and earns a small salary for taking care of the property. As yardman, his primary job is to sell or otherwise get rid of whatever remains in a set of old sheds and then to burn them down, one by one. Most of the story unfolds at the old construction site, as Jerry observes the landscape, repairs the house, fights with his wife, and talks with an old friend, a former yardman who stops by to visit occasionally. But the landscape is not simply the place where Jerry's story occurs. His observations of and interactions with his surroundings reveal his character and change his perspective.

Campbell defines Jerry as a character through his relationship with the landscape. He loves looking at "the scrubby field scattered with locusts and maples, and dotted with the storage sheds, rusted hulks of defunct cranes, and piles of deteriorating I-beams and concrete blocks" (9). He takes comfort in the combination of the detritus from the old construction company and the natural elements that are at once present and elusive—the deer and wild turkeys that Jerry knows are there but can't see, a snake that he glimpses a couple of times and longs to see again, a beehive he discovers hidden in the bedroom wall. The return of nature to this site reflects its decline as a site of production, and this pleases Jerry even though it also demonstrates the contradiction inherent in his job. Destroying the sheds moves him closer to losing his job, since once the land is cleared, the owner of the property will no longer need a yardman.

Campbell emphasizes this contradiction but also frames it as a conflict of vision, contrasting Jerry's way of seeing the landscape with his wife's view. He is especially fascinated with the unusual and beautiful snake he spots near the garden, but Natalie screams when she sees it, frightening the reptile away before Jerry can get close enough to identify it. In their different responses, in this scene and in several others, Campbell contrasts Jerry's working-class perspective with Natalie's middle-class aspirations. She complains regularly about living in the deteriorating old house. She wants to move into a prefab home in a new development, and while Jerry wants to make her happy, he "preferred a beat-up house to a nice one where he had to worry about wiping his feet before he came inside" (15). Campbell makes clear, however, that neither of their desires is realistic. The local school district has just laid off Natalie from her job as an office clerk and cut Jerry's hours as a custodian. Nonetheless, his wife insists that they take a vacation and pushes for them to buy a new home, which she ultimately does with the assistance of her parents, leaving him behind. Jerry resists being drawn into her sanitized world, holding on to the more hands-on, make-do life in the yard, but that, too, is unsustainable. Campbell reveals the conflict in their marriage and the contradictions of their economic position through the incremental erasure of the industrial elements and the ambiguous return of the natural, which is beautiful but also mysterious and uncontrollable, as embodied by the snake and the bees. At the end of the story, Jerry remains in the yard, reflecting on his marriage and his situation, recognizing that, like the snake he hopes to see once more, he is "the last of his kind" (32). He wants to stay in his untenable position, slowly demolishing the industrial elements and becoming ever closer both to nature and to displacement. The deindustrializing landscape reflects the internal tensions of Jerry's situation and his acceptance of his inability to resolve them.

We see how subjectivity at once shapes and reflects a character's perception of the landscape in Christopher Barzak's 2007 book, *One for Sor-*

row. The young adult fantasy novel centers on the relationship between two high school boys—the narrator, Adam McCormick, and Jamie Marks, who has been murdered but returns as a ghost who resists "crossing over" into complete death. Jamie draws Adam into a strange symbiotic relationship in which the living boy enables the dead one to hold on to life for as long as possible by sharing his memories; his physical warmth and affection; and, as Jamie begins to forget language, his words. In the process, Adam is drawn toward death. In a long section of the book, they travel from their semirural Ohio home to nearby Youngstown, a place that Adam has been only once before but that he's heard about from his grandfather, who once worked in the steel mills there.[4] Adam's observations of the deindustrialized landscape deepen his attraction to death, but when he later interacts with present-day residents who are revitalizing the city by making use of abandoned buildings and objects, he is also drawn back toward life.

Barzak uses Adam's perception of the landscape to emphasize this shift. When he arrives in Youngstown, Adam initially sees only evidence of deindustrialization: "Vacant factories with smashed-up windows. Black scars on the ground where steel mills had been demolished by their owners years ago. Yellow-brown weeds and thorny bushes. Leftover machine parts. Rotting car frames and engines. Rusty metal workings." He then notices that the steel mill is not fully abandoned. Ghosts of former workers "wandered the rubble of the mills, leaving no footprints as they went. . . . Most were men wearing grease-stained jumpsuits; others were young women wearing long tweed skirts, carrying folders pressed to their chests." When a shift change whistle blows, the ghost workers "poured from the abandoned factories, and others materialized to take their places . . . even though it was clear that what they wanted didn't want them" (227). While the mill and its surroundings reveal the slow decay of long abandonment, the clothing evokes the heyday of the steel industry in the 1950s rather than the time when the mills closed. The ghosts thus represent an idealized memory of steelwork, an iconic image from an era of prosperity and growth, in contrast with the physical setting in which they appear, which reflects the ravages of more than thirty years of decay after the mill closed. The combination of these two pasts at once reflects and reinforces Adam's romantic view of death, which involves both hopelessness, as embodied in the deindustrialized landscape, and a pull toward belonging and purpose, which he finds in his relationship with Jamie and is echoed in the thousands of worker ghosts.

Barzak uses this and other scenes of deterioration to cast Youngstown as a liminal way station between life and death for the two boys. Like the dead who wander the mill, the boys spend much of their time wandering through a "world of cracked concrete . . . a world where the trees lining the streets rotted and buildings disappeared every day" (236). Walking through the deteriorating city makes Jamie "feel like maybe he could be more alive here" (237), but Adam feels less and less interested in life. He feels alone, uncared for, drawn to death because life offers so little. He loses weight, can't sleep, and no longer feels hunger or cold. He becomes ghostlike. Decay seems attractive, and his body is becoming, like so many of the buildings he walks past, abandoned. The deterioration and decay that he sees around him shape his subjectivity and his body.

Adam's observations of the deindustrialized landscape influence how he feels, but his subjectivity also shapes how he sees. As he embraces the idea of death, he becomes unable to see evidence of renewal. Jamie and Adam take refuge in a crumbling old church that, like the vacant factories and debris-strewn brownfields, embodies the city's decline and reflects the boys' depression. When they first explore the building, Adam sees no evidence of life. He focuses on the stripped floorboards and smoke-stained walls, but he fails to recognize the sawhorses in the chapel, a tool-strewn worktable in the basement, and carpenters' lights hanging from the rafters as "signs of life" (232). Although he sees primarily decay, he notices that the minister sees the same scene quite differently: "You could tell that he didn't even see the fire stains, that the broken stained glass window and empty bell tower didn't register with him. . . . he saw nothing but crowds of believers filling his church with their voices" (246). Even as Adam notices how the minister's perception differs from his own, depression reinforces Adam's negative view, and that in turn deepens his sense of being drawn toward death.

Barzak develops the mutuality of perception and subjectivity as he traces Adam's slow recovery after Jamie crosses over into complete death, enabled by interactions with local residents who see potential amid the ruins. Weak, tired, and sick, Adam collapses in the church, and the minister's daughter, Tia, takes care of him, providing food, medicine, and human connection. He also meets Kurt, the owner of a used bookstore, who invites Adam in for tea and shares his own stories. Their caretaking, like their projects, rejects the notion that the decay of the past represents an inevitable decline, either for Adam or for the community. Within a few days, Adam's view of death changes. He "gives up" the wish to die, recognizing that "in the end I didn't really want it. I wasn't sure what I was on my way to now, but it wasn't dying" (277). Tia and Kurt inspire Adam to embrace life by representing a different way of seeing and interacting with the material and economic conditions of Youngstown. Both the church renovation and the used bookstore suggest the potential value of things that have been abandoned. Their alternative vision engages with rather than being limited by the detritus of deindustrialization. Through these characters and by tracing Adam's changing perception as he recovers, Barzak shows how multiple ways of seeing the deindustrialized landscape construct but also reflect different attitudes and actions.

Campbell and Barzak use the deindustrialized landscape to frame narratives about perception and subjectivity, and while both reference the past, their stories focus on the present. But as we see in Zadoorian, Slezak, and Bell, past and present coexist within the deindustrialized landscape. The intersections between past and present are especially significant for individuals who have prior history with a place, as Angela Flournoy suggests in her 2015 novel, *The Turner House.* For her characters, the physical environment evokes tensions among varied ways of seeing their present circumstances, and it provides opportunities for characters to see themselves, their histories, and their relationships more clearly. The novel traces a large African American family's responses to the threatened foreclosure of their now abandoned house on the East Side of Detroit. Turner focuses on two central characters, Cha-Cha, the eldest of the thirteen Turner children, who works as a truck driver for Chrysler, and Lelah, the youngest, a gambling addict who has been evicted from her apartment and is squatting in the abandoned family home. Along with backstory and interactions with family members and friends, Flournoy develops her central characters through their observations of and interactions with the deindustrialized landscape. Both Cha-Cha and Lelah feel conflicted about the old house and neighborhood, but both also find in the familiar but deteriorated landscape of home opportunities to resolve conflicts rooted in their personal and family histories.

We see this most clearly in scenes when they return to the old neighborhood. As they observe the deteriorating landscape, both also reflect on the conditions of their lives, so that material conditions and subjectivity are linked. Cha-Cha has settled in the suburbs, living a middle-class lifestyle made possible by his long career at Chrysler, yet he also feels vulnerable, a feeling that is embodied in the unexpected return of a "haint," or ghost, that he first encountered as a child in the family house. Through most of the novel, Cha-Cha is on disability leave, imposed by the company after an accident that he blames on the haint. He is also struggling to manage the family's conflicts over what to do with their former home, tensions in his marriage, and his interactions with the therapist the company has required him to see. Conflicted and confused, he drives from his suburban home to the old house, a visit that reconnects him with this past, including his troubled relationship with his father. While Cha-Cha notices the deterioration of the neighborhood, he is not bothered by the "phenomenon of disappearing landmarks," because "memory needed no visual cue to do its work." Nor does he expect to find reassurance by returning home, which offers him "no illusion of safety" (Loc. 3324). Indeed, he sees the house as evidence of the problems with which he is wrestling. Its "crumbling façade," which he describes as "the Turner coat of arms," is "disintegrating," with "Mold in the basement, asbestos hiding in the walls, . . . one more blasted-out house in a city plagued by them" (Loc. 4053). The house is a material manifestation of the family's deteriorating relationships, but it is also the originating site of his role as responsible patriarch, a role he took on because his father was so often drunk and unreliable. To expel the haint Cha-Cha must resolve his internal conflicts, and he is surprised to find that returning home not only provides an opportunity to confront the past but also reminds him that, after years away, he still belongs there. Parked across the street in his nice car, he at first worries that he will be seen as an outsider, perhaps as an "over-the-hill undercover cop" (Loc. 3330), a fear that seems to be confirmed when another car pulls up and its passengers look him over. But when they "nod, and drive away," Cha-Cha remembers his claim to ownership here, not of the property but of belonging: "This was the street where the first thirteen plus two later generations of Turners had been known. A face like his must still have meant something to people around here" (Loc. 3337). His connection to the neighborhood and to his own past is embodied in the familiarity of the landscape as well as the way others recognize him there, and his visit to the house marks the shift in his plotline from conflict to resolution. After this chapter, he is able to return home and begin to address his personal and family tensions.

For Lelah, the house and neighborhood offer an equally conflicted emotional landscape. At first, after being evicted from her apartment, she feels ashamed but also relieved to have a place to stay. She is reassured to find the front porch light on: "A house with electricity couldn't be classified as abandoned, and an individual with a key to that house didn't fit the definition of a trespasser" (Loc. 206). Returning to the house highlights her sense of not fitting in with her family, though she also thinks that, as a member of the family, she has a right to be there.

She sneaks into the house, fears her family's judgment of her, and worries that neighborhood conditions put her "at risk of being struck by a stray bullet, or kept awake by intermittent car horns, hoots, hollers, and alley cat screeches." Despite her sense of vulnerability, she also feels protected: "having lived there in the eighties when the final, fatal arrival of crack cowed the neighborhood, Lelah felt Yarrow Street had already given her its worst" (Loc. 213). In contrast to her brother, she finds comfort in having survived the conflicts of the past, and for her the house and neighborhood represent a place of refuge and survival.

Like Cha-Cha, Lelah's observations of and interactions in the house and the neighborhood allow her to reconnect with the past and reconcile with her present. As she walks through the house, she notices the outlines on the living room walls where dozens of family photos once hung, commemorating graduations, weddings, births—the ghostly presence of family life in the abandoned home. She recalls sitting on the floor in front of her mother's chair, watching life on the street while someone "greased her scalp and combed her hair. The memory made her feel safe for a moment, like maybe she'd made the right choice coming back here" (Loc. 220). She notes signs of deterioration but also vitality in the neighborhood. The house across the street is boarded up, and the ones next door have been burned down, but blooming dandelions show that "the ghetto could still hold beauty, and that streets with this much new life could still have good in them" (Loc. 247). She also observes people returning to the neighborhood, especially on Sunday morning when "younger relatives in sedans and SUVs picked up their parents and grandparents for church service." Like the men who apparently recognize family resemblance when they scope out Cha-Cha, Lelah sees people on the street who seem familiar, "younger facsimiles who mirrored the gait of a person she used to know." Through her observations of the neighborhood as it is now and her memories of how it used to be, she begins to feel "possessive about the property, imagined her presence might be beneficial" (Loc. 1736). Returning to the house is also, of course, beneficial for her, not only because she needs a place to stay but also because it reminds her that memory and family can be sources of support and connection.

In these narratives, scenes from deteriorating neighborhoods, tours through abandoned buildings and empty lots, and images of landscapes populated with ghosts of the past help to establish mood and verisimilitude, as setting often does in realistic fiction. But landscape also serves to reveal subjectivity as these writers show how characters understand

and navigate their situations, relationships, and perspectives through the way they see the material world and their interactions with it. These narratives identify the challenges and occasional opportunities of living amid the ruins, and they afford new perceptions and changes for the characters. These uses of landscape in deindustrialization literature enact Wiley's claim that landscape is not only what we see but also how we see. Landscape also helps to locate these landscapes within broader economic and social geographies, tying what we see in the present, in a particular location, with the history of that site and the social history of industrial growth and decline. In the process, these narratives raise questions about how the present is shaped and, in some cases, limited by the past, which, because it is embedded in the landscape, cannot be left behind.

Palimpsests of Place

The past is inscribed on the landscape in material form, but its meanings and associations are rooted in memory—of events, of relationships, and even of the landscape itself. Dolores Hayden writes, "landscape is a storehouse for memory" (8), referring to the built environment, though landscapes also reflect what has been erased. It is the combination of material conditions and memory that allows a landscape to be seen as a place. Michel de Certeau describes place as a palimpsest (109) in which "fragmentary and inward-turning histories" can be glimpsed behind or within what remains. Places, he suggests, "can be unfolded . . . like stories held in reserve" (108). In the palimpsest of place, stories, subjectivities, and absences come together with the material, enabling a sense of place to be passed down, through stories and social memory. In deindustrialization literature, narratives often traverse the physical landscape of the present and the remembered landscape of the past, as in Barzak's image of the ghosts entering the abandoned steel mill in *One for Sorrow*. In its use of remembered landscapes, deindustrialization literature represents the deteriorating or abandoned landscape as at once a material product of the half-life and a conceptual space, a way not only of seeing but also of thinking—about past and present and about the personal and local embodiment of widespread economic and social change.

The physical environment intersects with memory through stories, and a sense of place is nurtured when stories are shared among members of a family or community. Derrick "D" Jones captures the power of memory to articulate place in his evocative 2009 short film, *631*, which traces the history of his African American family and their Youngstown home at 631 Ridge Avenue. While the film presents that history in very personal ways, through family photos and excerpts from interviews with family members, the story was shaped by the economic decline of the city and the racial wealth gap, such that an intimate, local narrative reflects a larger economic and social landscape. In addition, Jones produced the film in 2008 and released it in 2009, so the filmmaker, the people interviewed, and viewers would all have been aware of the Great Recession and the foreclosure crisis, major economic events that lurk in the background of the film even without any overt reference. The timing of the film adds yet another layer to *631*'s palimpsest of place, creating a narrative in which family history, shared memories, and economic struggle are woven together with images of and stories about one house.

The film opens with the story of Cecil Dial's purchasing the home in the mid-1950s, at the peak of the family's economic and social stability. His daughter, Joyce, recalls that Cecil held a middle-class job as a business agent for the City of Youngstown, while his wife, Naomi, was a stay-at-home mother. Cecil made many improvements to the home, building a retaining wall along the sidewalk, adding a patio and a garage, and finishing the basement. In telling the story, Joyce positions the house as one part of the family's middle-class lifestyle, during a period when her mother drove a "brand new Cadillac, had a mink coat," and "we were considered pretty well-to-do." The house was a gathering place for their friends, and as we hear Joyce's narration, the film shows photos of 1950s dinner parties, with women in cocktail dresses and men in suits. Stories and images of that era define the house as a place of community and pride, a way of thinking about the house that is echoed in comments from Joyce's children, who grew up there in the 1970s and 1980s. Decades later, long after the family has had to abandon the house, one of Joyce's children comments that she would like to "put it back to the way it was back when Mom was growing up in there." The house represents a period of prosperity and stability for the family, and the memory is valued even by later generations who never experienced that version of the home.

The younger generation also remembers losses, however—of the house but also of economic stability and, to a lesser extent, social solidarity. All these began to crumble when the Dials divorced in 1971, and the family's decline is reflected in the way Joyce and her children talk about the house. While Joyce remembers it as "a pretty nice house," one of her children recalls that "We didn't have the best cars, but we had cars.

We didn't have the best-looking home"—long pause—"but we had a house." While it had increasing problems—Joyce's children describe the ugly carpeting and pipes in the kitchen that were "not up to par, so every time we washed dishes we had to empty the bucket"—the family retains a sense of affection for the house, which represents a connection with the past and a desire for a more stable future. "I'd bring it back to life," one of the siblings says, clearly remembering 631 Ridge Avenue as a hub of social activity and family bonds. If he could bring the house back to what it was, he says, "I'd let my kids grow up in there, and they kids, and they grandkids." Even though his own memories reflect its deterioration over time, he sees the house as representative of family bonds and continuity.

This sense of place persists even though the decline of the house contributed to social disruptions for the family. When a fire temporarily displaced the family, Joyce and her daughter stayed with friends, but one of the sons remembers that he had nowhere to go, "so I was just basically left out on the street." The family returns to the house after a relative gives them money to make repairs, but about a decade later, an electrical fire causes more damage. By this time, the house has suffered further decline, and it needs a new roof that, as Joyce explains, she could "never afford." So they abandon their home. More recent video footage shows a crumbling structure, and voiceover comments from the family make clear that they still feel its loss. They also recognize that losing the house is part of a larger loss of economic and social power. As one of Joyce's sons comments at the end of the film, it feels "unfair that the only thing that's keeping you from preserving your history or building your legacy in that home is that you just don't have the money to do it. I don't mean the money to get something. I mean the money to keep what's yours." While this comment reflects this one family's experience, losing a home because people didn't have the money "to keep what's yours" was becoming increasingly common in 2008, when the interviews were recorded. Even without any explicit references to larger social patterns, this family's story is representative of the losses experienced by many families in the Rust Belt, especially urban, working-class African American families. Like the Dials, many saw the economic stability they had just barely achieved at the height of the postwar industrial boom erode bit by bit, starting in the 1970s. Across the region, neighborhoods like theirs, made stable and comfortable by steady employment, became increasingly marked by abandoned homes and empty lots where houses had been demolished. The film shows how stories "express something irreducibly particular and personal, and yet they can be received as expressions of broader social and political context" (Cameron 574). In the case of *631*, the place remembered is very specific—one family's home—yet it also reflects the broader contexts of Youngstown and the industrial region during the second half of the twentieth century and the economic crisis of the early twenty-first century.

As *631* demonstrates, a sense of place is rooted in what Mah calls "living memory," which she defines as "people's present-day memories of a shared past" (15). Further, as the younger family members in *631* demonstrate, living memory can be passed down, so that a sense of place incorporates both lived experience and inherited narratives. The thirteen-year-old narrator of Shauna Seliy's 2007 novel, *When We Get There*,[5] draws on this layered way of seeing the landscape of western Pennsylvania, where he lives with his grandmother after his father has been killed in a mine accident and his mother has disappeared. Although most of the local mines have closed and many of the structures associated with the industry have been torn down, Lucas constructs a mental map of the region rooted in his own explorations of abandoned mines and coke ovens and in stories told by his family. Near an old coke oven, he finds "left-behind blasting caps, lamps, hard hats, signs in ten different languages saying Danger, saying Watch Your Head" (69), and these items function as historical markers, providing evidence of the shared and contested history of the place. Lucas's sense of place also comes from family stories, like his grandmother's memory of how, when she was a child, she "thought the Luna fire was the fire she'd heard about at school that burned at the center of the earth, and that the center of the earth was not far from Banning; it was just up the road, roaring away like a furnace" (70). Drawing on family lore and the material remains of the coal industry, Lucas has a strong sense of place, embodied not only in the associations he has with specific locations but also in his awareness of the larger geography of the region. He describes how his town connects with "a line of towns on a crooked spine of hills that stretched up and down the coal seam" (69), all associated with elements of coal and steel production: "They used to cook the coal in [the ovens] and turn it into coke. They'd ship the coke to the mills in Pittsburgh or Wheeling, where they used it to cook iron ore and make steel. Once they had steel, they didn't need to turn it into anything; it was just itself, the thing they were after all along" (70). Through Lucas's geographic and industrial narrative of his home region, Seliy locates his story in multiple ways—in a region, within a set of industrial processes, during a period of decline, within the shared history of eastern European immigration, and as part of a particular family history. Seliy emphasizes the role of social memory in constructing this layered, multifaceted sense of place by presenting the landscape of the novel in the voice of an adolescent boy. For Lucas, memory, narrative, landscape, and place are interdependent.

In *When We Get There*, the integration of memory and landscape seems almost natural, embedded in everyday family life and in crumbling structures and discarded items. Yet, as Hayden argues, social memory can too easily be erased when landscapes are reshaped. To preserve a sense of place, she suggests, even "totally bulldozed places can be marked to restore some shared public meaning, a recognition of the experience of spatial conflict, or bitterness, or despair" (8). Although Hayden focuses on historical markers and physical memorials, literary narratives can also work to preserve social memory for a particular place. *From Milltown to Malltown*, a 2010 collection of poems by Jim Daniels and Jane McCafferty paired with photographs by Charlee Brodsky, performs this memorializing work as it explores the connections and conflicts between past and present in the landscape. *From Milltown to Malltown* looks at the material and remembered landscape of Homestead, Pennsylvania, where a historic U.S. Steel factory was torn down in 1988, two years after it closed. A decade later, a shopping mall opened on the same land, though a dozen smokestacks from the mill were incorporated into the reconstructed landscape. While most of Brodsky's black and white photos capture the faces of people who live or work in the area, she also highlights details from the streets of Homestead: empty storefronts, old metal mailboxes on the side of a building, the facade of a run-down church, a "Slow/Children at Play" sign on a light pole. Daniels and McCafferty wrote the poems in response to Brodsky's photos, and their words invoke memories of the earlier version of Homestead as a site of steelmaking and working-class life.

The volume opens with a Daniels poem that frames the project in relation to the past, defining Homestead as "the land of Used-Ta-Be," a place where "the ancients" remember not only the "fire rising into the night sky / tangible smoke and soot of livelihood" but also "the endless disappearance and reemergence of men. / Diminishing returns. The celebrations of enormity / and deterioration." What "used-ta-be" is not only the mental image of the steel mill but also the labor it represented and its decline, as well as the tension between the scale of the mill, its "enormity," and the loss of its "deterioration." In this dual vision of past and present, "the ancients" remember the "battles and blood" associated with the steel mill and "search the landscape for some sign / that it was not imagined" (3). The past remains central to how people see this place, even as the reconstruction of the landscape disrupts memory.

Other poems in the collection insist that even spaces that look empty contain their histories: "No such thing as a vacant lot," Daniels writes in one poem, "Every lot rubbled with sin" (21). In the reference to sin, he reminds us that the seemingly abandoned landscapes of the dein-dustrialized town bear the marks of previous lives. Many of these poems use the structures and signs that mark the landscape as entry points for considering how people's lives have or have not changed in this place. In "Fresh Fish," for example, Daniels imagines that the key to a boarded-up storefront "sleeps in the bottom of a drawer" but also that "Once some-body sincere held that key / on a ring of other keys and they made a sound / something like hope" (37). McCafferty takes this notion further in "On This Very Spot," insisting that "every inch of this geography / contains a blistered history." It is a site "where scalded ghosts / mingle, and speak." Much as Daniels imagines the unnamed person who held the old key, McCafferty makes the memory of "this very spot" specific, naming one individual, "Hank Kalvecic, father of eleven / steel-worker since 1951," who "knelt / down and tried to pray on this very / spot" (57). Through details like this, Daniels and McCafferty teach us to see what seems at first invisible in the landscape. By invoking the presence of people from the past, they also insist upon Homestead as a place rooted in social memory.

The history of this place is shared across time, these poems suggest, and the present is not as different from the past as it might at first appear. McCafferty ends "On This Very Spot" with a reference to the "young / professional" who lives in a new condo in what is now a "squeaky, fragile place" (57). The current resident may be vulnerable in different ways than his steelworker predecessor, but, she suggests, the two workers have more than a location in common. Daniels similarly invokes continuity by linking the remembered past, represented by the smokestacks, with the commercial structures and signs of the present. In "On This Site," which accompanies an image of a Longhorn Steakhouse sign in front of a long, straight row of smokestacks, Daniels notes "the symmetrical puffs of meat-flavored smoke" from the restaurant and the cars in the parking lot "in freshly lined spaces // symmetrical as smokestacks," a repetition that highlights a key similarity between the past and the present: "It all means money / to somebody" (45). As Daniels writes in a final poem, "Find the Steel Mill in This Picture," printed alongside a photo of a park-ing lot, "even on this manufactured flatness // the world spins." A single car parked in a far corner of the lot, so small that it might go unnoticed, "might be the missing piece / of the puzzle," Daniels suggests, or it could be "the abandoned piece // of another puzzle made long ago. If you searched / this lot, perhaps you'd find the keys peeking out // beneath a stray leaf, something glittering/something tarnished" (76). The past and the present coexist, it seems, though the connections are not always clear. The past might glitter or it might be tarnished and abandoned. The "manufactured flatness" of the new landscape cannot be entirely separated from the landscape of the past, even if it hides in a corner or "beneath a stray leaf." By presenting both the past and present land-scapes of Homestead, Daniels, McCafferty, and Brodsky develop a sense of place based on social memory, insisting that shared history remains significant even when its material presence has been largely erased.

Christopher Barzak complicates the idea of place as a palimpsest in "The B&O, Crossroads of Time and Space." Instead of noting how the present is superimposed on the past, Barzak imagines a "perforation" that allows someone in the present to glimpse the scene Henry Miller would have seen from the Youngstown train station in 1940 of "two girls, heads wrapped in scarves, picking their way down the hill."[6] He describes their smoky, soot-dusted immigrant neighborhood, where "turkeys and chickens peck at the ground of back yards" and "mothers stand on square front lawns, wringing their hands in their aprons, waving to the girls as they approach." But Barzak also imagines how these figures in the past might have seen the future. While the speaker of the essay looks back through the perforation, the mothers see the girls climbing a rope to the future, "hand over hand, like sturdy athletes, until they see a man from the future looking through Henry Miller's spy-hole, and then the empty hillside behind him, the abandoned tracks of the B&O." In this image, Barzak challenges nostalgic views of the past that might cast the girls' lives in 1940 as the ideal. In the eyes of the mothers, that world was just a starting place, and they at first imagine their daughters moving into better futures. But he also questions that progressive narrative. The mothers expect great things, but the abandoned rail line reminds us that their hopes would not be fulfilled. As the mothers' view of a deindustrial-ized future makes clear, what lies ahead may not be what we desire. If we look carefully, Barzak seems to suggest, we can see the past clearly and through it, perhaps, gain awareness of our position in the present and the uncertainty of the future. As he writes at the end of the piece, "My back is to the future, the wind blowing my hair forward in waves toward the past. I dare not look over my shoulder."

Where "The B&O, Crossroads of Time and Space" imagines connections across time from a single spot, in "Map for a Forgotten Valley" Barzak links memories of the past with social relations in the present. In one section, "The Feral Houses of Youngstown," he calls on readers to appreciate the beauty in the deindustrialized landscape, but even more important, he draws attention to the memories these houses contain. Despite the gaps where aluminum siding has been stolen, leaving "silver insulation wrap to flicker in the sunlight" (21), an old piano with useless wires coiling out of the lid bears witness to the family that once lived here. Instead of evoking nostalgia for an idealized past, Barzak invites us to embrace the connection between the past and the present, to "find decay and disintegration, the coming apart of what was once composed, a beautiful process, a return rather than a disappearance" (22). For all its deterioration, this is a place of belonging: "In their disintegration these abandoned houses have been found: we measure love by its absence. We see what we have by what we have lost" (21). Barzak shows how this sense of place enables what Svetlana Boym describes as a "reflective nostalgia" that "dwells on the ambivalences of human longing and belonging and does not shy away from the contradictions of modernism" (2001, xviii). As in "B&O," and despite the warning that we "dare not" imagine that we can see the future, Barzak links the social memory of a more prosperous past with the deterioration of the present and also with the possibility of return, represented by evidence of residents reclaiming empty space in the city:

> What used to be a city is disappearing, and in its place are backyards with vegetable gardens, and down the street a new farmer's market, and across the way, a ragtag community theater is going to do Shakespeare in the park, even if the park has been abandoned by the city, and there are women now, three or sometimes four of them, who stand on corners singing spirituals, and a group of African American teenage boys, who tap dance down the main street of downtown, where no bowling ball will ever touch them. (14)

In Barzak's representation, Youngstown is at once "an emptied-out place, a hollowed place" (13) and a city that is "becoming itself" (15). The past is firmly embedded in the landscape, even if only as a matter of memory, and within the deindustrialized landscape people are already constructing new possibilities and thus reclaiming this place. By revealing the interconnections between past and present, Barzak implicitly challenges those who encourages residents to "get over" the past.

While these texts locate a sense of place in social memory and relationships, they also emphasize class conflict as an element of both landscape and place. As we have seen, conflicts over work, identity, and power thread throughout deindustrialization literature, and some texts trace how these conflicts play out within landscape and place. Yet even as capitalism involves both local, workplace conflict and global shifts and as the neoliberal ideology that contributed to economic restructuring integrates class conflict into public policy and international relations, deindustrialization literature almost never makes direct reference to globalization, politics, or policy. Instead, these narratives locate large-scale conflicts in particular physical settings and show how they intersect with the social memories that define place. In doing so, they remind us that people experience large-scale, globalized economic, social, and political conflicts through their immediate experience, within particular landscapes and specific places.

We see this in Flournoy's approach to foreclosure, a widespread economic and political issue that animates the family drama of *The Turner House* but that within the novel is represented through its personal, familial effects, not as a social or political concern. Even when Flournoy addresses the broader landscape of gentrification and racism, she does so through an individual's experience, complementing the family narrative at the heart of the novel with the conflicted views of a family friend who has been buying foreclosed houses, hoping that their value will eventually increase. David's story provides a wider context for the Turner family's problem, and it complements the family's personal ambivalence about their house with a conflicted view of the opportunities and problems that coexist in Detroit's struggling East Side. David recognizes that the houses he is buying had been family homes, "places where people had once worked hard, hazardous jobs to pay their mortgages," but he also sees little hope for the old neighborhood: "Words like *ghetto, dilapidated,* and *run-down* were inadequate to describe this portion of the city." One of the guys he hires to repair the old houses for rental offers an even grimmer description: "'This isn't postindustrial, post-white-flight, or post-automobile boom,' Kyle had said. 'It's like, post-zombie-fucking-apocalypse'" (Loc. 2400). David's perspective on foreclosures, gentrification, and neighborhood decline reminds readers that these widespread social and economic issues generate varied responses and effects, even among people with personal ties to a place. At the same time, Flournoy suggests that ties to personal history are not easily broken. While David insists that he has no interest in remaining connected to the neighborhood—he returns only to manage his properties and to visit his mother—he recognizes that "he was not from anywhere else, either" (Loc. 2417).

David's story also highlights the continuing racial conflicts in Detroit, a theme that Flournoy traces back to the 1940s, when Cha-Cha and Lelah's father, Francis Turner, first came to the city, hoping to find opportunity and freedom he could not get in Arkansas but instead encountering racism and economic struggle. In the present, David has moved to a new waterfront condo, literally buying in to the city's gentrification, even though he recognizes that in some parts of the city, "the all-white patrons" of hip new restaurants view him "with suspicion, as if his very presence suggested that they weren't as close to 'revitalizing' the area as they'd hoped" (Loc. 2420). David's perspective on the state of Detroit, together with the foreclosure narrative, emphatically reminds us that the landscape in which the characters operate and the sense of belonging they find in family and neighborhood reflect both personal and social histories. Through David, Flournoy provides a wider but still personal background for her primary narrative, and his ambivalence reveals how conflict can be embedded in the meaning of place.

The dual intersections of racial conflict and economic struggle and personal and political tensions frame a number of Detroit texts. For example, in the title story of *The Lost Tiki Palaces of Detroit*, Zadoorian connects the narrator's personal memory of place with the city's history of economic decline and racial division. As in most of Zadoorian's stories, the narrator is a white man who grew up in Detroit and now observes and interacts with both the continuing deterioration of the landscape and signs of revitalization. The story unfolds as the narrator rides the bus along Woodward Avenue, on his way to an unidentified job in the city. He passes the sites where three Polynesian-style restaurants once "nestled among the cathedrals of twentieth-century V-8 Hydraulic Commerce" (193), and he remembers the conflicts that explain their development and their decline. He recalls how the first "tiki palace" was built at a moment of economic expectation in the late 1960s, "to be the largest South Seas supper club of its kind in the Midwest," with a "lavish . . . Lucite bar-top with 1,250 Chinese coins embedded in it and bar tables made from brass hatch covers from trading schooners . . . a mountainette of volcanic lava . . . a grotto lush with palm trees and flaming tikis" (193–94). That opening, a sign of Detroit's prosperity, occurred "barely a month after the worst race riot in Detroit's history" (194). The restaurant, which invited patrons into an imagined version of an exotic culture, closed just two years later, reflecting the anxieties many felt about real encounters with racial difference as "the white folks disappeared from downtown Detroit at the end of the workday in the seventies" (199). In the present, the landscape has been both preserved and demolished, so that behind the famously restored Fox Theatre, "save for a fire station and an abandoned party store, there are mostly empty fields" (196). As in "Spelunkers," the narrator of this story notes signs of revitalization: "New buildings push out the grand old ones, like bullies in a big rush. When you go downtown at night there are people there now, suburban people, city people, doing things, spending money" (199). In these two sentences, Zadoorian highlights the narrator's ambivalence. The new buildings are "bullies," but there is also new economic activity as people return to the city, including, presumably, the narrator himself, riding the bus to work. In this story, the landscape of Detroit reflects the collision between the past, evident in both physical signs of what has been lost and the narrator's memory of what was once there, and a potential but uncertain future.

Along with contemplating the contested history and present of the Detroit landscape, the story shows how past conflicts play out in interactions among residents. Zadoorian interweaves his description of the view from the bus with a story about an African American man—the narrator describes him as homeless—who is also riding the bus. Soon after he boards the bus, the man begins to say, repeatedly, "I'm invisible," a claim that the other bus riders enact by doing their best to ignore him. Even as the narrator avoids making eye contact with the man, he reflects that the statement is "strange and existential—an awl to the heart," and he thinks that the homeless man "*understands his condition*" (195). The moment captures both the narrator's discomfort and his desire to distance himself from the situation by intellectualizing and thus rationalizing it. As the bus continues along Woodward, the homeless man begins to focus his attention on the narrator, the only white person on board, announcing that there's a "motherfucker on our bus" (197). While other riders sigh in exasperation at the man's taunts and one woman scolds him, no one takes action until he drops his pants and waves his penis around, at which point the bus driver kicks him off. The story closes with everyone on the bus laughing together about the incident, and while that may defuse the tension on the bus, it does not erase the significance of the racial and economic conflicts, deeply rooted in the city's history, that frame the story and, Zadoorian hints, complicate its efforts to revitalize.

Throughout the story, Zadoorian juxtaposes the deindustrialized landscape and the story of its decline, including its difficult history of racial conflict, with evidence of both change and persistence. New buildings and restorations, the return of economic activity, and even the white narrator's presence on the bus as he rides to work all suggest a city that is beginning to recover, while empty lots, abandoned buildings, and the tension between the African American homeless man and the white narrator, who is educated but does not appear to have a professional job, make clear that the city's past is still very much present. Change may well be coming, but the racial conflict and economic challenges of the city's history threaten efforts to create a bright new future. Demolition and erasure will not make the past invisible here. The living memory of Detroit will persist no matter how many big skyscrapers replace fondly remembered old buildings, and as this story reminds us, this includes memories of the conflicts and struggles that were also part of that past. This is reinforced by the persistence of the city's history in the landscape.

The persistence of personal memory and shared, conflicted history, both embedded in the physical and social elements of place, threads through Ken Meisel's poems about Detroit as well. Throughout his 2009 collection, *Beautiful Rust*, he invites us to look at the deindustrialized landscape of Detroit as both evidence of and a shaping influence on key conflicts in the city, past and present. Detroiters remember the prosperous, lively city where "supper clubs and lounges glowed like waterfalls of gold coins," but, Meisel warns, that is "a legend you must forget," pointing us instead to evidence of the city's decline: "the old woman whose grocery cart rattles over the road / shaking a cane at someone dead you can't even see," an "old tramp's battered bicycle wheel" that "hacks a rusty melody," and "the dark hulls of ransacked cars" (66–67). Elsewhere, he describes how residents search for "evidence there could be something / greater to the demolished cement / of the city's bridges and puddles. / For we were looking for proof / of life amidst this beautiful rust. / For something worth our loving, / here in the ruin" (15). In these lines, Meisel traces the conflicted intersection of the search for hope for this struggling city, a sense of connection to this place, and the material and social problems embedded in the landscape.

Signs of life are not hard to find in these poems, however, and Meisel's descriptions of the landscape are often populated with both present residents and those who are long gone, so that social memory remains even as buildings are demolished. In "Marvin Gaye and the Wrecking Ball," for example, Meisel tells us that both the singer and the city were "ruined" by gunshots and are now "under the wrecking ball" (35). In "Elegy for the Residents of the Niagara Apartments," he describes the former residents "huddling around an egg white electric burner / with burnt coffee on it, in winter," the "stale liquor // on your breath, and the stench of cigarettes / and the urine in the hallway where one light bulb // blown out, look[s] like an extinguished planet" (48). He also names the people who lived there, noting "Norm's filthy converse sneakers and his TV" and "Mary's silver walker and Rosie's key set," and he speculates that "the last drunken quarrel between Don & Marilyn / was echoing through the steel girders and the window moldings // as they ripped them down and they fell into dirt and concrete, / and into the walls with wiring scoring out of them like hair." Like Slezak and Campbell, Meisel references signs of nature returning, but he links this new life with the memory of the former neighbors, connecting the "yellow // flowers blooming wildly in the spring grasses on 3rd Avenue" with the "yellow construction hats" of "city workers" who were "collecting invisible bits of someone else's soul" (50). In responding to the erasure of the building from the landscape, Meisel insists on the significance of those whose lives were largely invisible even before their home was destroyed.

As in Zadoorian's stories, Meisel's poetic landscapes serve as reminders of the city's history, including its industrial past, its long-term economic struggles, its racial conflicts, the local music scene, and a sense of place that involves all of these. For Meisel, the social and material landscape of Detroit is complicated and conflicted, revealing divides of race and class while also providing opportunities to bridge them. In "He Helps Me Count What's Left Behind," for example, the speaker asks an African American cab driver to take him to Black Bottom, "where the jazz clubs were, / and where John Lee Hooker lived." But the speaker notes that the area was also home to "the old Fisher Plant #21," which is now a "white, abandoned" building (64), characteristics that contrast with the neighborhood's name and with its cultural history as a center of African American life. At the same time, their drive through the old neighborhood uncovers common ground between the two men: the speaker's father played music and the driver's aunt danced in one of the long-gone jazz clubs there. When they embrace at the end of the poem, this sense of shared history allows the speaker to imagine them as "old friends, / long lost brothers in arms / or refugees of this sad city, / counting all that's left behind" (65).

If this ending feels idealistic, elsewhere Meisel seems less hopeful about the potential for racial reconciliation in Detroit. "Our Common Souls" links the city's racial divide with economic struggle and violence through the physical and social environment. The poem juxtaposes a celebratory picnic at a storefront urban church with the house across the street, "blackened by arson, and gutted / down to floor planks and sooty half-walls." While the white speaker describes being "fed and welcomed and tended to / by black folks as sunny as this May light" (61), he also recognizes the depth of the divide in the pastor's comments that the city is split "from both this side and that; and you're cut in two halves, / like that burned house across from us." The divisions are also internal, the pastor suggests: you "never get right" with "the street you and your people were born / on" (62). The divide between people, these lines suggest, parallels the split between past and present, and neither can be fully separated or fully bridged. Meisel presents the racial divide even more starkly in "Elegy for Whatever Isn't Right," which juxtaposes the rise of the auto industry with the boredom, frustration, and violence of a group of contemporary teenage African American boys, "boys with nothing better to do. / Nothing greater to believe in," positioning both narratives in the context of Detroit's landscape. The landscape where the boys now fight with each other was once full of "iron manufacturers, gear shops, markets, / transmission shops, iron works, cigar stores and dime stores" (77), but that productive, industrial version of Detroit means nothing to these boys, "because it seemed / like ancient history" (75). Their landscape holds "the wreckage of an old house banged empty" alongside small, struggling storefront businesses, "everything, all of it . . . smoke / now and the ruined pieces of a city, all formed the puzzle / pieces of a road map, a collection of stories being sold off" (76). In both poems, Meisel uses the past and present landscapes of Detroit to position the city's racial divisions within its economic history.

Unlike most of deindustrialization fiction, which addresses societal concerns through individual perspectives, Meisel puts the focus on a larger narrative about Detroit as a place. Still, like deindustrialization literature generally, although these poems suggest broader economic and political dynamics, they do not overtly reference the broader context of globalization and neoliberalism. Like Meisel, Mark Nowak situates his documentary poems on a social level, revealing personal responses but focusing his attention on how deindustrialization affects communities, but he also references broader social conflicts. In his 2004 collection, *Shut Up Shut Down*, Nowak connects individual stories and specific, localized landscapes with explicit references to more global economic change and conflict. The book presents five sequences of poems reflecting working-class history, including several that examine the experience and effects of plant closings. The last section, "Hoyt Lakes/Shut Down," clearly locates its narrative in a specific place, an emphasis that is highlighted by accompanying but not directly referenced photographs, yet Nowak also suggests, at least briefly, that the local experience is part of a broader national pattern with global implications.

Although the photographs suggest specific locations, with images of closed industrial sites, locked gates and doors, and abandoned storefronts, the poems are not so much about the landscape as about what happened in these places and the losses that the scenes in the photographs represent. Each poem in this sequence has five sections, one quoting a news story about the shutdown, often featuring a quote from a laid-off worker or family member, followed by a section that seems to be an excerpt from an oral history interview and another more fragmentary, emotion- or sense-based response.[7] A few blank lines down, an epigrammatic line also responds to the story, and at the bottom of each page, we see a text box, with the name of a section of the mill and the number of people who lost their jobs. For example, the first poem in the sequence, "05.25.2000," appears alongside a black and white photograph of a sign indicating that the "main gate" for LTV Steel is "straight ahead." Behind the sign, we see several electricity poles and a few trees but also what appears to be a largely empty landscape of fields that are partially covered by snow. The poem begins with a quote from a news story reporting that "The shutdown will mark the first closing of one of the Iron Range's behemoth taconite plants since the 1980s." The middle section, in bold type, is a first-person description of someone's response to hearing that news: **"My stomach dropped to the floor. It was like my stomach was hit by a 10-ton brick."** In the third paragraph, the poem moves from the event and immediate response to a wider perspective that discursively locates the closing factory both spatially and temporally. The speaker lists work sites that have been affected by shutdowns over time: "*The factory of my father [reduced to rubble]. Factory [after factory (shut down)]. Seventeen stories. The blast furnace of my grandfather. The slaughterhouse across from the railroad [terminal] where my father's aunt used to work. Seventeen stories, and every single window shattered [shut up].*" This section invokes what we cannot see in the photo: the mammoth structures that made up the mills and factories; buildings that seemed too big to disappear; and the relationships, memories, and family economy connected with those sites. These lines also reinforce the point made in the opening section of the poem, that the Hoyt Lakes shutdown is a repetition of a familiar pattern, which is again represented in the epigram for this page: "workers / words / worth / [repeating]." By developing the narrative of what happened in this place across the dozen poems in the sequence, "Hoyt Lakes/Shut Down" defines the experience of the mill closing as at once communal and personal, deeply rooted in a particular place and its people.

At the same time, the sequence complicates this sense of locality by incorporating references to the opening of a Walmart store, a move that allows Nowak to connect the local story explicitly with economic changes happening across the United States and globally. In "02.27.2001–02.28.2001," Nowak quotes Sam Walton, founder of Walmart, promising that his company would "lower the cost of living for everyone" (151). Beneath the quote, Nowak inserts images of ads from local fast-food franchises that welcome Walmart to Hibbing, followed by a paragraph about members of a United Food and Commercial Workers local picketing at the opening. These references connect the Hoyt Lakes shutdown to broader economic patterns, and the poem links the specific local experience with the familiarity and repetition of shutdowns. The Hoyt Lakes closing is occurring in a specific place, where residents and workers see not only the locked gates and boarded-up doorways of the present but also the blast furnaces and packing plants of their parents and grandparents, but this specific shutdown is being repeated in multiple places and reflects a global economic change, as Walton signals in his statement that his company will show the entire world "what it's like to save and have a better lifestyle" (151). This link between the local and the global, appearing in the middle of a sequence focused on a specific site, highlights a tension within deindustrialization literature. Although place and landscape are often represented as if they were unique to particular locations, they are also, always, reflective of broader patterns.

While Nowak's work is unusual in connecting the local explicitly with the global, the personal and local narratives of deindustrialization literature reflect global economic, social, and political conflicts. While characters wrestle with their immediate circumstances—making sense of their lives, figuring out how to survive in a struggling city, navigating family relationships—they are also embedded in both the deteriorating landscape that embodies the half-life of deindustrialization and the more distant and less concrete neoliberal ideologies that contributed to deindustrialization and that exacerbate its social costs. At the same time, deindustrialization literature represents the half-life as a matter of lived experience, within particular landscapes and places. By locating narratives about economic conflict in local landscapes and social memory, these writers and filmmakers insist that the political is deeply personal and the global plays out locally.

The Lived Landscape

The stories, films, poems, and essays examined in this chapter represent the deindustrialized landscape as the material product of the half-life but also as productive, evocative spaces within which characters develop and conflicts are revealed if not resolved. They complement the many visual representations of the deindustrialized landscape, filling in the seemingly empty, abandoned spaces with stories that reimagine the ruins not as objects for observation but, to use Alice Mah's phrasing, as "forms and processes . . . experienced by people," including those who "identify them as home" (9). But they do more than populate the deindustrialized landscape. They also treat that landscape as a rich, multilayered, and dynamic setting that, as Mah suggests, reveals relationships "between forms and processes, between the spatial and the temporal, and between social, historical, economic, cultural, and urban dynamics" (133). Abandoned factories, deteriorating buildings, even seemingly empty lots where (sometimes pretty) weeds hide the remnants and detritus of the past result from economic restructuring and neoliberal politics, but they also shape how people see themselves, their communities, and the larger social and political forces that affect them. By telling stories about those who live amid the ruins, deindustrialization literature reveals these multiple dimensions.

Like the visual images of "ruin porn," these narratives reflect the "anxiety of decline" that, Apel suggests, many feel in the early twenty-first century (5). Like Apel, Tim Edensor and Tim Strangleman both read images of industrial ruins not only as evidence of decline but also as potential sources for critique. In part because its narratives offer more personal, intimate views of the deindustrialized landscape, the literature of the half-life creates a space for critique based on how economic restructuring and neoliberalism have affected ordinary people in their everyday lives. Where visual images often emphasize the contradictions of capitalism writ large, as in the grand, rubble-filled empty space of the old Michigan Central Terminal or the dramatically crumbling remains of the Packard plant, these narratives show us the outlines of old family photos on the walls of abandoned houses, the tools and scaffolds being used to renovate an old church, and the connection between a locked gate and an ad for a new Walmart. Even more important, they show us all of this through the eyes of individuals, people who are living with the effects of economic restructuring. In their stories, we see the landscape of the half-life, in all its beauty and with all its conflict.

FOUR

Rust Belt Chic

Reclaiming Working-Class Culture

Rust Belt chic sounds like an oxymoron. How could struggling midwestern cities known for long-term economic problems, deteriorating infrastructures, high crime rates, abandoned factories, and boarded-up shops possibly be chic? Nonetheless, writers from places like Cleveland, Buffalo, and Youngstown have embraced the idea, producing blogs, essays, fiction, poems, and memoirs that challenge long-standing images of the deindustrialized city as a place of failure and boredom. Where outsiders see civic dysfunction and dramatic deterioration, these writers see creative potential rooted in appreciation for local history, the resilience of communities that have survived decades of decline, the creative and economic potential of abandoned buildings, and the values of working-class culture. Richey Piiparinen, a cofounder of Belt Publishing, producer of *Belt Magazine* and a series of anthologies of writing about deindustrialized cities, describes Rust Belt chic as a funky mix of historic and hip:

> Rust Belt Chic is churches and work plants hugging the same block. It is ethnic as hell. It is the Detroit sound of Motown. It is Cleveland punk. It is getting vintage t-shirts and vinyl for a buck that are being sold to Brooklynites for the price of a Manhattan meal. It is babushka and snakeskin boots. It is babushka in snakeskin boots. It is wear: old wood and steel and vacancy. It is contradiction, conflict, and standing resiliency. But most centrally: Rust Belt Chic is about home, or that perpetual inner fire of longing to be comfortable in one's own

skin and one's community. Yet this longing is less about regressing to the past than it is finding a future through your history. ("Rust Belt Chic")

As Piiparinen's description suggests, Rust Belt chic is an attitude but also a lifestyle. It envisions a future that builds intentionally and appreciatively on the material and cultural remains of the past. Like the deindustrialized landscape, Rust Belt chic is a product of the half-life, but, like all deindustrialization literature, it is also a response to the long-term effects of economic restructuring. Rust Belt chic resists the "deep mourning" of nostalgia and instead exemplifies the "play that points to the future" that Svetlana Boym argues makes "reflective nostalgia" productive (55). As an alternative perspective on the continuing influence of deindustrialization, Rust Belt chic intervenes in the civic culture of the half-life.

Rust Belt chic is also a body of writing, a subset of deindustrialization literature. Through commentary and narrative, produced by journalists and creative writers but also urban planners and local activists, Rust Belt chic advocates for the value of the industrial and deindustrial past as a cultural legacy and a basis for personal and civic reinvention. It is a cultural version of what some have called adaptive resilience, staking a claim to the potential of the half-life despite, and often because of, its challenges.[1] Through their writing, the mostly middle-class white contributors to the Rust Belt chic also reclaim, reimagine, but also appropriate working-class culture.

Rust Belt chic is rife with contradictions. It is at once idealistic and cynical, nostalgic and strategic. In its reclamation, or some might say recuperation, of "Rust Belt" as a positive identification, these writers defend their cities from denigration and dismissal, even as they often idealize both the past and the potential for improvement. In embracing the hard work, toughness, and belonging of industrial culture and the persistence and loyalty of those who stayed in these cities even as they declined, Rust Belt chic embraces but also reinvents working-class identity. However, the working-class culture imagined by these mostly white middle-class writers too often downplays the conflicts of the past and largely ignores the struggles of working-class people in the present. It also reinforces racial divisions. The contradictions of Rust Belt chic become especially clear in the genre's claims to authenticity, a concept that, as Sharon Zukin has argued, is inherently problematic both in its definition and in its uses. While many of its contributors and readers find solace in Rust Belt chic, a critical analysis reveals a conflicted mix of productive engagement with the past and a problematic idealism based on a selective and romantic view of working-class struggle.

Defining the Genre

As a literary genre, Rust Belt chic takes several forms that roughly parallel its history. It first emerged in blogs, where journalists, planners, activists, and others posted their own writing, photographs, and sometimes videos. Geographer Jim Russell credits John Slanina's *I Will Shout Youngstown* blog, which started in 2006 and ran until 2014, as the first example of Rust Belt chic, though the themes can be traced back to Detroit artist Lowell Boileau's "Fabulous Ruins of Detroit," begun in the mid-1990s. Although "Fabulous Ruins" might be seen as an early example of "ruin porn," and Boileau has since appeared as a local tour guide to the ruins in several documentaries, his website was also a social art project that combined photos of abandoned and decaying buildings with writing about their place in Detroit's history and opportunities for readers to add their comments and stories. "Fabulous Ruins" includes one of the first Rust Belt online discussion boards, and Boileau also organized face-to-face meetings where regular readers traded stories and advocated for the preservation of significant sites. A decade later, Slanina, a policy analyst and engineer, also posted images of decaying buildings, but his site also included profiles of local activists, reports on urban redevelopment efforts from cities around the world, stories about local community groups, and responses to media coverage of Youngstown. Like Boileau, Slanina did not limit his efforts to his online presence. His blog was just one element of a larger practice of civic engagement. In the mid-2000s, he organized regular "thinkers and drinkers" gatherings where locals discussed ideas for revitalizing the city over beer in a downtown bar. He was also a driving force behind the formation of a west side neighborhood association and the creation of Simply Slavic, an annual downtown festival. For Slanina, *I Will Shout Youngstown* provided a forum for reflecting on but also advocating for his vision of Youngstown's potential, one that he often tied to the city's industrial, working-class, and ethnic past.

Slanina was not alone. Other young professionals across the Rust Belt, mostly white college-educated men, were creating blogs about other cities, documenting and commenting on the relationship between local history and economic development. By 2007, a network of Rust Belt bloggers began to meet face-to-face and post links to each other's sites. By 2009, journalists Angie Schmitt and Kate Giammarise had created

Rustwire, which republished online reports from a dozen cities in an effort to "consolidate thoughtful, constructive stories about post-industrial cities across the Rust Belt." It organized stories under the headings of "economic development," "good ideas," "green jobs," and "real estate," maintaining a strong focus on strategies for revitalizing the Rust Belt. In its earliest forms, then, Rust Belt chic writing was both journalistic and personal, combining news reports with commentary and reflection. Some of its producers identified as reporters, while others were advocates and interpreters. Few would have described their work as literary.

The genre became more of a hybrid of journalism and literature as it expanded, however, as memoirists, essayists, fiction writers, graphic storytellers, and poets began to contribute to online and print publications. That expansion was nurtured by Belt Publishing, created by Piiparinen and Anne Trubek, a writing professor at Oberlin College near Cleveland, in 2012. Their first book, *Rust Belt Chic: A Cleveland Anthology*, collected personal essays highlighting the qualities the contributors value in their often-ridiculed and long-struggling city. A year later, Piiparinen and Trubek started *Belt Magazine*, a website featuring essays, news stories, and interviews about cities across the Rust Belt, as well as some videos and photo essays. *Belt Magazine* drew national attention as the *New York Times*, the *Columbia Journalism Review*, and *American Prospect* published stories about its approach. By 2016, Belt Publishing had produced local collections on Buffalo, Cincinnati, Detroit, Flint, Pittsburgh, and Youngstown, with anthologies of writing about Akron and Chicago in the works. The Belt Publishing website describes these books as gathering community stories "by professional authors, college students, or public servants. The essays, photographs, and poems that comprise the final product are impassioned, emotional, visceral tales of individual lives lived in places that have been too often overlooked, stereotyped and misrepresented elsewhere." The online magazine and the print anthologies feed each other, as essays from the collections often appear on the website and pieces that began on the website are reprinted in the books. Belt is not the only publisher of regional and local anthologies, though. In 2013, for example, The Head and The Hand Press in Philadelphia published the *Rust Belt Rising Almanac*, which, the press's promotional description promises, offers "escapes, remains, and models of growth" in the form of stories, poems, and images. Local organizations have also published collections, such as *Eddie Loves Debbie*, a collection of stories, poems, essays, and photographs from both established writers and students associated with the Northeastern Ohio MFA program based at Youngstown State University.

Across these volumes, Rust Belt chic emphasizes personal essays, but it has expanded to include a range of forms, so that a short story often appears beside a reflective essay or an interview. Rust Belt chic takes multiple forms, and like deindustrialization literature more generally, it is defined by a shared theme rather than common elements of form.

Several journalists from the region have also published books that combine memoir with history and reporting, and while they may not view their work as part of Rust Belt chic, their books reflect the genre's themes and have been embraced and promoted by *Belt Magazine*. Mark Binelli returned to Detroit, his hometown, after the auto bailout and during an era when the city was the focus of countless news stories and documentaries about its long-term struggles. After writing a cover story for *Rolling Stone*, he lived in the city for a year, writing about his experiences in *Detroit City Is the Place to Be: The Afterlife of an American Metropolis*. Flint native Gordon Young felt pulled back to his hometown after years as a journalist and professor in San Francisco, and in *Teardown: Memoir of a Vanishing City*, he chronicles the city's history and its continuing struggles as well as his own ultimately unrealistic plan to contribute to the community's revitalization by buying and renovating a house there. In *The Hard Way on Purpose*, David Giffels recalls growing up in Akron, Ohio, as the local economy struggled with economic decline in the 1980s, and he reflects on the city's more recent history, including, among other things, its association with local sports teams and figures, especially native son LeBron James. The books complement the anthologies and websites, providing more fully developed and critical histories and sometimes raising questions about the idea of the Rust Belt as chic or cool. They also exemplify the genre's central themes: the intersections of past and present, community and individual, loss and possibility.

Remaking Place

While a sense of place runs through all of deindustrialization literature, in Rust Belt chic it is the dominant concern. In telling stories about the history, culture, and material conditions of Rust Belt cities, these writers engage in cultural place making or, perhaps more accurately, remaking. Rust Belt chic overtly articulates the character of deindustrialized cities and advocates for greater appreciation of their unique cultures among both locals and outsiders (though the qualities these writers identify are remarkably consistent across different locales, as we will see). Indeed, Rust Belt chic can be read as an effort to redefine the identities of Rust

Belt communities in response both to the disruption of deindustrialization itself and to largely negative representations of the region that appeared over subsequent decades, many of which focus on its failure to bounce back. As Giffels writes about Akron, these communities were "stripped" of their identities "by virtue of swift and profound industrial collapse." That economic loss also brought a deeper, more cultural displacement, he suggests: "We were something, we were Known [sic], like Firestone, and then, in a few years, we found ourselves with no idea of who we were or what was to become of us" (67). That uncertainty, together with economic decline, enabled media reports to redefine these cities as sites of failure and shame, though some reports exaggerated claims of recovery, creating new but contradictory identities for Rust Belt communities. As John Russo and I argued in 2003, the media have used deindustrialized cities to tell stories about economic restructuring, urban decline, and both the resilience and the failures of contemporary cities. Places like Cleveland, Youngstown, and Pittsburgh have appeared on lists of both the best and the worst places to live, to raise a family, or to start a business. Detroit, especially, has become a popular backdrop for apocalyptic films. From news stories about why industrial workers are wary of going on strike to reports on the promise of urban agriculture, from ads that associate blue jeans with the industrial history and deindustrial struggles of Braddock to coffee-table books with beautiful but depopulated images of Detroit's iconic ruins, deindustrialized cities have been objects of fascination, examples for analysis of what has gone wrong with the U.S. economy or with working-class culture, and evidence of both the intractability and the manageability of various social and economic problems.

Rust Belt chic rejects these external narratives, insisting that locals understand these places better than outsiders—including the contradictions at work in their cities and their region. As Giffels writes, many in the Rust Belt "have a perpetual reflex of self-explanation, a desperation of identity, an instinctive yearning toward legitimacy and a kind of pride that is a far piece from Chamber of Commerce jingoism" (12). Rust Belt chic rejects outsider narratives even when they focus on the cultural wealth of these communities. For example, Trubek, the editor of *Belt Magazine*, criticizes pieces like Alec MacGillis's 2013 *Slate* story about Baltimore, "The Rust Belt Theory of Low-Cost High Culture," which, she argues, "position those living in the Rust Belt as the simple locals . . . and the Rust Belt a new territory to be 'discovered.'" She defines such narratives as "post-colonial" because they emphasize the economic opportunities of deindustrialized cities, "the hint of profit down the line" as "coastal elites trek off to exploit the cheap charms of the Rust Belt." Of course, contributors to and leaders of Rust Belt chic sometimes deploy these tropes themselves in essays that emphasize the economic or cultural potential of these cities. The difference is not necessarily the representation of these places as cool or as culturally engaged but rather who has the right to make such claims.

The tension between insider and outsider views of the Rust Belt can be traced back to the origin of the term—a 1995 WNYC radio interview with Harvey Pekar, whose *American Splendor* comics captured the decline of Cleveland in the 1970s and 1980s, and his wife, Joyce Brabner. When interviewer David Garland asked about the relationship between New York and Cleveland, Brabner responded with disdain that Cleveland is where "all those anorexic vampires with their little black miniskirts and their black leather jackets" come with "video cameras to document Rust Belt chic" (51). They come looking for photos of "Harvey emptying the garbage" (51) or "footage of us going bowling. But we don't go bowling, we go to the library, but they don't want to shoot that" (52). This origin story dismisses Rust Belt chic as the invention of misguided outsiders, while the term's reclamation a decade later reflects a regional habit of resisting but also appropriating external narratives. Rust Belt chic has claimed ownership of the local narrative, insisting that the problem with outsider stories is not accuracy. It is that the observers are not locals. Even when outsiders "get it exactly right," Giffels acknowledges, "I don't want them to interpret me" (239). Detroit blogger Jim Griffoein puts it more explicitly: "We're not gonna let New York City reporters come here and define us!" (quoted in Binelli 281).

Along with articulating insider perspectives and claiming ownership of local stories, Rust Belt chic often explicitly addresses local readers. It thus goes beyond describing these communities to actively striving to construct or recuperate a sense of place. As Anna Clark writes in the introduction to *A Detroit Anthology*, "much is written about our city these hard days," but "it is typically oriented to those who are not from here." The anthology offers "a collection of Detroit stories for Detroiters. . . . These are stories addressed to the rhetorical 'you'" (9). Jacqueline Marino and Will Miller similarly identify local readers as the audience of the volume they edited about Youngstown. They argue that sharing local stories can "help those of us who consider ourselves part of Youngstown nation understand our past, so we can move thoughtfully into our futures" (9). In framing their collections as offering local readers new ways of understanding and connecting with their cities, these editors suggest that Rust Belt chic both defends deindustrialized communities from outsider misrepresentation and contributes to local solidarity and agency.

This investment in place is rooted in personal and community history. In essays in the anthologies and in book-length memoirs, especially, writers often share personal memories—riding a particular bus line to and from school, a grandmother's garden, a grandfather's hardware store, street corner kickball games. Some also reinterpret their own memories, implicitly inviting readers to recognize the value in ideas about these cities that they, like the writers, once rejected. For example, Marino recalls that as a child she didn't like visiting her grandparents, but looking back, she not only recalls the warmth and pleasure of being in their kitchen, but she also understands that her grandparents offered a model of a "loving, happy, and gender-equal" place. That, in turn, helps her recognize that Youngstown was not only a city troubled by "steel, corruption, racial and class division and, most distinctively, the weight of others' condemnation" (2015, 90), but also a place with many "oases" that were "not recorded or celebrated" (95). In her essay, Marino demonstrates the potential power of reinterpreting the meaning of place. For local audiences, she seems to suggest, reconsidering the history of a place can help residents to rethink their connection with it and balance the negative or oversimplified views of outsiders.

Although these personal and local stories often focus on the particular people, neighborhoods, music, restaurants, or stores that, the writers suggest, define each of these cities, they are also generic, with similar motifs emerging in tales set in different places. Each specific reference, like each city, has meaning for its long-time residents, yet all are described in terms of social networks and personal ties to local history. We see this combination of specificity and commonality in writing about food, a common place-making theme. Memories of specific local foods assert the uniqueness of each of these cities, yet all reflect the influence of local ethnic groups and the centrality of food to a sense of place. Clare Malone remembers Geraci's pizza and Presti's doughnuts in Cleveland's Little Italy. Nikki Trautman Baszynski opens her essay in the Youngstown anthology with a short list of local staples: "Wedding soup. Brier Hill pizza. Monkey salad" (79), and she traces her family's connections with local foods and a well-known local restaurant, including the pepperoni roll her grandmother would "tuck" into her bag whenever she came home to visit. As these personal references suggest, Rust Belt chic locates the source of community identity in the past, in everyday life, but also, crucially, in the sense of connection to other people that defines place.

Personal memories of families, neighborhoods, shops, bars, and amusement parks define these places, but industrial history underlies all of those stories. As Binelli, Giffels, and Young suggest in their memoirs, we cannot understand the culture of these places without knowing something about the history of the industries that shaped them and about how the communities were affected by the downsizing of those industries. Each of these memoirs traces the history of its city's relationship with the auto industry, which attracted workers to the area and exerted a strong influence on the patterns and relationships of workers' lives—where they lived, the rhythms of their days, the sense of belonging that workers felt. The shorter pieces in the anthologies and online also reference history, though usually with a narrower focus. For example, Diane DiPiero links industrial labor with Rust Belt culture in a short piece about her grandfather, a steelworker at the largest mill of Youngstown Sheet and Tube in Campbell.[2] According to DiPiero, her grandfather's "salt-of-the-earth disposition and a get-it-done attitude" not only "made it tolerable to work in the sweltering blast furnaces of the steel mills. They also produced a culture of people who spoke plainly but passionately about everything from national politics to neighborhood disputes" (82–83). In Rust Belt chic, writers use such memories of industrial labor to articulate the qualities of local culture.

The legacy of industrial work remains central to Rust Belt identity, in part because it is visible in the landscape and available as memory—often as inherited memory, based in family stories and old photographs. When the narrator of William R. Soldan's short story "Sad Beauty" visits a long-abandoned steel mill, he recalls "the pictures I've seen of this place, back when it was the place to be." Based on this second-hand knowledge, he imagines scenes from

> before my time: vats of liquid fire, blast furnaces, massive hearths lighting up the night. Men in sooty clothes, bustling back and forth, their grimy skin thick with sweat; some merely silhouettes, outlines against the raging flames. Sounds—the chugging, hissing, clanking of creation—soon join the images, and as this prosperous inferno blazes through my occipital lobe, illuminating my brain, my body can almost feel the heat. (64)

While Soldan suggests the persistence of sensual memory—even memories from a previous generation—as an element of place, other writers, like Giffels, emphasize cultural inheritance, a set of ideas and attitudes based in industrial labor that continue to define these cities long after the plants closed. Giffels points out that he is "of the first generation that never saw" Akron when it was a fully active factory town (23), yet his view of his hometown is nonetheless shaped by its industrial past. "Factory towns, places that make things, are defined by work," he writes (13). The experience of "making things" generates a tough, can-do spirit. Factory work "insinuates into the pores the same way soot once did. Here, uniquely, we do things the hard way on purpose. We recognize a virtue and a necessary creativity in choosing to do things that way" (13). By using present tense, Giffels suggests that long after most factory work disappeared from Akron, the community retains its cultural legacy.

For the writers of Rust Belt chic, however, deindustrialization is also central to that cultural legacy. Plant closings and the decline of these cities are as important as industrial history in forming Rust Belt culture, and Rust Belt chic takes pride in the grit and resilience of people and communities that persisted through decades of economic struggle. Rust Belt chic acknowledges that the loss of industry left workers without jobs and incomes and undermined the cities' ability to maintain public services, contain crime, or support deteriorating neighborhoods. But these writers, many of them the children or grandchildren of workers who were displaced by deindustrialization, also remember finding opportunities for pleasure that fostered an attitude of defiance and toughness. Several writers recall local music scenes that flourished despite of, and often in response to, their cities' economic struggles. Elaine Arvan Andrews remembers downtown Youngstown in the 1990s as "a destination for blue-collar bohemia" (31), which fostered "a fierce pride in my hometown, which, at the time, was well over a decade in fallout from Black Monday 1977" (29). Denise Grollmus remembers lying to her mother in order to make the trek to an underground Cleveland indie club, Speak in Tongues, located in "a dangerous neighborhood, where, more than once during a show, there was a shooting or break in a few doors down" (104–5). For these writers, the deteriorating and contested physical spaces of their cities offered creative potential. In decaying, abandoned old buildings, musicians and artists translated the experiences of loss and struggle into cultural expressions, and their fans reveled in opportunities to enact their own versions of grit and identification.

As these stories suggest, Rust Belt writers often define their individual identities through the character of their cities, linking their own claims to resilience and toughness to the struggles of their hometowns so that the articulation of place identities overlaps with claims about localized cultural identity. Writers from across the Rust Belt describe the people of their communities and sometimes themselves in terms that echo themes used to define place. For example, in an essay addressed to Pete Rose, the Cincinnati Reds baseball player and manager who was barred from the sport because of gambling, Jack Heffron identifies Rose as a "living metaphor for your hometown" because "you did far better with less talent than most of your opponents." This reflects the local character, Heffron writes, noting that it is "the Cincinnati way" to compensate for "what we lack in size and speed and pedigree" with "hard work and determination" (144). Rose also represents the community's need to find something to feel good about. Cincinnati fans could not help but "forgive" him, Heffron writes, "because we need you. When you were a winner, we were too. Nobody before or since made us feel quite so good about ourselves" (145). Heffron's characterization of community culture mixes negative and positive traits—a sense that the city "lacks" qualities that would help it succeed but that both the city and Rose made up for these gaps by working hard.

A number of writers deploy this kind of redefinition, noting how problematic qualities of their cities provide a basis for a positive cultural identity. Young describes the "perverse pride" he takes in stories about crime in Flint and the "exuberant recklessness" of the local character (44). In the Detroit and Youngstown anthologies, several writers reflect a similar contradictory pride in their community's well-known criminal patterns—Detroit's fires and Youngstown's history of mob violence, including the car bombs referenced in the Youngstown anthology's title, *From Car Bombs to Cookie Tables*. Sports and crime come together in a piece by former Ohio State football star and ex-convict Maurice Clarett, who defines himself as the "epitome of Youngstown." He has "fulfilled every good and bad stereotype of the city: raised in the hood. Local football star. National football champion. Convicted felon. Entrepreneur. Advocate for social change. I reflect Youngstown—the city I love. I've made mistakes. More than my fair share. But I strive to be a good individual" (184). Clarett claims that this mix of success and self-inflicted failure makes him, like his hometown, "too complex to be judged in broad strokes." Youngstown, he claims, is "more than its gangster history or steel folklore. It's a city where your word still matters and character means something" (186), but he is also identifying himself as someone whose life reflects both the struggles of his community and the strengths gained through the process of overcoming those struggles. Defining local culture through the examples of people who made mistakes but also worked hard emphasizes the toughness and resilience of the Rust Belt and its people. People in this region are resilient, these narratives suggest, because they have grown up in struggling communities, and they appreciate even failed efforts to make things better. As Youngstown pastor Nate Ortiz puts it, "I work hard, and I don't quit. Youngstown's the same way. That spirit lets people born here know they can rise above tough circumstances no matter where they are" (172). Rust Belt chic traces that sense of struggle and toughness to both the hard work of industrial labor and the losses of deindustrialization. Giffels suggests that an appreciation for difficulty and loss is part of his cultural inheritance as an Akron native; reclaiming the ruins of that city reflects a determined, hard-working "Calvinist instinct adapted into the genetic code by way of the repetition of a three-shift factory town" (17).

This version of Rust Belt culture has its roots in working-class culture, which also values connecting with family and good neighbors, working hard, persisting through difficulty, taking pride in resilience, but also maintaining—and even embracing—low expectations. These qualities reflect not only the industrial era of working-class history but also the loss and persistence of deindustrialization. Della Rucker argues that "the elder children of the rust belt," the generation who watched closings disrupt their parents' lives and who grew up in the first decade of deindustrialization, developed a worldview that expects uncertainty and distrusts both the American Dream as a concept and social institutions, which proved unable to help struggling families. Rust Belt identity involves a sense of belonging to a particular cultural group but also the low expectations of people who have experienced significant losses. As these qualities suggest, Rust Belt identity is inextricably linked with working-class culture, even though these writers rarely use the phrase "working class."

Creativity and Commerce: Rust Belt Aesthetics and Marketing

Rust Belt chic redefines the loss and struggle of the half-life as an opportunity, not only as a matter of local and individual character but as a resource for creativity. These writers see creative potential in the combination of industrial working-class culture, including not only the memory of old factories and neighborhoods but also the material detritus left behind, and a present-day landscape of unoccupied, affordable, and inspirational spaces. In recalling how he and his friends viewed the abandoned buildings of downtown Akron when he was a teenager,

Giffels writes that they were aware of both the "recently departed humanity" in the old buildings they explored and the potential these unused spaces represented: "fifty-two places we could get cheap. We could start a magazine, make documentaries, build a sculpture garden. // It was all possibility" (159). The buildings and storefronts had lost their identities as banks or shops or factories, which allowed Giffels and his friends to reclaim and redefine them: "They were exclusively ours because they had lost their exclusivity. In many ways, within the central city, we felt like the luckiest generation ever to have lived here. Everything was left to us and was ours to reinvent" (155–56). In describing the economically devastated landscape of his hometown as a resource for creative work and the property of his generation, Giffels connects the idea that deindustrialized cities provide the conditions for experimentation and play with the feeling of belonging to a place. As he puts it, "consciously choosing" to claim these abandoned sites "seemed like a membership" (150). For Giffels and others, economic displacement can be transformed into creative opportunity, and that, in turn, enables a new sense of place identity, based in industrial and deindustrial history and in postindustrial potential.

In articulating deindustrialized cities as places of creative reclamation of the industrial and deindustrial past, Rust Belt chic embraces the liminality of the half-life. These writers do not long to return to or reconstruct past conditions; they want to adapt the values and culture of the past as resources for responding to the challenges of the present. They acknowledge loss, but they also find inspiration in deterioration and persistence. Further, they define deindustrialized places as sites of potential in part because they are available to be reclaimed and reimagined. As Giffels writes, the "void" of "empty buildings and the general diaspora of people my age, . . . who'd hightailed it to more promising lands, . . . felt like something to be filled. And it felt as if it were exclusively my own" (24). This passage reflects Giffels's awareness of three distinct but interrelated elements: the loss of people but also of economic opportunity; the potential uses of abandoned spaces; and his own sense of ownership of place, which is possible only because of the losses that left these buildings empty.

In writing about the creative endeavors emerging in deindustrialized cities, Rust Belt chic highlights the development of a Rust Belt aesthetic. Not only have artists created studios, galleries, or creative businesses in abandoned buildings, but they have also repurposed the remnants of industry into artistic expression, as we see in films and photographs that capture the evocative beauty of industrial ruins. Binelli describes a number of such projects, including the work of his neighbors, Steve and Dorota Coy, who moved to Detroit and made the city the canvas and backdrop for their "Hygienic Dress League" art project, which features photographic and video images of them and their friends wearing gas masks and carrying machine guns (36).[3] He also discusses the more home-grown Heidelberg Project, Tyree Guyton's ongoing work that transforms a block of abandoned houses into an art installation, and a film and performance art piece by Matthew Barney that was staged at various sites around Detroit and included a fake assembly line where artists posing as factory workers made viols out of junk. While some tout the economic promise of such efforts, Binelli is skeptical, noting that "any potential Detroit arts renaissance" is "more about real estate opportunities and the romantic vision of a crumbling heartland Berlin—basically, vicarious wish fulfillment by coastal arts types living in long-gentrified cities" (265).[4] Artistic representations of deindustrialized cities can be exploitative at worst, especially when created by outsiders who, like Barney, treat the city as an exotic backdrop. In a passage that reflects ambivalence about the idea of a Rust Belt aesthetic, Giffels comments that "*postindustrial* is a rangy and encompassing and provocative adjective" that describes "a genre of music, a manner of dress, a style of art, a sociological term, a well-worn neologism, the end of the American century, an entire lifestyle" (23). While the idea that the region has its own aesthetic inspires some of these writers and generates skepticism in others, many have embraced the broader notion that the deteriorating and affordable built environment of deindustrialized cities can foster creativity and innovation.

As Binelli's skepticism about the economic and social impact of arts projects in Detroit suggests, Rust Belt chic at once contributes to and documents but also critiques efforts to revitalize deindustrialized cities. No doubt, Rust Belt chic has a strong element of boosterism and optimism. The Youngstown anthology illustrates this emphasis on hope in its structure. It opens with a section subtitled "Loss," but its final section, entitled "Rise," features essays that emphasize the promise of the city. Former mayor Jay Williams writes about the city's much-lauded 2010 Plan, the first public statement out of any American city focused on planning for shrinkage rather than growth. Local activist Phil Kidd, who came to Youngstown in part because he was inspired by the 2010 Plan, encourages area residents to "acknowledge the past" but also to "Be realistic about the challenges of the present. Get informed and involved if you want to change the trajectory of the future" (159). The Detroit anthology includes articles on the potential of urban agriculture and alternative organizing, including an inspiring if idealistic piece by activists Grace Lee Boggs and Scott Kurashige proclaiming a vision of a "twenty-first century city, a city both rural and urban, which attracts people from all over the world because it understands the fundamental needs of human beings at this stage in our evolution to relate more responsibly to one another and to the Earth" (222). Along with outlining their work on Detroit Summer, a youth-run project that involves both hands-on work and "intergenerational dialogues on how to rebuild Detroit," they describe the "thousands of family gardens, more than two hundred community gardens, and dozens of school gardens" that have been created in the city as evidence of the potential of "living on the margins of the postindustrial capitalist order" (224). These leaders hope to solve the problems facing their cities by capitalizing on the combination of grit and do-it-yourself spirit, inexpensive and historic vacant properties, and the loyalty that long-time residents feel toward their communities. Community organizers like Kidd, Boggs, and Kurashige, especially, represent an idealized vision of the future of deindustrialized cities, yet their sense of the rich potential of these places suggests the inspirational and aspirational vision of Rust Belt chic.

In contrast to this idealism, other contributors explicitly define Rust Belt chic as a marketing tool, an effort to "rebrand" struggling cities to attract new business and engage the local community. Piiparinen, a researcher in the College of Urban Affairs at Cleveland State University, explains that "At its most basic, Rust Belt Chic is about defining the factory coast's culture and aesthetic as a means to attract those longing for a dose of authenticity and usable space. Miami we are not. Buffalo doesn't need to be" ("Rust Belt Chic"). In a commentary on Rust Belt chic on the *Newgeography* blog, Aaron M. Renn, a senior fellow at the Manhattan Institute for Policy Research, describes Rust Belt chic as a "first attempt" by the region to offer its own definition of what a city should be, "rooted in a unique, local history, culture, geography," and this, he suggests, provides "a unique market positioning that's real to the place and has at least some competitive advantage in the marketplace." For these writers, if not for most contributors to the genre, Rust Belt chic is a practice of place making with decidedly commercial aims.

These two approaches are not necessarily antithetical, and Rust Belt chic not only incorporates both but also directly addresses the relationship between them. Community activism and economic development often complement each other. The subtitle of Slanina's *I Will Shout Youngstown* blog is "a forum on economic development and urban design in the city," while his interest in strengthening the city's economy has made him a successful organizer of community projects. Rust Belt chic also includes essays that question the effectiveness of revitalization efforts. Early in the Youngstown anthology, for example, Sarah Sepanek argues that "The Pro-Yo Movement Needs to Get Real." She recalls finding used syringes in the dirt as she helped to build one of the city's first urban gardens:

> Then I remembered that a community garden doesn't mean shit to many people in Youngstown. The transparency of this symbolism bowled me over—a feel-good community project literally covering up a real, underlying epidemic that was eating our town alive. The drug crisis can seem like an insurmountable problem, but ignoring it in favor of pet PR projects wouldn't help. Where was the call for volunteers to start a needle exchange? These peppers and squash can't be better than that for the city. (53)

Although she acknowledges that the neighborhood did improve over time, she also worries that "perception is only half the battle. Some improvements merely play a shell game, repackaging 'problem areas,' especially those close to campus. So one street is a little better. What about the next block? And the next?" (54). Similarly, in *Teardown*, Young examines both "smart shrinkage" and grassroots efforts to clean up neighborhoods, plant community gardens, and mentor young people, and he concludes that neither approach is sufficient. Flint will survive, he tells us, because it has many "tough people fighting . . . in their own ways" (240). We should not, he suggests, expect a triumphant conclusion to the battle. Similarly, in an essay about a visit to Buffalo, Detroit native Bill McGraw reminds readers that, in both cities, many people are still "suffering, unemployed, and have little hope of securing the kind of jobs that will lift them out of poverty. Neither city has anything on the horizon that will fundamentally transform its economy. Neither place is able to provide an adequate education to everyone who needs one." All of this reflects the region's experience with survival rather than recovery and the belief that struggle is a source of strength. As Giffels writes after warning us away from the expectation of a "redemptive ending" to his narrative of Akron, "Redemptive endings are easy, and we're not wired that way" (227).

As these comments show, Rust Belt chic is a basis for boosterism for some, an effort to find hope amid the ruins for others. Equally important, especially given decades of media scrutiny and arguments that deindustrialized communities need to redefine themselves, Rust Belt chic finds inspiration in linking the past and the future. Across the genre, writers define the identities of their cities by referencing their industrial histories and their experiences of loss and decline, but they also add a crucial theme that outsiders often miss: local culture. Rust Belt chic tells stories that highlight the social relations, shared memories, and attitudes that define a sense of place and belonging for local residents. These social and cultural elements of place have their roots in industrial culture but have persisted and adapted through decades of uncertainty and hardship. Rust Belt chic reclaims the cultural legacy of deindustrialized cities, and by addressing local audiences and creating opportunities for people to share their views, these online and print publications suggest that remembering and storytelling can remake these long-struggling places.

The Contradictions of Authenticity

In their use of the past as a source for art and commerce, these texts lay claim to the authenticity of both deindustrialized cities and their residents. Although *Belt Magazine* editor Anne Trubek told a *New York Times* reporter in 2013 that she "cringes" at "words like authentic," she also insists that Rust Belt chic is interested in things that are tangible, local, and real—"boots on the ground and things hidden in grandma's attic" (quoted in Schuessler). Trubek's resistance to the term and embrace of the idea that some things are "real" reflect the problem of authenticity, which is a cultural construct that carries contradictory meanings. As sociologist Sharon Zukin argues, the authenticity of place is a "social product" that, in the context of urban experience, has multiple, often contradictory meanings (17). To claim a place as authentic can be a way of acknowledging and expressing appreciation for its past, which often involves romanticizing past struggles. Authenticity can also be a matter of style or taste, and, Zukin suggests, a group's claim to "the authenticity of its tastes" implies their "moral superiority" (3). Given the tensions inherent in the word *authentic*, it is easy to understand why Trubek would cringe to hear it applied to the Rust Belt, yet Rust Belt chic uses the term in all of these ways—as a statement about the realness of both idealized and more critical local history and as a claim of authority for people defending their right to define their region and its culture.

As some Rust Belt chic writers note, the material conditions of deindustrialized cities embody the idea of authenticity, because the residue of history has not been erased or replaced with newer, apparently more generic buildings or businesses. Old warehouses and downtown storefronts retain links to the past even when they are repurposed as bars, small art galleries, coffee shops, or used bookstores, which provide opportunities for profit along with human interaction. Such businesses foster a sense of place because they are small, unique, and set in sites with specific historic resonance. Giffels contrasts such businesses, which reflect the specificity of place, with national chains, which erase locality: "If the Walden-books self-help aisle in Denver was identical to the one in Milwaukee and identical to the one in Jacksonville, then the idea of being *somewhere* was more like being *anywhere,* which is uncomfortably close to the idea of being *nowhere,* or of *where* being an irrelevant notion altogether" (149). Rust Belt cities are *somewhere* because their unique old places remain, even if many are boarded up. Embedded in this notion is not only a claim about remaking place in deindustrialized cities but also a claim to authenticity. Such businesses represent continuity with local history and resistance to erasure. These are recuperative claims that reframe a city's economic history, including the declines that, over time, become opportunities for redevelopment, as evidence not of weakness but of strength.

The idea of authenticity also reframes engagement with the past not as a simplistic nostalgia but as a productive, positive source of meaning and identity. Like the "urban authenticity" Zukin describes, Rust Belt authenticity becomes a source through which these writers "find their subjective identity" (18). Claiming authenticity valorizes the experience of struggle and appreciation for local history, translating a sense of belonging in a place and the persistence of those who stay in struggling communities into statements of moral authority and civic ownership. Piiparinen incorporates this appreciation for the realness of growing up in a Rust Belt city into his definition of Rust Belt chic. He cites an essay by *New York Times* columnist David Brooks on Bruce Springsteen, in which Brooks describes the benefits of growing up in a "specific place" with "hard boundaries": "you are going to have more depth and definition than you are if you grew up in the far-flung networks of pluralism and eclecticism, surfing from one spot to the next, sampling one style then the next, your identity formed by soft boundaries, or none at all" (quoted in "Anorexic Vampires" 20). For others, authenticity establishes the right to define local culture. In one of many passages in which Giffels defends Akron's authenticity "not because it compares favorably to other cities—places I also love—but because it doesn't," he offers a similarly modest claim for his own authenticity: "if my having never left doesn't at least provide me with some version of authority, then what have I got?" (226–27). Several of the Detroit writers make similar claims, including Shannon Shelton Miller, who draws a distinction between "real" Detroiters and pretenders who claim allegiance but did not fully live in or experience the city. Such statements define authenticity as rooted in persistence and loyalty, which earns long-time residents not just civic pride but a sense of ownership.

Even as these writers insist on the authenticity of their cities and their perspectives, they approach the concept with some irony, acknowledging doubts about its content, form, and basis. Writing about Cleveland, for example, Piiparinen insists on the city's authenticity but also struggles to articulate its central qualities. He writes that "Cleveland is a somewhere and has a something," a statement of specificity phrased in notably vague terms. The language remains abstract as he elaborates on the nature of "this thing": it is "part cultural, part aesthetic, part historical, and part a consequence of having to go on in the face of adversity." In the same passage, Piiparinen acknowledges the mix of commitment and distance involved in Rust Belt chic: "it is part wit, part ironic, part self-deprecating," even as it means being willing to "stand your ground in the defense of where you came from" ("No Reservations Cleveland"). To be at once "real" and ironic seems contradictory, yet it is central to Rust Belt chic. Giffels suggests why in writing about his efforts as a teenager (in the 1980s) to display his authenticity by wearing an old-style bowling shirt: "I recognized something authentic about such a shirt, something tangible and true, and also something circularly ironic, that it was the costume of some other culture than my own that was in fact the culture of which I was made, and to which I now aspired with what I imagined was irony" (89). He and his friends were "teenagers in a city that was fast losing its identity, ourselves just beginning to seek identities of our own. We needed outfits" (91). As in Piiparinen's description of Rust Belt chic in terms of cheap vintage T-shirts and vinyl records or "babushka in snakeskin boots," authenticity here involves style and consumption. At the same time, by casting authenticity as something that can be purchased, these writers acknowledge and even poke fun at the contradictions of their own claims to authenticity. As Chicago-based writer Ben Schulman has argued, when Rust Belt chic is articulated as a source of economic opportunity, it undermines its own claims to authenticity. If Rust Belt culture is up for sale, how authentic can it be?

The commercial value of authenticity can be seen beyond Rust Belt chic in ad campaigns in which major corporations use Rust Belt settings and narratives about the hard work and resilience of working-class communities to promote consumer goods. Chrysler used this trope in its 2011 "Made in Detroit" Superbowl ad, which described Detroit as "a city that's been to hell and back" but that also represents "hard work and conviction, and the know-how that runs generations deep in every last one of us." Similarly, a 2010 Levi's Jeans campaign, "Let's Go Forth to Work," featured the deindustrialized landscape and residents of Braddock, Pennsylvania, with a voiceover of a child describing how "a long time ago, things got broken here. People got sad and left." As the scenes shift to images of young people of color enjoying family interactions, digging gardens, and repairing old buildings, the child suggests that "Maybe the world breaks on purpose so we can have work to do." Where the Chrysler ad foregrounds images of renovated places in Detroit, the Levi's ad emphasizes the deterioration of Braddock, but it redefines the city as a "frontier." Both ads use the authenticity of the Rust Belt, as reflected in images of and claims about how these places embody history, grit, and belonging, to invite consumers to purchase goods that represent these qualities.

If authenticity is part of what makes Rust Belt places attractive, it is also undermined by its own effectiveness. As Zukin writes, the appeal of authenticity is a central theme in gentrification, which in turn usually leads to the erasure of the very conditions that made a place authentic. Zukin traces this shift as it played out in once declining ethnic working-class neighborhoods in Brooklyn and Harlem, where faltering hardware stores are replaced first by small artisanal cheese shops but then by Best Buy or other large chain stores. Gentrification is generally slower and less dramatic in places like Flint or Youngstown, where even the most modest transition from abandoned office building to hip lofts can seem like a stretch.[5] But even small-scale gentrification changes not only the economic and physical landscape but also the mix of people who live, work, or hang out in a neighborhood, and that in turn changes the cultural character of a place. If the very conditions that define deindustrialized cities as authentic—the availability and low cost of a historic but dilapidated built environment, the social memory of strong and hard-working communities, the lived experience of long-term economic struggle—make them attractive for new development, this will, in turn, attract more outsiders who share neither personal connections with nor informed appreciation for local history. If Rust Belt cities succeed at attracting entrepreneurs and artists, and if these newcomers succeed in transforming once largely abandoned downtowns and residential neighborhoods into cool places to be, then not only will long-term residents be priced out, but the cultural conditions that define Detroit or Cleveland or Pittsburgh as authentically Rust Belt could be lost.

Rust Belt chic's claims to authenticity are also undermined by its partial but unnamed appropriation of working-class culture. Rust Belt chic is a primarily middle-class genre. Most of these writers have college educations, often including graduate degrees, and while their economic positions vary, and quite a few hold professional positions, many are part of what Richard L. Florida has called the "creative class." They include writers, musicians, organizers, teachers, and professors, though often in contingent academic positions. Many grew up in middle-class households, with parents who were also educated and held middle-class jobs. Yet, as their stories suggest, they identify as much with their working-class grandparents as with their middle-class parents. In describing and claiming affiliation with the working-class roots of their communities, these writers reinvent working-class identity, much as white ethnics reclaimed Italian, Irish, and other cultural identities in the 1970s.[6] Some make the comparison explicit, as in Cleveland boomeranger Sean Watterson's comment that "Cleveland-ness is like Polish-ness or Irish-ness. It's an ethnicity" (quoted in Frolick). Rust Belt chic reimagines the working-class identity of previous generations, highlighting belonging and translating struggle into resilience, and links it with the contemporary "creative class" to invent Rust Belt identity. Like white ethnicity, Rust Belt chic takes pride in the economic and social struggles of earlier generations. It is also, like white ethnicity, a way of claiming a productive and meaningful otherness for middle-class white people. In addition, it is also, like Irish or Italian identity, an optional and largely invented concept, based not on the writers' own experiences but on the reconstruction of a place-, race-, and class-based identity, rooted in the past but also redefined in relation to the conditions of the present.

Given the economic uncertainty many younger Americans face in the early twenty-first century, a reinvented working-class identity might well appeal to the middle-class children and grandchildren of industrial workers. It is easy to see how they would be drawn to the kind of working-class history that Giffels describes:

> the working class had for decades been the most stable, most prosperous, most highly regarded local demographic. In Akron, tire builders referred to themselves as the "kings" of the rubber industry, without

irony. They were highly paid, backed by an extraordinarily powerful labor union, and thanks to years and years of hard-nosed contract negotiations, they enjoyed exceptional job security and benefits. In Akron, the working-class families were the ones with the Cadillacs and the vacation homes and the high-end kitchen makeovers. (36–37)

In a period when college graduates struggle to find secure jobs that pay enough to cover high levels of student loan debt, a home mortgage, or other trappings of a middle-class lifestyle, the memory of industrial labor and its loss, the dilapidated but affordable and useable landscape, and discourse about the creative potential of these places and their people all provide inspiration. Rust Belt chic embraces belonging and resilience not only as shared characteristics of the people in deindustrialized communities but also as productive responses to the economic uncertainty of younger freelancers and indebted professionals.

That said, these writers almost never name the working class explicitly as a source of inspiration. Rust Belt chic constructs a hybrid class identity that links working-class family stories and local history with an ethos of preservation, involvement in economic development and urban planning, and creative work, much of it precarious. To adapt Florida's familiar concept, Rust Belt chic imagines a "creative working class" that gains authenticity from its local roots and appreciation for the aesthetic and evocative power of industrial ruins as well as consumer choices like vintage clothing and local beer. Identity is always constructed and performed, of course, and to claim any identity as authentic is problematic. But this is especially true when the claim applies to an identity that so clearly appropriates the history and style of a cultural group that has been displaced and destabilized, like the white working class in the United States.

Read in this way, Rust Belt identity represents a kind of cultural gentrification, and as with the gentrification of old working-class neighborhoods, as Zukin argues, its claims to authenticity reflect contradictory ways of relating to working-class culture. Authenticity draws people to gentrifying areas, yet despite their appreciation for working-class culture and their sometimes idealistic engagement with class politics, they nonetheless contribute to its displacement. Zukin articulates this in personal terms, reflecting on her own experience of moving into what was once a solid working-class neighborhood. She wants, on the one hand, "to offer an objective standard of authenticity that defends their right to the city" and to define her own "identity in terms of the same subjective kind of authenticity," yet she also recognizes that she contributes to the displacement of poor people "by constructing the habitus, latte by latte, of the new urban middle class" (18). Rust Belt chic writers display a similar set of contradictory desires. They appropriate elements of working-class history and culture with almost no overt attention to class, defining the qualities they embrace as reflections of place. Even when they write about the hardships of their grandparents' working-class experiences and the devastation of plant closings, they barely acknowledge the struggles of earlier generations of industrial workers to gain economic or safety protections, much less the role of corporations in shaping industrial conditions or in choosing to close plants and displace a generation of workers. By incorporating working-class culture into Rust Belt identity, they acknowledge its strengths while cherry picking a largely conflict-free version of the working-class past.

This, too, is ironic, since many of the middle-class writers who contribute to Rust Belt chic are, in economic terms, downwardly mobile if not exactly working class, and the industries in which they work are turning increasingly to freelance and contingent labor. Put simply, the conflicts and downturns they experience at work are not unlike what workers of previous generations contended with. Giffels acknowledges this, noting how his own profession, journalism, is contracting and downsizing like Akron's rubber industry had thirty years earlier (229–30). Quite a few Rust Belt chic writers are part of the educated precariat who, as Hannah Woodroofe has argued, struggle to get by economically, define themselves around their avocations rather than paid employment, and are often actively involved in barter economies. For some, Rust Belt chic may offer a kind of compensatory identity, an alternative cultural position for those with uncertain professional positions. Their appropriation of working-class culture enables them to construct a subjective identity that validates resilience, which has clear relevance for people scraping by in a freelance and adjunct economy. Like their grandparents, they recognize the value of belonging as both a source of meaning and an important element of economic survival. Given their economic and social positions, we can see why these writers and their readers would see the old working class as a source of inspiration. Their appropriation embraces the positive values of working-class life.

Yet even as Rust Belt chic identifies with the working class of the past and promotes the conditions created by long-term economic struggle as opportunities for development, it also largely ignores working-class experience in the present. No doubt, contemporary representations of working-class life, from pop culture icons like Honey Boo Boo to news reports on rising rates of addiction and death among the white working class, do not seem as inspirational as images of neighbors helping each other through hard times or the collaborative and productive manual labor of manufacturing.[7] Worse, the persistent economic struggles of those who are left out of the economic renaissance of Rust Belt cities contradict claims that these places are recovering or even that they have great potential. Rust Belt cities regularly appear on national lists of the places with the highest rates of poverty, crime, foreclosure, and segregation. Such problems are not part of the cool vibe that excites most Rust Belt chic writers, and the anthologies and web publications that publish most work in the genre rarely feature working-class voices. This absence may reflect not the blind spots of the editors of these publications but rather a lack of excitement about Rust Belt chic among working-class people, who face both economic constraints and cultural denigration. Nonetheless, by embracing the memory of earlier working-class experiences and ignoring the lives of workers in the present, Rust Belt chic at once appropriates and erases working-class culture.

Race and Conflict

The remembered ideal of industrial working-class identity is also, of course, almost entirely white, as are the overwhelming majority of writers contributing to Rust Belt anthologies and web publications. Although editors occasionally acknowledge that this is a problem, the erasure of the racial diversity of these cities, the racial conflicts of their history, and the segregation of the present undermines Rust Belt chic's claims of authority and authenticity. Indeed, the very idea of "Cleveland-ness" as a kind of ethnicity, comparable to "Polish-ness," as Watterson phrased it, emphasizes this, especially given the contested history of white working-class ethnicity in the United States. Most Rust Belt chic writing not only reflects the perspectives and experiences of white people but also too often erases racial conflict along with conflicts over work, religion, and political control. As with the absence of contemporary working-class voices, this may reflect the conflicted relationship that people of color have with the history and present conditions of these cities. Jimmy Izrael articulates the racial gap of most Rust Belt chic in stark terms in his contribution to the Cleveland anthology:

> I have never, ever met any single person of color with any great passion
> for this city. . . . Most of the Cleveland lovers are white, half-monied,

often tethered to the city by some financial interest, and more than a few are invested in giving the city any variety of media handjobs. They wear tee shirts and tattoos, tributes to Cleveland. Those people are insane. (130)

Izrael's rejection of the proponents of Rust Belt chic as white, middle-class, and foolish reflects long-standing racial divisions as well as different perceptions of and interests in promoting the city. The grandchildren of white industrial workers can look back on a working class that enjoyed stability and solidarity, as Giffels's articulation of rubber workers as "kings" suggests, while African American workers in these communities look back on a more conflicted past. A long history of economic and social marginalization might well make writers of color less likely to embrace Rust Belt heritage, especially if it is compared with white ethnicity.

While most Rust Belt chic writing ignores the experiences of people of color and the history of racial conflict, the intersection of race and class plays a central role in writing about Detroit. This is not surprising, given that the city's decline is widely understood to have begun with racial conflicts of the 1960s, which, as Thomas J. Sugrue has argued, reflected the movement of auto plants to the suburbs. While the history and persistence of racial divisions are reflected in and contribute to the problems facing other Rust Belt cities, Detroit's identity and its residents' articulation of the issues and attitudes that shape their identities as Detroiters are inextricably linked with race. A Detroit Anthology includes a number of narratives that view the city through the lens of race, from the perspectives of both white and black writers. For example, Miller describes how, because she is white, most people assume that when she says, "I'm from Detroit," she really means that she comes from a suburb of Detroit. She also expresses frustration at white suburbanites who claim Detroit as their hometown. The anthology also includes poems that capture the fearful assumptions of a white man when he is approached by a young black man at a gas station (Olzmann 36); define the city in terms of the 1967 uprising—"a riot I fit into" (Jess 49); comment on the city's high murder rate and "ghost factories" (Osayande 158–59); and describe the complex mix of "Financial divides, color lines and imagined issues" (Leonard 211). As these pieces suggest, conflicts around race are deeply embedded in this city's identity, in ways that rarely emerge in writing about other parts of the Rust Belt, even though other cities have experienced similar tensions.

At the same time, some Detroit writers embrace the city's diversity as productive. J. M. Leija acknowledges the divisions but also suggests that Detroiters sometimes overcome their differences. The city is "ripped down the middle . . . two-parts post-apocalypse and three parts stubborn as hell," and it is "sprinkled with the long-term poison of racism." But "my Tigers," Leija writes, "bring together almost 42,000 people every time they play," and at the ballpark, "My dad, the old Mexican, teases the young white girls who come for social Friday nights and icy daiquiris and have no idea how batting average is computed" and bonds with "the Arabic man in front of us who put a cap back on his young daughter's head" (190). Where writers from other cities reference white ethnic diversity, noting the influence of Italian, Polish, German, and other European immigrant cultures, Leija's story is unusual and significant in its focus on interactions among immigrants who are not white.

Most important, some contributors comment on how racial tensions play out within efforts to address Detroit's problems, a move that raises questions about the viability of Rust Belt chic as the basis for urban redevelopment. The tension is reflected especially well in two essays in the last section of the book. White writer Shaun S. Nethercott says that she caught the "Detroit virus" when she moved to the city because she felt that she could "do really important work here that makes a real difference in people's lives and the shape of the city" (216). A few pages later, in the closing essay in the anthology, Marsha Music offers an ambivalent discussion of the return of whites to Detroit, people who "proudly [proclaim] their Detroit provenance and [revel] in their new urban life." While some "recreate suburban segregation in the heart of the city," wanting "life in Detroit—without Detroiters," others view it as "the most exciting place in the world to live in diversity" (230). In *Detroit City Is the Place to Be*, Binelli reports on an interview with Music in which she complains that some of the young white people who have come to Detroit "bring a sort of bacchanal spirit—like they're out on the frontier and they can do anything." When Binelli remarks that they do seem arrogant, she responds that the right term is "white supremacy." "Detroit isn't some kind of abstract art project," she tells Binelli. "It's real for people. These are real memories. Every one of these houses has a story" (285).[8] In her essay in the anthology, published several years after her conversation with Binelli, Music acknowledges that the relations among longtime residents, who are mostly African American, and returnees and newcomers, who are mostly white, reflect tensions that are rooted in history but also current circumstances. Yet she also calls for reconciliation between the two groups: "I believe it is the responsibility of the rest of us—those who, like me, never left—to welcome them; to tell our new residents the real city narratives, to share the truths of what happened here from all sides." She encourages the new arrivals "to actually *see* longtime residents, *for we are not invisible.*" They should "learn from our history" and "work alongside our earlier residents and their children in Detroit's renewal" (231). That the collection ends with this call to collaboration and renewal reflects both the persistence of racial division in the city and the way it has been incorporated into Detroit's version of Rust Belt identity.

Reclaiming Steeltown

At the end of *Steeltown USA: Work and Memory in Youngstown,* John Russo and I wrote that the city had a "problem with memory" (245). Around 2000, as we were completing that book, a modest local cultural war was erupting over how Youngstown should deal with its past. Some planners and developers argued that the community needed to "get over" the past. The problem with Youngstown, they claimed, was its inability to redefine itself as anything other than a steel town or a place that had failed to recover after the mills closed. Others argued that the community should embrace its history with pride. Youngstown had a culture of hard work and commitment, some great old houses and neighborhoods, a downtown full of cheap space in architecturally significant office buildings, and a beautiful park running for twelve miles through its heart. Residents also had a strong sense of belonging and connection, organized around ethnic churches and festivals as well as affinity with the local college football team and many active civic and arts groups. Youngstown, they suggested, just needed to return to its roots, to focus on unity and capability.

We argued that neither option would resolve the city's long-standing problems. Youngstown could not simply leave its history behind, but it also could not advance without dealing more critically with the divisions and conflicts of its past. The community should, we wrote,

> embrace pride in what was produced here—not just steel but also a strong working-class community—and accept the failure to deal with conflicts involving race and class. . . . It must never forget the harm inflicted by corporate irresponsibility, yet it must also accept responsibility for tolerating corruption and division. (247)

Youngstown's strong, supportive ethnic communities had fostered a sense of belonging and helped people survive through tough economic times, but they had also reinforced boundaries within the larger community, especially along racial lines but also politically, reinforcing competition and distrust among the many small cities and townships of the Mahoning Valley. Residents and especially community leaders also needed to recognize that the economic structures that had built the city's industrial economy had changed dramatically. Youngstown's problem was not that people still thought like steelworkers but that capitalism had changed. Youngstown could not be saved by building prisons or casinos or by attracting high-tech companies that would hire a few hundred workers in a city with persistent double-digit unemployment, especially if many of those workers came from outside and lived in the suburbs. If the Youngstown metro area was going to persist in the face of these changes, it would have to deal with its history, not just celebrate it. It had to acknowledge and understand the way historic divisions of race, class, and place had contributed to problems that many preferred to ignore, problems that would not be solved by revitalizing the downtown area.[9] Youngstown needed a critical conversation about its own history.

At its best, Rust Belt chic takes up this challenge. Although some of this writing still ignores or downplays conflicts of class and race, and while it often views the past in idealized ways, Rust Belt chic also offers examples of more critical reflection. Binelli and Young, especially, trace historical conflicts and critique contemporary efforts to address the continuing economic and social challenges facing Detroit and Flint. In the blogs and anthologies, younger writers find inspiration in the struggles of the past, not just the memory of happier times. While some want to let readers know about old neighborhood bars or reminisce about local bands, others advocate for preserving and repurposing historic buildings. Over time, *Belt Magazine* has increasingly mixed stories about the history of Rust Belt cities with commentary on current issues, from the water crisis in Flint to Cleveland's struggling school system to the 2016 presidential race. Although Rust Belt chic is sometimes overly optimistic about economic development projects, and while the genre's claims about revitalization can seem exaggerated, these writers are not wrong to take note of real improvements in their cities. As John Slanina told me in a 2006 interview, Youngstown was at that point the best it had been in his lifetime, and he wanted to contribute to making it even better. Writing was just one of the ways he began to do that.

Will Rust Belt chic generate enough interest in and appreciation for deindustrialized cities to achieve the kind of economic revitalization that Piiparinen and others envision? That seems unlikely, in part because the challenges facing these cities are part of a global economic shift and will not likely be resolved solely through the gentrification of old warehouse districts or downtowns. But Rust Belt chic may be able to accomplish something more significant than making Cleveland—or any other city— cool. It can push readers to wrestle with three central questions that define not only the challenges facing the Rust Belt but also the problems facing a whole generation, nationally and beyond. How do we deal with the past? How do we envision the future? And who do we think we are?

Like all of deindustrialization literature, Rust Belt chic has a contested relationship with the past. It rejects calls to "just get over" the past or to "move on," as if the past had not happened. Yet it also recognizes that the past of deindustrialized cities includes not only the good old days of the industrial heyday but also the long painful period of loss and struggle after shutdowns. These writers find value in the resilience and struggle of the half-life. By embracing this very mixed understanding of history, Rust Belt chic avoids what Jefferson Cowie and Joseph Heathcott call "smokestack nostalgia" (15). The best work of this genre instead exemplifies what Fred Davis identifies as "third order" or "interpretive" nostalgia: it goes beyond remembering and raises questions about the past and contemporary engagement with it. Rust Belt chic demonstrates how nostalgia can, as Tim Strangleman has suggested, serve as a "vehicle for reflection or critique rather than uncritical celebration" (2013, 33). By resisting its own tendency to idealize the past but also by refusing to simply "get over it," Rust Belt chic insists that the relationship between past and present can be at once critical and productive.

Because the genre includes a range of perspectives, Rust Belt chic also reflects contemporary debates about how to imagine the future. While some contributors insist that the "spirit" of their deindustrialized communities ensures some unspecified and intangible future success, for the most part, Rust Belt chic also invites us to stop expecting that modernity will necessarily yield a better future. Even when writers tout the potential of the Rust Belt to attract economic development, most resist "solutionism." Detroit writer John Patrick Leahy borrows the term from Belarusian critic Evgeny Morozov, explaining that, in Detroit, solutionism "combines a utopian idealism with the technocratic fantasy that systemic problems can be managed away with the right experts and right digital tools." Most contributors to Rust Belt chic advocate for more modest expectations. They validate the resilience of deindustrialized cities, which have been surviving the legacy of economic restructuring for decades already.

These writers present varied ways of articulating the value of that resilience, reflecting both accommodation and resistance to neoliberalism. Some argue that the region has great potential both to attract new business and to foster alternative models, as in Akron urban planner Jason Segedy's buzzwordy call for "economic development and public investment to be hyper-nimble, hyper-scalable, hyper-neighborhood-focused, and ultra-diverse." Others reject such visions, urging their communities to pursue more modest but also more socially oriented goals. As Young suggests at the end of *Teardown*, Flint will never again be what it was in the 1950s, "a bastion of the middle class," but it could become a "different place that still had pride and dignity" (241). Rust Belt chic also embraces radical visions that overtly reject neoliberal capitalism, as in Boggs and Kurashige's vision of an alternative communal economy emerging from Detroit's urban agriculture movement. Rust Belt chic does not, in other words, offer any single view of how to respond to economic restructuring. Rather, at its best, as exemplified by the Detroit anthology and the book-length journalistic memoirs, it invites readers to think critically about what we can learn from the resilience of deindustrialized cities. By including this range of perspectives, Rust Belt chic highlights the contested contemporary discourse of economic change, in which some promise a renaissance of creativity, flexibility, and growth while others critique such a vision as the "cruel optimism" of false promises that distract us from the way economic restructuring contributes to increasing inequality and destabilization.[10]

No doubt, the concept of authentic places and identities is problematic, and because most Rust Belt chic contributors are white and middle class, their work offers an incomplete and selective portrait of the region. Rust Belt chic sometimes appropriates elements of working-class culture in problematic ways, especially when it is embodied through style and consumption. Rust Belt chic also ignores the current conditions of the American working class and often reinforces the inaccurate image of the working class as white. However, as *A Detroit Anthology* demonstrates, it can also be self-critical about its own claims and about what— and who—it excludes.

But Rust Belt chic also embraces a value shift that trades individual striving and the pursuit of the American Dream for the working-class values of belonging and grit, even though these qualities are rarely articulated overtly as "working class." Sometimes, Rust Belt chic's retelling of the past can romanticize poverty and struggle, but at the same time, it engages with and often reconsiders the working-class past, identifying insights and models in a way of life that most of these writers are two generations removed from. As the contradictions of authenticity and whiteness make clear, this vision is as problematic as are claims for the value of resilience, but the hybrid class identity articulated in Rust Belt chic also offers an alternative cultural location for writers and readers for whom the old suburban, professional version of middle-class life is largely out of reach. For people living in a contingent economy, where the middle class is—together with the working class, of course—on the losing end of the expanding inequality gap, reclaiming the values of belonging and grit may not only offer a way to reconcile the contrast between the promise of the American Dream and the reality of the contemporary economy; it may also serve as a first, if very modest and incomplete, move toward solidarity and resistance.

Rust Belt chic engages with these questions in diverse and contested ways, and that is one of its strengths. This writing deserves critical attention not only as reportage or as a collection of local voices but as a many-voiced narrative about how a region long defined by loss and often accused of being stuck in the past can find meaning in its history and reconcile its past and its potential. Rust Belt chic is an interpretive genre, responding to, building on, and wrestling with the continuing influence of deindustrialization. It is also a genre of advocacy, focused on defending the region from narratives that dismiss it as stuck in the past, cite it as evidence of both specific local failings and a frightening future for the rest of the country, or celebrate limited improvements as evidence of widespread revitalization. Finally, in the context of the half-life of deindustrialization, Rust Belt chic shows that the economic, social, and cultural shifts that began with plant closings continue to ripple through American life decades later. The legacy of displacement and decline lives on, in the landscape, in how communities define themselves, and in how, regardless of their education or position, people have learned to expect uncertainty.

CONCLUSION

The Half-Life Goes Public

Why Deindustrialization Literature Matters

In a June 2016 essay, David Brooks ponders the "anomie, cynicism, pessimism and resentment" that, he says, was clear to "anyone who spends time in the working-class parts of America." He acknowledges that "part of this pain arises from deindustrialization," but he immediately dismisses its significance. After all, he writes, "Life in, say, a coal valley was never a bouquet of roses." The real problem for working-class people, he argues, is the loss of "social institutions and cultural values." Workers, he laments, no longer take pride in being "loyal, tough, hard-working, resilient and part of a good community." While Brooks notes the influence of "the modern meritocracy, which . . . devalues the class of people who work with their hands," he underestimates, like too many middle-class commentators and scholars, the role of deindustrialization in shaping not only economic conditions but also working-class culture. No doubt, as he admits, working-class life was never easy, but Brooks glosses over the contrast between the industrial era and the early twenty-first century. Most important, he does not seem to understand that it was deindustrialization that undermined the institutions and values he worries about, both directly, by cutting jobs despite the hard work and loyalty of workers, and indirectly, as the half-life has continued, by disrupting working-class communities and demanding a different kind of toughness, resilience, and loyalty. In dismissing the continuing significance of deindustrialization, Brooks echoes the call that working-class people should "just get over it."

He also echoes the concerns expressed in several books and commentaries published between 2012 and 2016 that describe contemporary working-class culture as struggling with moral, social, and psychological failures. Charles Murray and Andrew Cherlin see evidence of moral decline in reduced rates of marriage and increased rates on out-of-wedlock births. Robert Putnam traces the loss of social networks, an observation echoed by Jennifer Silva. Anne Case and Angus Deaton's study of rising death rates among middle-aged white people notes that the rates were especially high for those with a high school diploma but no college experience (a typical, though problematic, stand-in for class in many studies and polls).[1] In 2017 they described the problem as "death by despair." While these studies acknowledge the real economic constraints at play in contemporary society, they don't always recognize that today's challenges reflect not only the loss of good jobs and the social benefits they provided but also the long-term struggle to adapt to an economic and political culture that does not value working-class lives.

When we read contemporary working-class culture as evidence of the half-life of deindustrialization, however, we can see that what some diagnose as failures of morality or character are actually responses to and even ways of resisting changes that threaten not only people's livelihoods but also their way of life. Many working-class people recognize and resent the challenges that contemporary neoliberal ideology presents to the values of grit, hard work, and community. Good jobs have become scarce in the contingent, often precarious service economy, but many workers still display the resilience and grit to show up day after day, shift after uncertain shift, at jobs that don't pay enough to lift them above the poverty line. And yes, some see that their hard work won't pay off and are making different choices, ones that look self-destructive or even immoral to some observers. If working-class people seem to be leaning more toward the hard-living end of the spectrum of family cultures that Lillian Rubin described in the 1970s, that does not reflect a moral shift but a realistic response to economic restructuring. Settled living is not only an attitude; it is an option made possible by steady employment and decent incomes. Social networks have frayed, and some have embraced self-reliance and individualism or have lost their faith in institutions, but many still work hard to create and sustain solidarity. They recognize the value of community as a source of personal and political agency. For others, both self-efficacy and collective power seem out of reach.

Deindustrialization literature offers an important counterpoint to the public narrative of the failure of working-class culture by examining contemporary working-class lives from the inside, through the perspectives of people who must navigate the day-to-day insecurity and disrespect of service jobs and the deteriorating landscapes of deindustrialized cities. By making the subjectivity of working-class people visible, these narratives reveal both the hidden injuries of deindustrialization and the tenuous resistance that is also emerging in the half-life. Deindustrialization literature shows how workers continue to seek meaning through work despite declining real wages, shrinking benefits, manipulative corporate rhetoric and control, and doubts about the value of the work itself. In narratives about working-class people struggling to construct stable lives as economic uncertainty undermines their situations, identities, and affiliations, we see how the already conflicted relationships among class, gender, and race become even more contentious in the contingent economy. Where pundits too easily assign racism and xenophobia exclusively to the white working class, novelists, filmmakers, playwrights, and poets show us the pain and discomfort of diverse working-class subjectivities as people wrestle with competing loyalties, fragmented workplace networks, and economic precarity. Yet these texts also remind us that, beneath these conflicts of identity and affiliation, many working-class people retain a sense of mutual responsibility and connection. Family and community still matter, even as they have become harder to maintain.

Deindustrialization literature also takes us inside the deteriorating spaces of the deindustrialized landscape, revealing the everyday material reality of living amid the ruins. Where documentary filmmakers and photographers often show depopulated and spectacularly decaying landmarks, literary narratives emphasize subjectivity rather than spectacle. It may be tempting for outside commentators to ask—as experts and residents in several of the documentaries do—what is wrong with communities that let grand buildings crumble or people who burn down houses in their own neighborhoods, but deindustrialization literature shifts the focus, showing how, for long-term residents, those spaces represent contested personal and communal histories. These stories show not only the struggle of living in hollowed-out and crumbling places but also the complex meanings embedded in the landscape. The losses, the struggles, the conflicts of the past remain present in both decaying physical structures and memories of earlier times and people. Deindustrialization literature also identifies an important tension in the landscape, which seems open to new interpretations and uses, even as signs of new growth just barely mask the hard foundations and conflicted memories that resist erasure and continue to shape contemporary experience.

As deindustrialization literature makes clear, the past remains present in material reality and subjectivity. While some of these narratives recall the pride and solidarity of earlier eras, the past of the half-life does not involve a simple nostalgia for the good old days of the industrial heyday. Across the genre, we encounter a range of memories, many of them focused on difficulty and loss, as well as evidence that history shapes the present, for good and for bad. These stories reveal how prior experience, including stories handed down from previous generations, shapes the way characters see themselves and their situations. Some writers and their characters look back on the work, relationships, and places of the past to understand just how much has been lost, while others recognize the continuing exploitation of capitalism or trace how people's perspectives on work, identity, and place reflect the history of racial conflict over access to jobs and union representation. These stories also suggest that the past can provide inspiration for responding to new challenges, even if it does not always point to strategies that allow for real agency.

In deindustrialization literature, the past includes success and failure, growth and loss, industrial pride and deindustrial struggle. In part because of this complexity, memory and history also function as tools for examining and critiquing the present, including, in many cases, raising questions about the continuing influence of the past itself. Indeed, deindustrialization literature reminds us that memory and history are themselves narratives that can and sometimes must be retold and reinterpreted. Deindustrialization literature suggests that working-class people are not clinging to an idealized version of the past, nor are they mired in self-pity and picking at old scabs. They recognize that the past cannot be escaped or erased. In its complex engagement with the past, deindustrialization literature presents a productive, critical nostalgia.

In other words, memory and history remain active elements of working-class culture as people respond and adapt to the economic and social changes wrought by deindustrialization and the post-Fordist, postindustrial era that is still emerging. We can usefully imagine the half-life of deindustrialization as the liminal period during which working-class culture is adapting to the insecurity and fragmentation of the postindustrial economy. In that process, the past is at once a conceptual frame, a residual structure of feeling through which people make sense of new conditions, and a source of critique and tension, a means of resisting change. That said, liminality suggests transformation, from one state to another, and while we may be able to describe the material and structural conditions of postindustrial life, we cannot yet identify the contours of the working-class culture that is emerging in relation to those conditions. When historians look back at the working class of the twenty-first century, what will stand out? As economic insecurity erodes the possibility for working-class people to construct settled lives, how will the meaning of work shift? Will class activism and solidarity develop in a growing working class[2] despite the contingency and fragmentation of working life? How will gentrification, crime, and crumbling infrastructures affect local economies but also community life in deindustrialized cities? How will the appropriation of working-class culture by marketers, civic boosters, and artists address economic inequality and the continuing struggles of Rust Belt cities to "recover" from deindustrialization? Will precarious workers become, as Guy Standing has suggested, a new "dangerous" class, the Precariat? Deindustrialization literature may not offer definitive answers to these questions, but its attention to subjectivity and experience provides insight that we find in few other sources.

It can also help us make sense of the present. Around the time I began studying deindustrialization literature, journalists were starting to pay closer attention to white working-class voters, especially in Rust Belt swing states like Ohio and Pennsylvania. In 2008 and 2012, John Russo and I—then codirectors of the Center for Working-Class Studies at Youngstown State University—fielded hundreds of queries from journalists around the world seeking insight into working-class voters. Some asked for assistance in reaching out to these voters. Media interest spiked again in 2016, but with a new urgency, as both Bernie Sanders and Donald Trump seemed to appeal to the kinds of people whose stories and voices we hear in deindustrialization literature, people who have been left behind by the U.S. economy, some since factories and mines shut down in the 1970s and 1980s but some with more recent losses, rooted in the Great Recession of 2008. Political rhetoric channeled the anger and resentment of many in the white working class in various directions—at Wall Street; at Washington; toward immigrants, people of color, or Muslims. Trump's campaign, especially, turned up the dial on resentment, division, and anxiety, which played out against the backdrop of increasing violence, as a young Muslim man killed dozens in a gay nightclub in Orlando, as police shot black men in a dozen American cities, as a couple of mentally ill black men turned their guns on police officers, and as terrorists attacked civilians across Europe and the Middle East. In a frightening period, some worried about the return of fascism, including Brooks, who described how it could take hold:

You start with a fundamental historical transformation, like the Great Depression or the shift to an information economy. A certain number of people are dispossessed. They lose identity, self-respect and hope. . . . They become mired in their resentments, . . . They fall for politicians who lie about the source of their problems and about how they can surmount them.

Although Brooks went on to assure readers that the United States is not yet "close to that kind of descent," he also suggested that "we're closer than we've been" (12 July 2016). Journalists and commentators, Brooks among them, often blamed the working class—especially the white working class—for being duped by Trump's divisive populism and deceptive showmanship, ignoring the link that Michael Parenti has made between fascism and corporatism.[3] Still, many also clearly wanted to understand the experiences and perspectives that were generating so much resentment.

As an English professor, I often tell my students that literature can help us understand how people are shaped by and respond to the economic, political, and social forces around them. People interpret and act on the world by telling stories, and literature preserves and makes those stories accessible. In addition, as the centrality of cultural representations in Working-Class Studies suggests, narratives not only reflect but also comment on, interpret, and influence social patterns. Deindustrialization literature sheds light on the experiences and perspectives of working-class people in the twenty-first century. The few dozen examples discussed here represent just some of the thought-provoking, insightful, and often entertaining writing that deserves more public as well as critical attention. In tracing the central themes of deindustrialization literature, I have had to leave out many examples, such as Richard Russo's *Empire Falls*, poems by Jessica Care Moore, films like *Up in the Air* about middle-class experiences with restructuring, and recent television programs focused on health care and retail work, such as *Getting By* and *Superstore*, not to mention the graphic novel *The Adventures of Unemployed Man*. In the last months of my work on this book, Russo and Jennifer Haigh both published new novels, and we will see more as writers and publishers respond to the cultural and political tensions that are making the half-life increasingly visible and troubling.

These narratives matter because the half-life of deindustrialization continues to shape working-class lives. Certain radioactive substances have half-lives lasting thousands of years, remaining potent and toxic long after their existence has been forgotten. The half-life of deindustrialization may well last for decades and across generations, and as this literature shows and as we see in contemporary American culture, the heyday of the industrial working class, the devastation of shutdowns, and their long, slow aftermath all remain potent influences, not only for the working class but also for many in the middle class. For those who want to understand how individuals, communities, and working-class culture more broadly are responding to and resisting the effects of the half-life, deindustrialization literature should be required reading.

Notes

INTRODUCTION

1. See the 2015 report by Anne Case and Angus Deaton, who, in a 2017 commentary on the study, identify rising death rates among middle-aged white people without college degrees as reflecting "diseases of despair" (2017, 3).

2. Like some of the early work by feminist scholars who uncovered long-forgotten women writers of the past, this book argues for the significance of these texts, with the goal of fostering further research by other scholars. That seems a lofty aim, but it has shaped some of my choices in writing this book, such as the regional emphasis or the inclusion of texts in varied forms (with little discussion of how the ideas of this literature play out in form).

3. Jim Daniels offers a useful overview of worker poetry and poetry about work, including a historical overview, in his essay in Russo and Linkon's *New Working-Class Studies*.

4. Two recent dissertations have addressed some of this literature, both with a strong regional focus. Asynith Helen Palmer's 2014 project, "Re-Constructing the Rust Belt: An Exploration of Industrial Ruin in Blogs, Fiction, and Poetry," focuses on what she terms "rust belt literature." Matthew Martin Holman's 2012 dissertation examines Rust Belt gothic fiction.

5. Within literary studies is a long history of debates about how to define literature, and the debate is far from resolved. See, for example, the dozen articles in "What Is Literature Now?" a 2007 special issue of *New Literary History*. Social scientists have also taken up the debate, and cultural geographers have been especially interested in the value of storytelling and literature as sources for thinking about place, space, and planning. See, for example, essays by Angharad Saunders and Emilie Cameron.

CHAPTER 1

1. For a useful summary of critical discussions about changes in work, including the idea that new forms of work would improve workers' lives, see Strangleman, "The Nostalgia for Permanence at Work? The End of Work and Its Commentators."

2. Daniels has spoken about the connections between his life and his writing in several pieces, including a 2012 profile by Bill Castanier in the Lansing, Michigan, *City Pulse*, and an undated interview with Tim Ross in *The Artful Dodge*.

3. The poems from *Digger's Blues* were republished in a 2003 collection of new and selected poems, *Show and Tell*.

4. Several of Romero's films as well as other zombie movies have been set in deindustrialized places, perhaps because such settings highlight the continuing and contested connections between past and present.

5. For a fuller discussion of absent fathers in deindustrialization literature, including in this novel, see my article, "Men without Work: White Working-Class Masculinity in Deindustrialization Fiction."

6. While Bakopoulos could not imagine a Black Friday strike actually happening, six years after the novel was published, it did. In 2012 and again in the next few years, workers at Walmarts around the United States went on strike on Black Friday.

7. This discussion of *The Wire* is drawn from an article on the series I coauthored with Alexander Russo and John Russo, "Contested Memories: Representing Work in *The Wire*."

8. The concept of "community of memory" applies here. Developed by Robert Bellah et al., in *Habits of the Heart*, their 1985 study of individualism and community in American culture, "community of memory" describes the way shared memories, good and bad, can help to create and maintain social networks but also provide agency.

CHAPTER 2

1. In "Labor History and the 'Sartre Question,'" Gutman quotes Jean-Paul Sartre as noting that "The essential was not what 'one' has done to man, but what man does with what 'one' has done to him" (326). Gutman suggests that this question "redefines the important questions we should ask in studying the history of dependent American social classes" (326), including enslaved people, immigrants, and workers.

2. See, for example, Lois Weis's *Class Reunion: The Remaking of the American White Working Class*; Linda McDowell's "Masculine Identities and Low-Paid Work: Young Men in Urban Labour Markets"; Anoop Nayak's "'Boyz to Men': Masculinities, Schooling and Labour Transitions in De-industrial Times"; and Valerie Walkerdine and Luis Jimenez's *Gender, Work and Community after De-Industrialisation: A Psychosocial Approach to Affect*. It is worth noting that most of these studies examine white working-class men in the United Kingdom.

3. Earlier studies had shown similar patterns among African Americans, especially younger men, during the 1990s. For example, Charis E. Kubrin, Tim Wadsworth, and Stephanie DiPietro traced suicide rates among young black men, a study that aimed to provide an empirical test of William Julius Wilson's argument that deindustrialization undermined not only economic but also social stability in black

communities. As several commentators noted in 2015, when the Case and Deaton study was attracting major attention, the link between economic struggle and rising mortality was old news for blacks. Equally important, high rates of drug overdoses and suicides among African Americans had not been treated with the same kind of public hand-wringing as the studies of white death rates.

4. For a fuller discussion of tensions among workers around race, gender, and immigration status, see Bruce Nelson's *Divided We Stand: American Workers and the Struggle for Black Equality*; Alice Kessler-Harris's *Out to Work: A History of Wage-Earning Women in the United States*; and Robert H. Zeiger's *For Jobs and Freedom: Race and Labor in America since 1865*. David R. Roediger's *The Wages of Whiteness: Race and the Making of the American Working Class* is a foundational text for discussions of racial tensions around access to jobs. Bill Fletcher Jr. and Fernando Gapasin offer a more contemporary take on divisions within the labor movement in *Solidarity Divided: The Crisis in Organized Labor and a New Path toward Social Justice*.

5. Geographer Linda McDowell, sociologist Anoop Nayak, and educational psychologists Valerie Walkerdine and Luis Jimenez found that constructing masculinity in the absence of blue-collar work requires alternative means and venues for performing physical and psychological toughness and claiming social power. McDowell shows that young men have found new ways of expressing masculinity through crime, drugs, and suicide (832), and Nayak traces a similar pattern, showing how white working-class men find spaces for performing masculinity in bars and on the street rather than at work. Walkerdine and Jimenez argue that psychological investment in the "hard body" of steelwork, the image of the tough, productive laborer that is deeply embedded in local cultures, explains young working-class men's refusal to accept service industry jobs that would put them on display doing "feminine" work in public places such as grocery stores. Not only has economic change affected the kinds of work men do; it has also created conditions that have required men to expand their roles within the family, beyond breadwinning to more active caretaking. Lois Weis found in the United States that the now grown sons of displaced steelworkers have embraced a more androgynous version of working-class masculinity, not only because work has become more service oriented, as Walkerdine and Jimenez suggest, but also because family economies now rely on multiple incomes and shared family responsibilities.

6. In a review of the novel, Stacey D'Erasmo suggests that O'Nan was hampered by his effort to treat his working-class African American characters with respect: "While there is no reason that a white man shouldn't write about African-Americans, or vice versa, O'Nan appears to have been waylaid in his fictional mission by the sneakiest of demons: politeness. Tentative, almost fatally respectful, he treats his characters very gingerly, as if he were afraid he might break them. . . . There's no doubt that O'Nan means well, but the lack of surprise and psychological inventiveness inadvertently suggests that people with less money have fewer, and less complicated, emotions."

7. See, for example, Eric King Watts's "Border Patrolling and 'Passing' in Eminem's *8 Mile*"; Roy Grundmann's review of the film from *Cineaste*; and Russell White's essay on *8 Mile* as an example of "postindustrial minstrelsy."

8. See Thomas J. Sugrue, *The Origins of the Urban Crisis: Race and Inequality in Postwar Detroit*.

9. A number of scholars have traced and critiqued rap as a response to deindustrialization, including most notably Robin D. G. Kelley in *Race Rebels: Culture, Politics, and the Black Working Class*; Tricia Rose in *Black Noise: Rap Music and Black Culture in Contemporary America*; and Lester Spence in *Stare in the Darkness: The Limits of Hip-hop and Black Politics*.

10. As White and others have suggested, Eminem has successfully claimed the power to define himself in the hip-hop world, but his ability to do that is based, in part, on advantages of whiteness. He is seen as having succeeded not only because of the quality of his work, which critics agree is strong, but also because, as a white man, he was a more acceptable representative of hip-hop and added to the genre's crossover appeal.

11. It is worth noting, of course, that two of the writers most directly addressing race, O'Nan and Mathers, are white, and both, in very different ways, could be described as performing a contemporary version of blackface. O'Nan presents African American characters, while Mathers appropriates an African American art form. It is important for white writers to engage with the way race shapes working-class identities, yet, as these texts show, that can be tricky, especially when addressing race involves taking on African American voices or styles. Critics have noted the difficulties and problems these writers encounter. Reviewer Stacey D'Erasmo suggests that O'Nan treats his characters with a "politeness" that is "almost fatally respectful." Eminem, on the other hand, has been criticized for "pitting race and class against each other in rather problematic ways" (Grundmann 32).

12. *Sweat* was originally jointly commissioned and produced by the Oregon Shakespeare Festival and Arena Stage in Washington, D.C. In 2016, it was staged at the Public Theater in New York, and it opened on Broadway in March 2017. Along with winning the Pulitzer Prize for Drama that year, it was nominated for a Tony Award for Best Play.

13. See Barbara Jensen's *Reading Classes: On Culture and Classism in America* and Jack Metzgar's "Politics and the American Class Vernacular."

14. Silva also finds that this "therapeutic model of selfhood" is enacted not only internally, in the way people make sense of their experiences and relationships, but also externally, through telling their stories. As Silva writes, this therapeutic narration functions as a means of validation, replacing the "normative and socially recognizable transition[s] to adulthood," such as marriage or having children, as a way of "perceiv[ing] themselves as adults" (2012, 506). While deindustrialization literature certainly includes narratives in which working-class people struggle with family traumas and internal demons of the kind that Silva identifies, these texts only rarely show characters telling their stories. Nonetheless, we might read deindustrialization literature as a social, public, fictionalized version of therapeutic narratives.

15. In her review of Hodgen's novel, Sarah Banse claims that the unnamed town in the novel is actually Worcester, Massachusetts. While this may be accurate, Hodgen explicity avoids naming the town, a move that helps to suggest that its condition as a deindustrialized city matters more than any particular historical or contextual detail.

16. See Sonali Perera's *No Country: Working-Class Writing in the Age of Globalization*.

CHAPTER 3

1. Detroit has been the subject of many documentaries, including *Deforce*, *Detroit: Wild City*, *Grown in Detroit*, and *Detroit: Ruin of a City*, as well as photography exhibits and books, including Dan Austin and Sean Doerr's *Lost Detroit: Stories Behind the Motor City's Majestic Ruins*; Yves Marchand and Romaine Meffre's collection (published with essays by Robert Poliardi and Thomas J. Sugrue), *The Ruins of Detroit*; and *Detroit Resurgent*, a more people-centered collection featuring photos by Gilles Perrin. As Strangleman notes in a 2014 essay on visual representations of deindustrialized landscapes, "nowhere is more 'explored' than Detroit" (26).

2. The site seems to be modeled on Lowell Boileau's "Fabulous Ruins of Detroit," which combines images of decaying and repurposed old buildings with a narrative about their history and a very active discussion forum focused on remembering the city's past and advocating for preservation (www.detroityes.com/home.htm).

3. Cutting off city services to neighborhoods deemed not "viable" was a strategy included in several Rust Belt city plans that focused on accepting the idea that these cities would continue to lose population. Youngstown, Ohio, and Detroit both drew international acclaim for such plans, but neither city has been able to implement the concept, because long-term residents in the least "viable" neighborhoods have refused to leave their homes. Bell's novel imagines what might happen if a large city like Detroit had actually followed through on this idea.

4. The novel was made into a film, *Jamie Marks Is Dead*, in 2014, but the film left out the Youngstown section.

5. The novel was published in the United Kingdom under the title *The Trials and Tribulations of Lucas Lessar*.

6. In an email responding to my query about this reference, Barzak writes: "Henry Miller really did stop off in Youngstown. He writes about it in his travel memoir, *The Air-Conditioned Nightmare*, which he was commissioned to write as a kind of cultural tour of the U.S. as it continued to industrialize. The trip was taken in 1940 and 1941. Youngstown was I think his second stop, after Pittsburgh. He didn't stay long, and maybe only has about a page and a half or two pages of writing about it in that book, fairly early on in its opening. . . . He describes those girls that I re-describe in my piece, and in many ways what I've written in that piece is mainly a kind of retelling or revisionistic effort to take what Miller described about Youngstown then, and turn it into a piece that connects the visions of Youngstown past and present, and then to talk about the future in all its nebulousness, and in a lot of ways to achieve a kind of justification for the sort of cynicism that a place like Youngstown breeds in its citizens, at least in the ones who are keeping a mental tally of all the losses and a register of all the various political corruptions that have torn the place apart over the years."

7. Nowak has described his writing as "multitrack recordings rather than poems" (2014 Lannan Seminar).

CHAPTER 4

1. For an example of how this concept has been used in discussions of Rust Belt revitalization, see Margaret Cowell's study, *Dealing with Deindustrialization: Adaptive Resilience in American Midwestern Regions.*

2. Campbell abuts Youngstown, though it operates as a separate entity.

3. The documentary *Detropia* includes scenes of one of the Coys' projects, and a still from that section of the film was used on posters, the DVD box, and other promotional materials for the film.

4. For a critical analysis of what arts projects can and cannot contribute to economic redevelopment in deindustrialized communities, see Maynard Seider's documentary *Farewell to Factory Towns?* (farewelltofactorytowns.wordpress.com). After telling the story of the development of a contemporary art museum and studio space, Mass MoCA, in North Adams, Massachusetts, Seider shows that the project made only a modest contribution to local economic conditions, and he argues that economic redevelopment requires more systemic change, including a national industrial policy.

5. Between 2005 and 2015 several old office buildings in Youngstown were converted to apartments, but the developers initially had difficulty recouping their investments because the local market would not support the high rents the developers wanted to charge. At least some residents wanted to live downtown, but they could not justify (or afford) to pay twice the rent to do so.

6. A number of scholars have traced the way working-class whites have used ethnicity as a way of both claiming belonging and negotiating political and economic issues. For a useful overview, see "The Invention of Ethnicity," by Conzen et al.

7. In 2016 the public image of the contemporary working class was further tarnished by association with the xenophobia, resentment, and anti-intellectualism reflected in Donald Trump's campaign for president, which was often described as having particular appeal for the white working class.

8. Binelli refers to Music as Marsha Cusic, which is her former married name. She prefers to use her pen name and asked me to do the same.

9. For a critical discussion of the limitations of downtown development, see "Shrinking 'Smart'?: Urban Redevelopment and Shrinkage in Youngstown, Ohio" by James Rhodes and John Russo.

10. See Lauren Berlant's book, *Cruel Optimism*, which explores how people hold on to fantasies of positive outcomes even in the face of what she calls "compromised conditions of possibility" (23). Berlant traces this concept through several cultural themes, including post-Fordism.

CONCLUSION

1. Jack Metzgar has published a series of critiques of these and other books and studies on the *Working-Class Perspectives* blog, workingclassstudies.wordpress.com. See especially his pieces from February 23, 2015; April 27, 2015; September 27, 2015; March 14, 2016; and May 2, 2016.

2. A 2015 Gallup Poll shows that the number of Americans who identify themselves as working class has risen from 33 percent in 2001 to 48 percent in 2015, while

the number who define themselves as middle class has fallen from 63 percent to 51 percent. Meanwhile, *The Guardian* reported in March 2016 that 56.5 percent of millennials in the United States—people between the ages of eighteen and thirty-five—identify as working class.

3. Parenti made this argument in his 1997 book, *Blackshirts and Reds: Rational Fascism and the Overthrow of Communism,* but he has continued making the case in recent years.

Works Cited

Andrews, Elaine Arvan. "The Mystique of Cedar's Piiparinen Lounge." In Marino and Miller, 29–35.

Apel, Dora, *Beautiful Terrible Ruins: Detroit and the Anxiety of Decline.* New Brunswick, NJ: Rutgers University Press, 2015.

Austin, Dan, and Sean Doerr. *Lost Detroit: Stories Behind the Motor City's Majestic Ruins.* Charleston, SC: History Press, 2010.

Bakopoulos, Dean. *Please Don't Come Back from the Moon.* Orlando, FL: Harcourt, 2005.

Bal, Mieke. "Introduction." In *Acts of Memory: Cultural Recall in the Present,* ed. Mieke Bal, Jonathan V. Crewe, and Leo Spitzer, vii–xvii. Hanover, NH: Dartmouth College, 1999.

Banse, Sarah. "Review: Elegies for the Brokenhearted." *Ploughshares* 114 (Spring 2011): 189–91. Web. 1 Mar. 2016.

Barzak, Christopher. *One for Sorrow.* New York: Bantam, 2007.

Barzak, Christopher. "Map for a Forgotten Valley." *New Haven Review* 7 (Winter 2010). Web. 12 Jan. 2011.

Barzak, Christopher. "The B&O: Crossroads of Time and Space." *Muse* 12 (Jan. 2011): 7. Web. 12 Jan. 2011.

Barzak, Christopher. "Re: Quick question." Email to author. 11 Dec. 2015.

Baszynski, Nikki Trautman. "Saudade." In Marino and Miller, 79–81.

Bell, Matt. *Scrapper.* New York: Soho Press, 2015.

Bellah, Robert N., et al. *Habits of the Heart: Individualism and Commitment in American Life.* New York: Harper and Row, 1985.

Belluz, Julia. "Nobel Winner Angus Deaton Talks about the Surprising Study on White Mortality He Just Co-Authored." *Vox,* 7 Nov. 2015. Web. 28 Nov. 2015.

Benjamin, Walter. *The Origin of German Tragic Drama.* London: NLB, 1977.

Berlant, Lauren G. *Cruel Optimism.* Durham, NC: Duke University Press, 2011.

Binelli, Mark. *Detroit City Is the Place to Be: The Afterlife of an American Metropolis.* New York: Metropolitan Books, 2012.

Boggs, Grace Lee, and Scott Kurashige. "Planting Seeds of Hope." In Clark, 222–24.

Boileau, Lowell. "The Fabulous Ruins of Detroit." *DetroitYES*. Web. 22 July 2016.

Bossen, Howard, John P. Beck, Gilles Perrin, and Nicole Ewenczyk. *Detroit Resurgent*. East Lansing: Michigan State University Press, 2014.

Boym, Svetlana. *The Future of Nostalgia*. New York: Basic Books, 2001.

Boym, Svetlana. "Ruinophilia: Appreciation of Ruins." *Atlas of Transformation*, 2011. Web. 14 June 2016.

Brooks, David. "The Revolt of the Masses." *New York Times*, 28 June 2016. Web. 28 June 2016.

Brooks, David. "Are We on the Path to National Ruin?" *New York Times*, 12 July 2016. Web. 12 July 2016.

Cameron, Emilie. "New Geographies of Story and Storytelling." *Progress in Human Geography* 36, no. 5 (2012): 573–92. Web. 7 Oct. 2015.

Campbell, Bonnie Jo. *American Salvage*. Detroit: Wayne State University Press, 2009.

Carroll, Hamilton. "Policing the Borders of White Masculinity: Labor, Whiteness, and the Neoliberal City in *The Wire*." In *"The Wire": Race, Class, and Genre*, ed. Liam Kennedy and Stephen Shapiro, 262–82. Ann Arbor: University of Michigan Press, 2012.

Case, Anne, and Angus Deaton. "Rising Morbidity and Mortality in Midlife among White Non-Hispanic Americans in the 21st Century." *Proceedings of the National Academy of Sciences* 112, no. 49 (2015). Web. 28 Nov. 2015.

Case, Anne, and Angus Deaton. "Mortality and Morbidity in the 21st Century: Post Conference Version." *Brookings Papers on Economic Activity* (Spring 2017).

Castanier, Bill. "Write to Work." *Lansing City Pulse*, 19 Jan. 2012. Web. 8 July 2016.

Cherlin, Andrew J. *Labor's Love Lost: The Rise and Fall of the Working-Class Family in America*. New York: Russell Sage Foundation, 2014.

Clarett, Maurice. "13 Staples." In Marino and Miller, 184–88.

Clark, Anna, ed. *A Detroit Anthology*. Cleveland: Belt Publishing, 2014.

Coles, Nicholas, and Peter Oresick, eds. *For a Living: The Poetry of Work*. Urbana: University of Illinois Press, 1995.

Conzen, Kathleen N., et al. "The Invention of Ethnicity: A Perspective from the U.S.A." *Journal of American Ethnic History* 12, no. 1 (Fall 1992): 3–41.

Cowell, Margaret. *Dealing with Deindustrialization: Adaptive Resilience in American Midwestern Regions*. New York: Routledge, 2015.

Cowie, Jefferson. *The Great Exception: The New Deal and The Limits of American Politics*. Princeton: Princeton University Press, 2016.

Cowie, Jefferson, and Joseph Heathcott. "The Meanings of Deindustrialization." In *Beyond the Ruins: The Meanings of Deindustrialization*, ed. Jefferson Cowie and Joseph Heathcott, 1–6. Ithaca, NY: Cornell/ILR Press, 2003.

Cresswell, Tim. *Place: An Introduction*. Chichester, West Sussex: Wiley Blackwell, 2015.

Daniels, Jim. *Places/Everyone*. Madison: University of Wisconsin Press, 1985.

Daniels, Jim. *Punching Out*. Detroit: Wayne State University Press, 1990.

Daniels, Jim. *M-80*. Pittsburgh: University of Pittsburgh Press, 1993.

Daniels, Jim. *Show and Tell: New and Selected Poems*. Madison: University of Wisconsin Press, 2003.

Daniels, Jim. "Work Poetry and Working-Class Poetry: The Zip Code of the Heart." In Russo and Linkon 2005, 113–37.

Daniels, Jim. *In Line for the Exterminator: Poems*. Detroit: Wayne State University Press, 2007.

Daniels, Jim, Jane McCafferty, and Charlee Brodsky. *From Milltown to Malltown: Poems*. Grosse Pointe Farms, MI: Marick Press, 2010.

Davis, Fred. *Yearning for Yesterday: A Sociology of Nostalgia*. New York: Free Press, 1979.

Dawn of the Dead. Dir. George A. Romero. Laurel Group, 1978.

de Certeau, Michel. *The Practice of Everyday Life*. Trans. Steven Rendall. Berkeley: University of California Press, 1984.

Deforce: The Past, Present, and Future of Detroit. Dir. Andrew Falconer. Detroit Documentary Productions, 2010.

D'Erasmo, Stacey. "Here Comes the Neighborhood: Stewart O'Nan's Novel Takes Place in an African-American Section of Pittsburgh." *New York Times*, 25 Feb. 2001. Web. 8 Feb. 2016.

Detroit: Ruin of a City. Dir. George Steinmetz and Michael Chanan, 2005.

Detroit Wild City. Dir. Florent Tillon. Ego Productions, 2011.

DiPiero, Diane. "The Only Chick in Town." In Marino and Miller, 82–84.

Douthat, Ross. "The Dying of the Whites." *New York Times*, 7 Nov. 2015. Web. 28 Nov. 2015.

Edensor, Tim. *Industrial Ruins: Spaces, Aesthetics, And Materiality*. Oxford: Bloomsbury, 2005. *eBook Collection*. Web. 23 June 2015.

Eddie Loves Debbie: The Youngstown Anthology. Youngstown, OH: Youngstown State University Student Literary Arts Association, 2013.

8 Mile. Dir. Brian Grazer et al. Universal, 2003.

"Employment for the Largest Occupations in the United States, May 2015." Bureau of Labor Statistics. Web. 7 July 2016.

Farewell to Factory Towns? A Documentary Film. Dir. Maynard Seider. 2012.

Fletcher, Bill, Jr., and Fernando Gapasin. *Solidarity Divided: The Crisis in Organized Labor and a New Path toward Social Justice*. Berkeley: University of California Press, 2008.

Florida, Richard L. *Cities and the Creative Class*. New York: Routledge, 2005.

Flournoy, Angela. *The Turner House*. Kindle ebook. New York: Houghton Mifflin Harcourt, 2015.

Foster, Catherine. "When the Jobs Leave Town." *Oregon Shakespeare Festival*, n.d. Web. 21 Feb. 2016.

Frolick, Joe. "Boomerangers Happily Return to Cleveland." *Plain Dealer*, 20 Nov. 2012. Web. 17 Feb. 2015.

Garland, David. Interview with Harvey Pekar and Joyce Brabner. WYNC *Spinning on Air*, 22 Aug. 2003. In *Harvey Pekar: Conversations*, ed. Michael G. Rhode, 34–55. Jackson: University Press of Mississippi, 2008.

Garrett, Bradley L. "Urban Exploration as Heritage Placemaking." In *Reanimating Industrial Spaces: Conducting Memory Work in Post-Industrial Societies*, ed. Hilary Orange, 72–91. Walnut Creek, CA: Left Coast Press, 2015.

Getting On. HBO Television, 2013–2015.

Giffels, David. *The Hard Way on Purpose: Essays and Dispatches from the Rust Belt*. New York: Scribner, 2014.

Gordon, Avery. *Ghostly Matters: Haunting and the Sociological Imagination.* Minneapolis: University of Minnesota Press, 1997.

Grollmus, Denise. "Speak in Tongues." In Piiparinen and Trubek, 103–7.

Grown in Detroit. Dir. Manfred Poppenk and Mascha Poppenk. Filmmij, 2009.

Grundmann, Roy. "White Man's Burden: Eminem's Movie Debut in *8 Mile.*" *Cineaste* 28, no. 2 (Spring 2003): 30–35.

Gutman, Herbert. "Labor History and the 'Sartre Question.'" In *Power and Culture: Essays on the American Working Class,* 326–28. New York: Pantheon Books, 1987.

Haigh, Jennifer, *Heat and Light.* New York: HarperCollins, 2016.

Hayden, Dolores. *The Power of Place: Urban Landscapes as Public History.* Cambridge, MA: MIT Press, 1995.

Heffron, Jack. "Pete Rose." In *The Cincinnati Anthology,* ed. Zan McQuade. Cleveland: Belt Publishing, 2014.

Hendrix, Grady. *Horrorstör.* Philadelphia: Quirk Books, 2014.

Hernandez, Lolita. *Autopsy of an Engine and Other Stories from the Cadillac Plant.* Minneapolis: Coffee House Press, 2004.

High, Steven. "'The Wounds of Class': A Historiographical Reflection on the Study of Deindustrialization, 1973–2013." *History Compass* 11, no. 11 (Nov. 2013). Web. 17 Mar. 2016.

High, Steven C., and David W. Lewis. *Corporate Wasteland: The Landscape and Memory of Deindustrialization.* Ithaca, NY: Cornell/ILR Press, 2007.

Hodgen, Christie. *Elegies for the Brokenhearted.* New York: Norton, 2010.

Hoffman, Nancy, Florence Howe, and Elaine Hedges. *Women Working: An Anthology of Stories and Poems.* Old Westbury, NY: Feminist Press, 1979.

Holman, Matthew Martin. "Rust Belt Gothic Fiction." Indiana University of Pennsylvania, May 2012. ProQuest Dissertations Publishing. Web. 29 Feb. 2016.

"Imported from Detroit." *Chrysler. YouTube,* 5 Feb. 2011. Web. 7 July 2016.

Izrael, Jimmy. "Not a Love Letter." In Piiparinen and Trubek, 130–32.

Jensen, Barbara. *Reading Classes: On Culture and Classism in America.* Ithaca, NY: Cornell/ILR Press, 2012.

Jess, Tyehimba. "Infernal." In Clark, 49.

Katznelson, Ira. "Working-Class Formation: Constructing Cases and Comparisons." In *Working-Class Formation: Nineteenth-Century Patterns in Western Europe and The United States,* ed. Ira Katznelson and Aristide R. Zolberg, 3–43. Princeton: Princeton University Press, 1986.

Kelley, Robin D. G., *Race Rebels: Culture, Politics, and the Black Working Class.* New York: Free Press, 1996.

Kessler-Harris, Alice. *Out to Work: A History of Wage-Earning Women in the United States.* New York: Oxford University Press, 1982.

Kidd, Phil. "Defending Youngstown." In Marino and Miller, 157–62.

Krugman, Paul. "Despair, American Style." *New York Times,* 9 Nov. 2015. Web. 28 Nov. 2015.

Kubrin, Charis E., Tim Wadsworth, and Stephanie DiPietro. "Deindustrialization, Disadvantage and Suicide among Young Black Males." *Social Forces* 84, no. 3 (Mar. 2006): 1559–79. Web. 5 Jan. 2016.

Lauter, Paul. "Under Construction: Working-Class Writing." In Russo and Linkon 2005, 63–77.

Leahy, John Patrick. "Detroitism." *Guernica*, 15 Jan. 2011. Web. 5 Mar. 2015.

Leija, J. M. "Playing Ball." In Clark, 189–91.

Leonard, Chantay Legacy. "Strange City." In Clark, 211.

Levi's Jeans. "Let's Go Forth to Work." *Vimeo*, 2012. Web. 22 July 2016.

Linkon, Sherry L. "Men without Work: White Working-Class Masculinity in Deindustrialization Fiction." *Contemporary Literature* 55, no. 1 (Spring 2014): 148–67.

Linkon, Sherry. "To Really Understand Working-Class Voters, Read These Books." *Moyers and Company*, 5 July 2016. Web. 22 July 2016.

Linkon, Sherry Lee, and John Russo. *Steeltown USA: Work and Memory in Youngstown.* Lawrence: University of Kansas Press, 2002.

Linkon, Sherry, Alexander Russo, and John Russo. "Contested Memories: Representing Work in *The Wire*." In *"The Wire": Race, Class, and Genre*, ed. Liam Kennedy and Stephen Shapiro, 239–61. Ann Arbor: University of Michigan Press, 2012.

"Lolita Hernandez." *Creative Mornings*, n.d. Web. 23 June 2014.

MacGillis, Alec. "The Rust Belt Theory of Low-Cost High Culture." *Slate*, 1 Jan. 2015. Web. 17 Aug. 2017.

Mah, Alice. *Industrial Ruination, Community, and Place: Landscapes and Legacies of Urban Decline.* Toronto: University of Toronto Press, 2012.

Malik, Shiv, Caelainn Barr, and Amanda Holpuch. "US Millennials Feel More Working Class than Any Other Generation." *Guardian*, 15 Mar. 2016. Web. 19 Apr. 2016.

Malone, Clare. "Little Italy's Shabby Chic." In Piiparinen and Trubek, 54–56.

Marchand, Yves, Romain Meffre, Robert Poliardi, and Thomas J. Sugrue. *The Ruins of Detroit.* Göttingen: Steidl, 2010.

Marino, Jacqueline. "A Comforting Kind of Shame." In Piiparinen and Trubek, 189–92.

Marino, Jacqueline. "A Girl's Youngstown." In Marino and Miller, 89–95.

Marino, Jacqueline, and Will Miller, eds. *Car Bombs to Cookie Tables: The Youngstown Anthology.* Cleveland: Belt Publishing, 2015.

Marino, Jacqueline, and Will Miller. "Sinkin' Down in Youngstown: An Introduction." In Marino and Miller, 7–10.

McAdams, Dan P., and Kate C. McLean. "Narrative Identity." *Current Directions in Psychological Science* 22, no. 3 (June 2013): 233–38. Web. 21 Sept. 2014.

McDowell, Linda. "Masculine Identities and Low-Paid Work: Young Men in Urban Labour Markets." *International Journal of Urban and Regional Research* 27, no. 4 (Dec. 2001): 828–48. Web. 23 Jan. 2014.

McGraw, Bill. "From Chopin to Craft Beer: A Buffalo Skeptic Sees the Light." *Belt Magazine*, 4 May 2015. Web. 29 June 2015.

Meisel, Ken. *Beautiful Rust: Poems.* Huron, OH: Bottom Dog Press, 2009.

Meitner, Erika. "This Is Not a Requiem for Detroit." *Virginia Quarterly Review: A National Journal of Literature and Discussion* 87, no. 2 (2011): 125. Web. 12 Jan. 2015.

Metzgar, Jack. "Politics and the American Class Vernacular." In Russo and Linkon 2005, 189–208.

Metzgar, Jack. "Class War and Sociology." *Working-Class Perspectives*, 23 Feb. 2015. Web. 23 Feb. 2015.

Metzgar, Jack. "Putnam's Poignant Folly: Empathetic Blaming." *Working-Class Perspectives*, 27 Apr. 2015. Web. 27 Apr. 2015.

Metzgar, Jack. "Human Tumbleweeds: Insecurity, Culture, and the American Working Class." *Working-Class Perspectives*, 27 Sept. 2015. Web. 27 Sept. 2015.

Metzgar, Jack. "Misrepresenting the White Working Class: What the Narrating Class Gets Wrong." *Working-Class Perspectives*, 14 Mar. 2016. Web. 14 Mar. 2016.

Metzgar, Jack. "Parts and Wholes: Unpacking Reports of White Working-Class Death Rates." *Working-Class Perspectives*, 2 May 2016. Web. 2 May 2016.

Meyer, Philipp. *American Rust*. New York: Spiegel and Grau, 2009.

Miller, Shannon Shelton. "I'm from Detroit." In Clark, 24–28.

Mitchell, Don. *The Lie of the Land: Migrant Workers and the California Landscape*. Minneapolis: University of Minnesota Press, 1996.

Moore, Andrew, and Philip Levine. *Detroit Disassembled*. Bologna: Damiani Editore, 2010.

Moore, Jessica Care. "Detroit Men." In Bossen and Beck, xiv–xvii.

Morisseau, Dominique. *Skeleton Crew*. Unpublished PDF, 2015.

Murray, Charles A. *Coming Apart: The State of White America, 1960–2010*. New York: Crown Forum, 2012.

Music, Marsha. "The Kidnapped Children of Detroit." In Clark, 225–31.

Nayak, Anoop. "'Boyz to Men': Masculinities, Schooling and Labour Transitions in De-industrial Times." *Educational Review* 55, no. 2 (2003): 147–59. Web. 23 Jan. 2014.

Nelson, Bruce. *Divided We Stand: American Workers and the Struggle for Black Equality*. Princeton: Princeton University Press, 2001.

Nethercott, Shauna S. "The Detroit Virus." Clark, 214–17.

Newport, Frank. "Fewer Americans Identify as Middle Class in Recent Years." *Gallup*, 28 Apr. 2015. Web. 19 Apr. 2016.

Nottage, Lynn. *Sweat*. Unpublished manuscript, 2015.

Nowak, Mark. *Shut Up Shut Down: Poems*. Minneapolis: Coffee House Press, 2004.

O'Dell, Tawni. *Back Roads*. New York: New American Library, 2001.

O'Dell, Tawni. *Coal Run*. New York: New American Library, 2005.

Olzman, Matthew. "Gas Station on Second Street, Detroit." In Clark, 26.

O'Nan, Stewart. *Everyday People*. New York: Grove Press, 2001.

O'Nan, Stewart. *Last Night at the Lobster*. New York: Viking, 2007.

Oresick, Peter, and Nicholas Coles, eds. *Working Classics: Poems on Industrial Life*. Urbana: University of Illinois Press, 1990.

Origen, Erich, and Dan Golan. *The Adventures of Unemployed Man*. New York: Little, Brown, 2010.

Ortiz, Nate. "Faith and Home." In Marino and Miller, 170–74.

Osayande, Deonte. "By the Time This Reaches You." In Clark, 158–59.

Palmer, Asynith Helen. "Re-Constructing the Rust Belt: An Exploration of Industrial Ruin in Blogs, Fiction, and Poetry." PhD diss., University of Michigan, 2014.

Parenti, Michael. *Blackshirts and Reds: Rational Fascism and the Overthrow of Communism*. San Francisco: City Lights Books, 1997.

Pearson, Jesse. "David Simon." *Vice* 16, no. 12 (Dec. 2009). Web. 12 Dec. 2011.

Perera, Sonali. *No Country: Working-Class Writing in the Age of Globalization*. New York: Columbia University Press, 2014.

Piiparinen, Richey. "Rust Belt Chic: Not Just for Hipsters." *Rust Wire*, 18 May 2012. Web. 7 July 2015.

Piiparinen, Richey. "Anorexic Vampires." In Piiparinen and Trubek, 17–21.

Piiparinen, Richey. "No Reservations Cleveland." *The Urbanophile*, 21 Nov. 2012. Web. 10 June 2014.

Piiparinen, Richey, and Anne Trubek, eds. *Rust Belt Chic: A Cleveland Anthology*. Cleveland: Belt Publishing, 2012.

Portelli, Alessandro. "The Peculiarities of Oral History." *History Workshop* 12 (Autumn 1981): 96–107. Web. 26 July 2016.

Portelli, Alessandro. "What Makes Oral History Different?" In *The Oral History Reader*, ed. Robert Perks and Alistair Thomson, 63–74. New York: Routledge, 1991.

Pugh, Allison J. *The Tumbleweed Society: Work and Caring in an Age of Insecurity*. Oxford: Oxford University Press, 2015.

Putnam, Robert. *Our Kids: The American Dream in Crisis*. New York: Simon and Schuster, 2015.

Renn, Aaron M. "The Promise and Peril of Rust Belt Chic." *Newgeography*, 27 Sept. 2012. Web. 16 Feb. 2015.

Requiem for Detroit? Dir. Julien Temple. Films of Record, 2010.

Rhodes, James, and John Russo. "Shrinking 'Smart'?: Urban Redevelopment and Shrinkage in Youngstown, Ohio." *Urban Geography*, 13 May 2013. Web. 17 July 2015.

Rich, Nathaniel. "Book Review: *Last Night at the Lobster*." *New York Times*, 5 Nov. 2007. Web. 18 Dec. 2014.

Roediger, David R. *The Wages of Whiteness: Race and the Making of the American Working Class*. London: Verso, 2007.

Rose, Tricia. *Black Noise: Rap Music and Black Culture in Contemporary America*. Hanover, NH: University Press of New England, 1994.

Ross, Tim. "A Conversation with Jim Daniels." *Artful Dodge*, 7 Sept. 1998. Web. 23 June 2014.

Rubin, Lillian B. *Worlds of Pain: Life in the Working-Class Family*. 1976; rpt., New York: Basic Books, 1992.

Rucker, Della. "The Elder Children of the Rust Belt." *Wise Economy*, 25 Oct. 2013. Web. 24 July 2015.

Russell, Jim. "Revenge of the Pittsburgh Potty." In Piiparinen and Trubek, 22–28.

Russo, John, and Sherry Lee Linkon. "The Social Costs of Deindustrialization." In *Manufacturing a Better Future for America*, ed. Richard A. McCormack, 183–213. Washington, DC: Alliance for American Manufacturing, 2009.

Russo, John, and Sherry Lee Linkon, eds. *New Working-Class Studies*. Ithaca: Cornell/ILR Press, 2005.

Russo, John, and Sherry Lee Linkon. "Collateral Damage: Deindustrialization and the Uses of Youngstown." In Cowie and Heathcott, 201–18.

Russo, Richard. *Empire Falls*. New York: Alfred A. Knopf, 2001.

Russo, Richard. *Everybody's Fool*. New York: Alfred A. Knopf, 2016.

Rust Belt Rising Almanac. Philadelphia: The Head and The Hand Press, 2013.

Saunders, Angharad. "Literary Geography: Reforging the Connections." *Progress in Human Geography* 34, no. 4 (2010): 436–52. Web. 7 Oct. 2015.

Schmitt, Angie, and Kate Giammarese, eds. *Rustwire*. Web. 17 Aug. 2017.

Schuessler, Jennifer. "New Magazine Celebrates 'Rust Belt Chic,' With a Wink." *New York Times*, 13 Sept. 2013. Web. 16 Feb. 2015.

Schulman, Ben. "This Ain't City Chicken: The Geography of Authenticity." *Belt Magazine*, 29 May 2014. Web. 16 July 2015.

Segedy, Jason. "Confessions of a Rust Belt Orphan (How I Learned to Stop Worrying and Love Northeast Ohio)." *Notes from the Underground*. 2 Nov. 2013. Web. 17 Aug. 2017.

Seliy, Shauna. *The Trials and Tribulations of Lucas Lessar*. London: Bloomsbury, 2007. Republished in the United States as *When We Get There*.

Sennett, Richard, and Jonathan Cobb. *The Hidden Injuries of Class*. New York: Knopf, 1972.

Sepanek, Sarah. "The Pro-Yo Movement Needs to Get Real." In Marino and Miller, 53–56.

Sheard, Timothy. *A Bitter Pill: The 6th Lenny Moss Mystery*. Kindle ebook. Brooklyn, NY: Hardball Press, 2013.

Silva, Jennifer M. "Constructing Adulthood in an Age of Uncertainty." *American Sociological Review* 77, no. 4 (June 2012): 505–22. Web. 6 Dec. 2013.

Silva, Jennifer M. *Coming Up Short: Working-Class Adulthood in an Age of Uncertainty*. New York: Oxford University Press, 2013.

Slanina, John. Personal interview. 23 June 2006.

Slanina, John. *I Will Shout Youngstown*. Web. 19 July 2016.

Slezak, Ellen. *Last Year's Jesus: A Novella and Nine Stories*. New York: Hyperion, 2002.

Soldan, William R. "Sad Beauty." In *Eddie Loves Debbie: The Youngstown Anthology*, 57–67. Youngstown: Youngstown State University Student Literary Arts Association, 2013.

Sollars, Werner, *The Invention of Ethnicity*. New York: Oxford University Press, 1988.

Spence, Lester K. *Stare in the Darkness: The Limits of Hip-Hop and Black Politics*. Minneapolis: University of Minnesota Press, 2011.

Springsteen, Bruce. "Youngstown." *The Ghost of Tom Joad*. Columbia Records, 1995.

Standing, Guy. *The Precariat: The New Dangerous Class*. London: Bloomsbury Academic, 2011.

Strangleman, Tim. "Nostalgia for Permanence at Work? The End of Work and Its Commentators." *Sociological Review* 55, no. 1 (2007): 81–103.

Strangleman, Tim. "'Smokestack Nostalgia,' 'Ruin Porn' or Working-Class Obituary: The Role and Meaning of Deindustrial Representation." *International Labor and Working-Class History* 84 (2013): 23–37.

Strangleman, Tim. "Deindustrialisation and the Historical Sociological Imagination: Making Sense of Work and Industrial Change." *Sociology* 51, no. 2 (2017): 466–82. Web. 25 July 2017.

Sugrue, Thomas J. *The Origins of the Urban Crisis: Race and Inequality in Postwar Detroit*. Princeton: Princeton University Press, 1996; reprinted with a new preface, 2005.

Superstore. NBC Television, 2015–2016.

Todorov, Tzvetan. "What Is Literature For?" *New Literary History* 38, no. 1 (Winter 2007): 13–32. Web. 23 Mar. 2016.

"Totally Wired." *Guardian Unlimited*, 13 Jan. 2005. Web. 11 Dec. 2011.

Trubek, Anne. "The Post-Colonial Theory of the Rust Belt." *Belt Magazine*, 2 Jan. 2015. 29 June 2015.

Up in the Air. Dir. Jason Reitman. DreamWorks, 2009.

Vance, J. D. *Hillbilly Elegy: A Memoir of a Family and Culture in Crisis*. New York: Harper, 2016.

Walkerdine, Valerie, and Luis Jimenez. *Gender, Work and Community after De-Industrialisation: A Psychosocial Approach to Affect*. Basingstoke, UK: Palgrave, 2012.

Walter, Laura Maylene. "Crossing the Ohio Border." In Piiparinen and Trubek, 184–88.

Watts, Eric King. "Border Patrolling and 'Passing' in Eminem's 8 Mile." *Critical Studies in Media Communication* 22, no. 3 (2005): 187–206. Web. 29 Dec. 2015.

Weis, Lois. *Class Reunion: The Remaking of the American White Working Class*. New York: Routledge, 2004.

"What Is Literature Now?" *New Literary History* 38.1, Special Edition (Winter 2007).

White, Russell. "'Behind the Mask': Eminem and Post-Industrial Minstrelsy." *European Journal of American Culture* 25, no. 1 (2005): 65–79. Web. 2 Feb. 2016.

Williams, Jay. "The Profundity of Youngstown." In Marino and Miller, 163–67.

Wilson, William Julius. *When Work Disappears: The World of the New Urban Poor*. New York: Vintage Books, 1997.

The Wire. HBO Television, 2002–2008.

Woodroofe, Hannah. Personal interview. 21 July 2014.

Wylie, John. *Landscape*. New York: Routledge, 2007.

Young, Gordon. *Teardown: Memoir of a Vanishing City*. Berkeley: University of California Press, 2013.

Zadoorian, Michael. *The Lost Tiki Palaces of Detroit*. Detroit: Wayne State University Press, 2009.

Zandy, Janet. "In the Skin of a Worker; or, What Makes a Text Working Class?" In Zandy 2004, 84–93.

Zandy, Janet. *Hands: Physical Labor, Class, and Cultural Work*. New Brunswick, NJ: Rutgers University Press, 2004.

Zandy, Janet, ed. *Calling Home: Working-Class Women's Writings: An Anthology*. New Brunswick, NJ: Rutgers University Press, 1990.

Zieger, Robert H. *For Jobs and Freedom: Race and Labor in America since 1865*. Lexington: University Press of Kentucky, 2007.

Zukin, Sharon. *Naked City: The Death and Life of Authentic Urban Places*. Oxford: Oxford University Press, 2010.

Index

addiction, working-class: among whites, 68; in deindustrialization literature, 86, 87, 88; to gambling, 70, 86

The Adventures of Unemployed Man (graphic novel), 168

aesthetics, Rust Belt, 142–47

African Americans: death rates of, 60; suicide rates among, 172n3. *See also* working class, black

agency, worker: in deindustrialization literature, 16, 48, 67; in deindustrialized communities, 164; economic undermining of, 46; in industrial labor, 17; limits of, 45, 46–53; the past in, 46; in working-class identity, 57, 94

Akron (Ohio): authenticity of, 148–49; industrial past of, 140; ruins of, 142

American Dream: distrust of, 142; economic restructuring and, 161

Andrews, Elaine Arvan, 140

Apel, Dora, 96, 129

"Arbeit Macht Frei" (Nazi slogan), 43

authenticity: commercial value of, 149–50; engagement with past, 148; in gentrification, 150; identity and, 148, 149; of local culture, 148; moral superiority in, 147; of place, 147, 160; in Rust Belt chic, 132, 145, 147–54, 160

auto industry: closings in, 21–22, 27; move to suburbs, 155; poetry of, 25; in Rust Belt chic writing, 139; social values of, 22; strikes in, 48; worker knowledge of, 21

automation: expansion of, 23; reduction in workforce through, 28

Bakopoulos, Dean: *Please Don't Come Back from the Moon*, 26, 46–49; agency in, 49; economic restructuring in, 49; erasure of race in, 68–69; industrial versus service work in, 47; the past in, 48; postindustrial workplace in, 53; solidarity in, 48, 49; strike plans in, 47–49; worker agency in, 48

Bal, Mieke, 4

Barzak, Christopher: Youngstown in works of, 120

—"The B&O, Crossroads of Time and Space," past and present in, 119

—"Map for a Forgotten Valley," past and present in, 120

—*One for Sorrow:* abandoned building use in, 108; deindustrialized landscape in, 107–10; fantasy in, 108; film version of, 175n4; ghost workers of, 108, 109, 113; romanticization of death in, 108–9; solitude in, 109; subjective perception in, 109; Youngstown in, 108–10

Baszynski, Nikki Trautman, 138

Bell, Matt: *Scrapper,* 11; abandonment in, 104; deindustrial aesthetic of, 104–5; deindustrialized landscape in, 103–5; poetic language of, 105; setting of, 103–4

Bellah, Robert, 172n8

Belt Magazine (online publication), 131,
134, 135; current issues in, 158; working-
class narratives in, 11
Benjamin, Walter: on ruins, 96, 100
Berlant, Lauren: *Cruel Optimism*, 176n10
Binelli, Mark, 176n8; *Detroit City Is the Place
to Be*, 135, 156; on economic challenges,
158; on industrial history, 139; on Rust
Belt creativity, 144
Black Friday, 47; strike (2012), 172n6
Boggs, Grace Lee, 145, 160
Boileau, Lowell: "Fabulous Ruins of Detroit," 133, 175n2
Bottom Dog Press, deindustrialization
literature in, 11
Boym, Svetlana, 35; on reflective nostalgia,
120, 132; "Ruinophilia," 96
Brabher, Joyce, 137
Brooks, David, 148; on fascist threat, 167–
68; on working-class attitudes, 163
built environment: affordances of, 105;
creativity in, 144; depopulated images
of, 99; deterioration of, 16, 18, 165;
gentrification of, 150. *See also* landscapes,
deindustrialized

Campbell (Ohio), 139, 176n2
Campbell, Bonnie Jo, 18; *American Salvage*,
86, 106; middle-class aspiration in, 107;
"The Yard Man," 106–7
capitalism: as agent of decline, 103;
changes in, 158; contradictions of labor
in, 26; exploitative, 57, 166; intractability
of, 52; social violence of, 24, 44; working-
class resistance to, 57
capitalism, global, 52, 53; in deindustrialization literature, 22; ideological power
of, 25; politics of, 98. *See also* globalization
Carroll, Hamilton, 50
Case, Anne, 60, 164, 171n1, 173n3
Center for Working-Class Studies, 55, 167
change, anxiety over, 36
Cherlin, Andrew, 164; *Labor's Love Lost*, xv
cities, Rust Belt: artistic representations
of, 144; authenticity of, 147–54; crime
in, 154; in deindustrialization literature,
11, 13; economic loss in, 136; economic
opportunities of, 136–37, 149, 154;
entrepreneurs in, 150; experimentation
in, 143; external narratives of, 136, 137;
global issues affecting, 159; idealized

future for, 145; identities in, 135–36;
local foods of, 138; material conditions
of, 135, 147–48; online reporting on, 134;
poverty in, 154; reclamation of, 143, 157–
61, 167; reinvention of, 143; resilience of,
159, 160; revitalization of, 108, 112, 123,
124, 146, 176n1, 260; Rust Belt chic writers on, 135; urban development of, 133.
See also communities, deindustrialized;
Rust Belt
Clarett, Maurice, 141
Clark, Anna, 137
class: in deindustrialization literature, xviii,
12; education in, xv; effect of gender on,
58, 70; effect of race on, xv, 58–59, 70;
and maleness, 12; Marx on, xiii; material
bases of, 57; in Rust Belt chic, 155; and
whiteness, 12, 77
class divide, geographic, xv
Cleveland (Ohio): authenticity of, 149;
local foods of, 138; Rust Belt authenticity
of, 151; underground scene of, 140
Clinton, Bill: resentment of, xvi
Clinton, Hillary: working-class voters on,
xvii
Cobb, Jonathan, xiv
Coles, Nicholas, 10
communities, deindustrialized: activism
in, 146; agency in, 164; arts projects in,
176n4; black, 72–73, 155, 172n3; contemporary life in, 8; cultural responses in,
73; decline of, 28, 90; in deindustrialization literature, 41; gambling in, 70; gentrification of, 150–51; identity in, 5, 19,
58, 87, 138–39; loss of identity in, 5; past
of, 1, 4; perseverance of, 19; personal
memories of, 139; reinvention of identity
in, 19; revitalization of, 18; Rust Belt chic
on, 138; smart shrinkage of, 146; white
males in, 65. *See also* cities, Rust Belt
communities, working-class, xiv; effects
of deindustrialization on, xvi; past
strengths of, 2; shared experiences of,
1–2; toughness of, 2
Cowie, Jefferson, 4, 159; *Beyond the Ruins*, 3
Coy, Steve and Dorota, 144, 176n3
culture, African American: hip-hop in, 77
culture, American: working-class perspectives on, xvi
culture, Rust Belt, 135, 137; defiance in,
140; industrial history in, 140; legacy of,
147; local character in, 141–42, 147; posi-

tive identity in, 141; toughness in, 140, 142; in working-class culture, 142. *See also* Rust Belt chic

culture, working-class: adaptations of, 59–60; appropriation of, 151; contingency in, 54; creative potential of, 142; deindustrialization in, 4, 13, 24, 56, 83, 163, 164, 168–69; elements of, 56; false consciousness of, 58; inheritance in, 140; loss of, 163; memory in, 166; past formations of, 5; pop culture icons of, 153–54; postindustrial, 7–8; reconstruction of, 8, 18; resilience in, xviii; response to change, 8, 10; response to community decline, 73; Rust Belt chic and, 152, 160; Rust Belt culture in, 142; in Rust Belt identity, 153; webs of significance in, 7, 54. *See also* identity, working-class

Daniels, Jim, 17, 172n2; remembered landscape in, 117–19; use of detail, 28; on worker poetry, 171n3
—Digger poems, 25, 27–32, 37–38; attachment to work in, 32; "Digger, Power, Speed," 30; "Digger, the Birthday Boy," 29; "Digger Goes on Vacation," 29; "Digger Laps at the Bowl," 30–31; "Digger on the Nature Trail," 30; *Digger's Blues*, 30–31, 172n3; "Digger's Melted Ice," 28; "Digger Turns in His ID," 31; displacement in, 31; dualities of work in, 28, 29–32; loss of work in, 30, 31; resistance in, 29; resistance to work in, 32; workplace connections in, 31
—"Find the Steel Mill in This Picture," 118–19
—"Fresh Fish," 118
—*From Milltown to Malltown*, 117–19
—*In Line for the Exterminator*, 27, 31
—*Places/Everyone*, 27
—*Punching Out*, 28–29
Davis, Fred, 23–24, 159
Deaton, Angus, 60, 164, 171n1, 173n3
de Certeau, Michel, 97, 113
decline, anxiety of, 96, 129
deindustrialization: abstract causes of, 3; civic dysfunction in, 131; continuing effects of, 5–6, 10; cultural responses to, 4, 13, 24, 56, 83, 163, 164, 168–69; definition of working class, 4–5; documentaries on, 11, 95–96, 100–101, 175n1; economic restructuring in, xviii,

3; effect on class solidarity, 6–7, 165; effect on white males, 61; elite observers of, xiv; intergenerational aspects of, 6; interracial bonds and, xvii–xviii; job loss in, 163; liminality of, 5–6, 8, 56–57, 166; long-term effects of, 10, 49; lost benefits of, 39, 54; material environment of, 99; neoliberalism and, 3, 128; persistent effects of, 3, 163, 169; personal perspectives on, 9; physical effects of, 2, 99; placing of blame for, 3; politics of resentment following, xvi–xvii; psychological effects of, 2; rap as response to, 174n9; shared injuries of, 6; socioeconomic effects of, xv–xvi, 2, 3, 5, 62; subjective experiences of, 15; tangible evidence of, 4; transformative moments in, 22, 166; of twenty-first century, 6; uselessness in, 40–41

deindustrialization half-life, 2, 5–8, 13; adjustments made in, 94; cultural, 24, 56, 164, 168–69; effect on middle class, 169; embodiment in landscape, 105, 128; identity in, 57; landscapes of, 96, 113; liminal period of, 56–57, 166; material realities of, 97, 106; persistence of, 163, 169; physical manifestations of, 99; Rust Belt chic in, 132, 161; social effects of, 106; worker doubt in, 85

deindustrialization literature: absent fathers in, 172n5; addiction in, 86, 87, 88; African American writers of, 11, 13; agency in, 16, 48; artistic aims of, 14; authors of, 9; black masculinity in, 71–76; capitalism in, 22; class consciousness in, 54; class divisions in, xviii, 12; communities in, 41; contemporary settings of, 9; corporate management in, 32–34, 42; critical attention to, 10; cultural context of, 14; daily life in, 8–9; decline of labor in, 27, 40; Detroit in, 99–105, 121–28; difference in, 12–13; dualities of work in, 23, 25, 32; economic displacement in, 12, 20, 68, 87–88; economic restructuring in, 12, 20, 68, 87–88, 90, 126; forms of, 11; friendship in, 33; globalization in, 22, 127, 128, 129; haunting in, 25–26, 35–45; health care in, 32–33; identity in, 17, 58–60, 84, 121; individual and community in, 59; inequality in, 12–13; interpretive nostalgia in, 23–24; landscape in, 18, 97, 106, 110, 129–30, 165; Latina writers of,

deindustrialization literature (*continued*)
96; lived experience in, 13; the local in, 13, 128, 129; masculinity in, 84; meaningful work in, 165; memory of labor in, 16, 23, 25, 36, 46–53, 165–66; non-white authors of, 12; nostalgia in, 26, 35–45; novels, xvii; the past in, 23, 25–26, 36, 39–45, 166; past and present in, 15–16, 35, 45, 113; perception narratives in, 110; the personal in, 15; plant closures in, 36, 45, 127–28; political dynamics in, 126; positive aspects of, 22–23; postindustrial-era authors of, 39; power of, xviii; pride in, 30; productive/problematic labor in, 32; and public perceptions, 164–65; race relations in, xviii, 12, 166; redemption in, 86–87; research into, 171n2; response to neoliberalism, 17; Rust Belt cities in, 11; settings of, 13, 99; sexuality in, 13, 70–71, 75; shaping of present, 113; social benefits in, 27; strikes in, 47–49; struggle in, 9; subjectivity in, 110, 165; temporality in, 9; therapeutic narratives of, 87, 93, 174n14; whiteness in, 12, 68, 69, 84; women authors of, 12; working-class perspectives in, 168; working-class solidarity in, 48, 49, 54; younger adults in, 8, 10. *See also* Rust Belt chic; working-class literature
D'Erasmo, Stacey, 173n6, 174n11
Detroit: apocalyptic films featuring, 136; authentic residents of, 149; in deindustrialization literature, 99–105, 121–28; deindustrialized landscapes of, 101, 102, 104–5, 122–24; deterioration in, 95–96; diversity in, 155–56; documentaries about, 96, 175n1, 176n3; economic expectation in, 122–23; factory closures in, 27; fires in, 141; murder rate in, 155; musical genres of, 77; past and future in, 123, 124; past and present in, 126; racial difference in, 122–26, 155–57; real estate opportunities in, 144; revitalization of, 123, 124, 156, 157; ruins of, 136; Rust Belt authenticity of, 151; in Rust Belt Chic writing, 135, 155; socioeconomic problems of, 70, 158; uprising of 1967, 155; urban agriculture in, 145, 160; white suburbanites of, 155
A Detroit Anthology, 156, 160; race in, 155
Detroit Summer (youth project), 145
Detropia (documentary), 176n3

DiPiero, Diane, 139
Douthat, Ross, 60

East Liberty (Pittsburgh): joblessness in, 73; working-class blacks of, 72
economic restructuring: American Dream and, 161; creative opportunities in, 143; cultural influence of, 9; decline of work quality in, 27–28; in deindustrialization literature, 12, 20, 68, 87–88, 90, 126; disruption caused by, 80, 93–94; effect on masculinity, 49; effect on working class, 7; mortality rates and, 173n3; under neoliberalism, 121; opportunities in, 153; racial divisions in, 72–73; undermining of agency, 46; undermining of stability, 83; working-class identity and, 57, 59, 87, 165
Eddie Loves Debbie (anthology), 134
Edensor, Tim, 96; on industrial ruins, 129
Eminem: advantages of whiteness for, 174n10; blackface charges against, 78, 174n11; claims for whiteness, 77; depiction of socioeconomic decline, 93
—*8 Mile*, 17; creative success in, 79; critics of, 78; hard-living life in, 78, 79; hard versus settled living in, 88; identity narrative of, 76; individual responsibility in, 59; intergenerational difference in, 77; past/present tension in, 76; race/class relationship in, 70, 78, 84; rap in, 77, 78; relational identity in, 79; service work in, 78; setting of, 76; settled-living life in, 78–79; success fantasies in, 79; "white trash" identity in, 70, 79; white working-class masculinity in, 58, 76–80; women in, 78
Equal Employment Opportunity, threat to white males, 61
explorers, urban, 99–100

factory closures: abandonment in, 104; in auto industry, 21–22, 27; cultural responses to, 10; in deindustrialization literature, 26, 45, 127–28; memories of, 1, 2; reflective nostalgia concerning, 36; steel mills, xvi. *See also* landscape, deindustrialized; ruins
Farewell to Factory Towns? (documentary), 176n4
fascism: corporatism and, 168; threat of, 167–68

identity: characteristics of, 57; construction of, 152; interior monologues of, 58; multifaceted, 57; performance of, 58; social networks of, 59

identity, Rust Belt, 135–36; belonging in, 142; community, 138–39; hybridity of, 152, 161; industrial work in, 139; positive, 141; in working-class culture, 153

identity, working-class, 51, 121; agency in, 57, 94; among millennials, 177n2; class in, 58, 59, 85; collective, 85; community in, 5, 19, 58, 87, 138–39; connection in, 85–93; construction through narrative, 58; contingency of, 17–18, 57, 94; contradictions in, 66; in deindustrialization literature, 17, 58–60, 84, 121; diversity in, 56, 94; economic aspects of, 57, 59, 87, 165; effect of neoliberalism on, 57, 59; in everyday life, 57; future of, 94; globalization in, 94; individual, 59, 85–86, 94, 164; isolation in, 85; loss of, 5; low expectations in, 91; material conditions in, 18; multifaceted, 58–59, 94; multiracial, 80; narratives of, 57, 60–68; negotiation of, 76; political aspects of, 57; in popular imagination, 56; race in, 68–85, 94, 173n4; reinvention of, 18–19, 151–52; relational, 79, 88; Rust Belt chic and, 132, 148, 151, 153; scholarship on, 56; self-defined, 76; self-management of, 59; self-reliance in, 59, 164; social categories in, 85; social networks in, 93, 94; socioeconomic disruption of, 93–94; solidarity in, 85, 94; sources for, 56; trauma in, 85–93, 174n14; of twenty-first century, 93–94; white, 154–57; white male, 60–62; younger people's, 85, 177n2. *See also* culture, working-class; masculinity, working-class

immigrants, 116; rights to jobs, 60–61

individualism, in working-class identity, 59, 85–86, 94, 164

industrial spaces, changing uses of, 8, 143, 148

Izrael, Jimmy, 154–55

James, LeBron, 135

Jamie Marks Is Dead (film, 2014), 175n4

Jensen, Barbara, 59

Jimenez, Luis, 58

Jones, Derrick "D": *631*, 11, 12, 113–16; community in, 114; decay in, 115; Great Recession in, 114; palimpsest of place in, 114; power of memory in, 113–14; sense of place, 114–16; socioeconomic loss in, 115; younger generation in, 114; Youngstown in, 114

Kasich, John, xvii

Katznelson, Ira, 6–7, 54

Kidd, Phil, 144–45

Kiely, Kathy, xvii

Krugman, Paul, 60

Kundera, Milan, 15

Kurashige, Scott, 145

labor: dualities of, 22, 23, 27–35, 43, 53–54; exploitative, 27, 44, 45, 53; fragmentation in, 26; meaning in, 25, 26–27; moral value of, 43–44, 45; new forms of, 172n1; pleasure in, 25; problematic, 32, 35; productive, 32, 35, 52, 53; social productivity of, 52; worker relationships in, 34, 36; working-class writing about, 22

labor, industrial: African Americans in, 81, 82; changing conditions of, 31; communal spirit in, 26; corporate management of, 32–34; decline in quality of, 27–28; half-life of dualities, 53–54; humiliation in, 29; identity in, 6; local culture and, 139; loss of, 152; material conditions of, 7, 28; material productivity in, 35; meaning in, xviii, 17, 22, 37–38; pride in, 4, 27, 29; Rust Belt chic and, 139, 142; self-definition through, 56; sensual memory of, 139; versus service work, 47; as site of resistance, 38; social productivity in, 35; temporal distance from, 39; transition to service work, 22, 23, 53; white male entitlement to, 61–62

labor, service: adaptations to, 26; benefits in, 34; commitment to, 34; dualities of, 22, 32; increase in, 53; versus industrial labor, 47; internalization of blame in, 44; meaning in, 34–35, 53; pride in, 27; problematic aspects of, 43; retail, 47–48; scarcity of, 164; transition from manufacturing, 22, 23

landscapes: conflict embedded in, 98; empty, 99; as how we see, 113; political, xviii; relationship to locale, 98; shared, xviii

landscapes, deindustrialized: anxiety over, 96; appearance and reality in,

102; creative potential of, 152; creativity concerning, 142–43; documentaries of, 95–96, 100–101, 175n1; economic loss in, 103; embodiment of death, 108–9; embodiment of socioeconomic change, 113; fabulous ruins of, 99–106; following Great Recession, 115; graffiti of, 100–101; human presence in, 97, 102, 129–30; in literature, 18, 97, 106, 110, 129–30, 165; lived, 129–30; material conditions of, 97, 105; meanings attached to, 99; media depiction of, 95; memory of, 97, 113; multiple readings of, 96–97; natural cycles in, 102–3; optimism concerning, 101, 102; past and present in, 99, 103, 110, 119; as place, 97; power conflicts in, 121; as product of half-life, 113; recovery of loss in, 100; relationships of, 97; residents of, 129–30; return of nature to, 107, 125; revitalization of, 108; as site of conflict, 121–29; socioeconomic symbolism of, 106; spatio-temporal relationships in, 129; subjectivity of, 112–13; unbuilt environment of, 105–6; urban explorers of, 99–100; visual representations of, 129–30; Walmart in, 128, 130. *See also* built environment; ruins

Lauter, Paul, 16, 17

Leahy, John Patrick, 159

Leija, J. M., 156

"Let's Go Forth to Work" (Levi's Jeans campaign), 150

Levine, Philip, 95

literature: audience perception of, 14; multiple readings of, 14; response to social forces, 168. *See also* deindustrialization literature; working-class literature

lockouts, industrial, 81–82, 83–84

MacGillis, Alec: "The Rust Belt Theory of Low-Cost High Culture," 136

"Made in Detroit" (Superbowl ad), 150

Made in Michigan (small press), 11

Mah, Alice, 129; on deindustrialized landscapes, 97; on living memory, 116

Mahoning Valley (Ohio), deindustrialization in, xvi

Malone, Clare, 138

Marino, Jacqueline: Youngstown anthology of, 137, 138, 144

Marx, Karl: on class difference, xiii

masculinity, working-class: African American, 58; androgynous version of, 173n5; class and, 12; in deindustrialization literature, 84; effect of economic restructuring on, 49; expression through crime, 173n5; models for, 62; narratives of, 58; performance of toughness, 173n5; relational meaning of, 75; traditional models of, 66; without labor, 78. *See also* identity, working-class

masculinity, working-class black: in deindustrialization literature, 71–76; stereotypes of, 72. *See also* working class, black

masculinity, working-class white, 8; in deindustrialized communities, 65; disruption of, 61–62; limitations of, 65–66; performance of, 65. *See also* working class, white male

Mass MoCA (North Adams, Massachusetts), 176n4

McCafferty, Jane: *From Milltown to Malltown*, 117–19; "On This Very Spot," 118

McDowell, Linda, 58

McGraw, Bill, 146

Meisel, Ken, 11–12

—*Beautiful Rust*: black frustration in, 126; class divide in, 125; deindustrialized landscapes in, 124–26; "Elegy for the Residents of the Niagara Apartments," 125; "Elegy for Whatever Isn't Right," 126; "He Helps Me Count What's Left Behind," 125; idealism in, 125; "Marvin Gaye and the Wrecking Ball," 124–25; "Our Common Souls," 126; racial difference in, 125; return of nature in, 125

memory: communities of, 172n8; idealized, 108; inherited, 139; of the past, 18; sense of place in, 119. *See also* the past

memory, working-class: in deindustrialization literature, 16, 23, 25, 36, 46–53, 165–66; of deindustrialized landscapes, 97, 113; narrative reinforcement of, 4; sensual, 139; of solidarity, 17; as source of resistance, 53–54; in United Kingdom, 172n2

Metzgar, Jack, 174n13, 176n1

Meyer, Philipp: *American Rust*, 11, 17; agency in, 67; economic decline in, 63; futility in, 67; generational difference in, 64–65, 66, 68; hard versus settled living in, 88; instability of labor in, 66; interior monologues of, 66–67; internal identity in, 63–64; internal narratives of, 65;

Meyer, Philipp (*continued*)
    performance of masculinity in, 65; physical masculinity in, 65; race in, 69; socioeconomic decline in, 93; violence in, 62–63, 67; whiteness in, 68, 69; women's opportunities in, 64–65; working-class masculinity in, 58, 62–68
middle class: in deindustrialization half-life, 169; in Rust Belt, 151; working-class aspirations for, xiv
Miller, Henry: *The Air-Conditioned Nightmare*, 175n6; Youngstown visit (1940), 119, 175n6
Miller, Shannon Shelton, 149, 155
Miller, Will: Youngstown anthology of, 137, 138, 144
Mill Hunk Herald (Pittsburgh), 10
Mitchell, Don, 97–98
Moore, Andrew: *Detroit Disassembled*, 95–96
Moore, Jessica Care, 168
Morisseau, Dominique, 11; depiction of socioeconomic decline, 93
    —*Detroit '67*, 70
    —*Paradise Blue*, 70
    —*Skeleton Crew*, 17, 70–72; black masculinity in, 71–72; class in, 70, 84; gender in, 70–71; race in, 70, 84; sexuality in, 70–71; violence in, 72; women characters, 71; working-class identity in, 70; working-class masculinity in, 58
Morozov, Evgeny, 159
Morrison, Toni: *Beloved*, 24
mortality rates, white working-class, 60, 68, 171n1
Moyers and Company, xvii
Murray, Charles, 164; *Coming Apart*, xv
Music, Marsha, 156–57, 176n8

narratives, working-class: of despair, 15; of hope, 15; reinforcement of memory, 4; subjectivity in, 8
nature: resilience of, 96; return to deindustrialized landscapes, 107, 125
Nayak, Anoop, 65
neoliberalism: cultural responses to, 13; culture of self-reliance, 93; deindustrialization and, 3, 128; deindustrialization literature and, 17; economic restructuring under, 121; effect on working-class identity, 57, 59; ideological power of, 25; internalization of, 85; intractability of, 52; resistance to, 160; undermining

of unions, 46; working class under, 7, 60, 164
Nethercott, Shaun S., 156
North American Free Trade Agreement, xvi
nostalgia: in deindustrialization literature, 26, 35–45; interpretive, 23–24; performance of, 37–38; productive, 24, 166; for productive labor, 53; reflective, 35–39, 120, 132; in Rust Belt chic, 159; "smokestack," 159
Nottage, Lynn, 11; depiction of socioeconomic decline, 93; Pulitzer Prize of, 79–80
    —*Sweat*, 17, 79; addiction in, 80, 86; class commonalities in, 80, 81, 83, 85; connections in, 85; disruptions to identity in, 84–85; gender in, 80; immigrants in, 81; industrial labor in, 80–83; interclass conflict in, 83; Latinx workers in, 81, 82–83; lockout in, 81–82; multigenerational characters of, 80; multiracial characters of, 80, 81, 82; perspective of "others" in, 82; productions of, 174n12; race in, 70; setting of, 80; solidarity in, 59, 83; unions in, 80–83; we/they relationships in, 80; white supremacy in, 83; worker exploitation in, 84; working-class masculinity in, 58
Nowak, Mark: on his writing, 175n7
    —"Hoyt Lakes/Shut Down," 127–28
    —*Shut Up Shut Down*: deindustrialized landscapes in, 126–28; local/global in, 127, 128; photographs of, 127; plant closure in, 127–28

Occupy Movement, xv
O'Dell, Tawni: substance abuse in, 86; violence in, 86
    —*Back Roads*, 10–11, 86
    —*Coal Run*, 11, 25–26; addiction in, 87; community in, 41, 87; haunting in, 39, 40; industrial/service labor in, 53; purposeful labor in, 45, 49; redemption in, 87; social violence in, 40; uselessness in, 40–41; value of labor in, 40–41
O'Nan, Stewart: depiction of black characters, 173n6, 174n11
    —*Everyday People*, 72–76; black working-class masculinity in, 58, 72–76, 84; community decline in, 72–73; construction of identity in, 76; fantasy/reality in, 74;

gang life in, 73–74, 75; internal narratives of, 74, 76; narrative strategy of, 73, 76; race in, 70; sexuality in, 75; socioeconomic decline in, 93; structural racism in, 72–73; traditional life in, 73, 74
—*Last Night at the Lobster*, 25, 32, 33–35; corporate management in, 33–34; meaning of labor in, 34; postindustrial workplace in, 53; worker relationships in, 34
oral histories, remembered actions in, 14, 38
Oresick, Peter, 10
Ortiz, Nate, 142

Palmer, Asynith Helen, 171n4
Parenti, Michael, 168; *Blackshirts and Reds*, 177n3
the past: collective, 38; in community identity, 138–39; as cultural legacy, 132; in deindustrialization literature, 23, 25–26, 35, 36, 39–45, 166; memories of, 18; as narrative resource, 15; power of, 16; reclamation of, 143; as resource, 25–26; Rust Belt chic and, 133, 135, 147, 159; as source for resistance, 52; as source of agency, 46. *See also* memory
Pekar, Harvey: *American Splendor* comics, 137
Pennsylvania, mines of, 116
Piiparinen, Richey, 134; on Cleveland authenticity, 149; on economic revitalization, 158; on Rust Belt chic, 131, 145
place: authenticity of, 147, 160; centrality of food for, 138; hard boundaries of, 148; landscape and, 98; palimpsests of, 97, 113–20; reinterpretation of, 138; relationship to locale, 98; in Rust Belt chic, 135–42; social meanings of, 98, 100–101, 147; in social memory, 121. *See also* landscape
Portelli, Alessandro, 14, 38
post-Fordism, 5, 166, 176n10
postindustrial era: adaptations to, 166–67; characteristics of, 144; working-class culture in, 7–8; working-class difficulties in, xvi, 166–67
precariat class, 153, 167
presidential election (2016): class divide in, xiv–xv; cultural divide in, xiii; populist messages in, 20, 167
Pugh, Allison J.: *The Tumbleweed Society*, xv
Putnam, Robert, 164; *Our Kids*, xv

race: in deindustrialization literature, xviii, 12, 166; in Detroit, 122–26, 155–57; effect on class, xv, 58–59, 70; role in identity, 57; Rust Belt chic and, 154–57; in working-class identity, 68–85, 94, 173n4
Reading (Pennsylvania), lockout in, 83–84
redemption: in deindustrialization literature, 86–87, 93; for younger working class, 87–88
Renn, Aaron M., 145
revitalization, 18; of deindustrialization landscapes, 108; of Detroit, 123, 124; of Flint (Michigan), 160; limits of, 176n9; Rust Belt, 112, 123, 124, 146, 176n11, 260; in Rust Belt chic, 146, 158–59
Rich, Nathaniel, 35
Roediger, David R.: *The Wages of Whiteness*, 173n4
Romero, George, 172n4; *Dawn of the Dead*, 42
Rubin, Lillian, 164; *World of Pain*, 64
ruin porn, 95, 129
ruins: ambivalence of, 100; appeal of, 96; haunting in, 96; symbolism of, 96
ruins, industrial, 99–106; artistic expression in, 143–44; as home, 129; life among, 113, 165; repurposing of, 143, 148; visual representation of, 103. *See also* landscapes, deindustrialized
Russell, Jim, 133
Russo, John, xvi, xvii, 19, 157–58, 167
Russo, Richard: *Empire Falls*, 168
Rust Belt: abandoned spaces of, 143; African American families of, 115; boosterism in, 146–47; city services in, 175n3; community activism in, 145; economic development in, 145–46, 159; insider/outsider views of, 136–37; loss of people from, 143; middle-class aspects of, 151; online discussions of, 133; opportunity loss in, 143; optimism concerning, 158; outsider narratives of, 136–37; professionals of, 133; resilience in, 142; ruined landscapes of, 96; self-explanation of, 136; "solutionism" in, 159; toughness in, 140, 142; unemployment in, 146. *See also* cities, Rust Belt; culture, Rust Belt
Rust Belt chic, 18–19; accommodation in, 160; activists of, 133; in advertising, 150; advocacy in, 161; aesthetics of, 142–47; aspirational vision of, 145; as attitude, 132; authenticity in, 132, 145, 147–54,

Rust Belt chic (*continued*)
160; authority in, 154; on auto industry, 139; blogs, 133–34; on character of cities, 140–41; on cities' potential, 137; class in, 155; commitment in, 149; on community identity, 138–39; community in, 135, 138–39; contradictory desires in, 153; critical reflection in, 158; cultural appropriation in, 151; debates over future, 159; definition of city, 145; deindustrialization legacy of, 140; depiction of working class, 154; downwardly mobile writers of, 153; economic opportunity in, 149; engagement with past, 133, 135, 147, 159; fashions of, 149; hard work in, 141; home in, 131–32; hybrid identity in, 152, 161; identity in, 148; the individual in, 135; industrial labor and, 139, 142; as interpretive genre, 161; journalism of, 134; as lifestyle, 132; as literary genre, 133–35; local character in, 141, 147; local narratives of, 137; local readers of, 137; loss in, 135; as marketing tool, 145–46; nostalgia in, 159; past and present in, 135; past/future links in, 147; personal writing of, 134; place in, 135–42, 145; possibility in, 135; race and, 154–57; resilience in, 150, 152, 159; resistance to neoliberalism, 160; response to uncertainty, 152; revitalization in, 146, 158–59; romanticization of poverty, 160; self-criticism of, 160; storytelling in, 147; whiteness in, 154–55, 161; and working-class culture, 152, 160; working-class identity and, 132, 148, 151, 153; Youngstown in, 137–38. *See also* deindustrialization literature
Rust Belt Chic: A Cleveland Anthology (Piiparinen and Trubek), 134
Rust Belt Rising Almanac, 134

Sanders, Bernie, 167
Saunders, Angharad, 15
Schmitt, Angie: *Rustwire*, 133–34
Segedy, Jason, 160
Seider, Maynard: *Farewell to Factory Towns?*, 176n4
selfhood, therapeutic, 85, 174n13
self-reliance: in neoliberalism, 93; in working-class identity, 59, 164
Seliy, Shauna: *When We Get There:* family in, 117; immigration in, 116; publication of, 175n5; sense of place in, 116–17; social memory in, 117

Sennett, Richard, xiv
Sepanek, Sarah, 146
sexuality: in deindustrialization literature, 13, 70–71, 75; role in identity, 57, 94
Sheard, Timothy: *A Bitter Pill*, 32–33; on friendships, 33; mystery novels of, 25
Shelley, Percy Bysshe: "Ozymandias," 95
Silva, Jennifer, 59, 94, 164; *Coming Up Short*, 85; on therapeutic selfhood, 85, 174n13; on working-class trauma, 87, 93; on younger working class, 60, 85, 86, 91
Simon, David, 54–55. See also *The Wire*
Simply Slavic festival (Youngstown), 133
Slanina, John: *I Will Shout Youngstown*, 133, 146
slavery, in fiction, 24
Slezak, Ellen: "Here in Car City," 102–3
Soldan, William R.: "Sad Beauty," 139–40
solidarity, working-class: in deindustrialization, 6–7, 54, 165; in deindustrialization literature, 48, 49, 54; disruption of, 3, 6–7, 85; fragility of, 59; memory of, 17; in working-class identity, 85, 94
Speak in Tongues (Cleveland club), 140
Springsteen, Bruce, 2, 19, 148
Standing, Guy, 167
steel mills: closing of, xvi; idealized memory of, 108
Steeltown USA: Work and Memory in Youngstown (Linkon and Russo), xvi, 157–58
Strangleman, Tim, 5, 7, 8; on industrial ruins, 129; on nostalgia, 23–24, 159; on structures of feeling, 35; on visual imagery, 104
strikes: Black Friday (2012), 172n6; in deindustrialization literature, 47–49; Flint (1937), 48
Sugrue, Thomas J., 155, 173n8
Superstore (television program), 168

Temple, Julien: *Requiem for Detroit?*, 95
Todorov, Tzvetan, 14
Traficant, Jim, xvi
Trubek, Anne, 134, 147; on outsider narratives, 136–37
Trump, Donald J.: divisive populism of, 20, 168; elite supporters of, xiv; working-class support for, xiii, 167, 176n7

unions: African Americans in, 80–81; benefits for workers, xiii; decline of, 46;

exclusions from, 61; fights within, 4; ideologies opposing, 7
Up in the Air (film), 168

Valenzuala, Luisa: *Como en la Guerra*, 24
Vance, J. G.: *Hillbilly Elegy*, xv
violence, social: in American cities, 167; of capitalism, 24, 44; in deindustrialization literature, 40
voters, working-class, xvii, 167

Walkerdine, Valerie, 58
Walton, Sam, 127, 128
Watterson, Sean, 151
Weis, Lois, 58, 173n5
"What Is Literature Now?" (*New Literary History*, 2007), 171n5
White, Russell, 77–78
whiteness: class and, 12, 77; in deindustrialization literature, 12, 68, 69, 84; in Rust Belt chic, 154–55, 161
white supremacy, 83, 156
"white trash": black ethnicity and, 77; identity, 70, 79
Williams, Jay, 144
Williams, Raymond, 5; *Border Country*, 98
Wilson, William Julius, 172n3; *When Work Disappears*, 73
The Wire (HBO), 11, 17, 49–53; death of work in, 50–52; global capitalism in, 52, 53; industrial/service labor in, 53; meaningful labor in, 52; memory in, 49, 50–51, 52–53; the past in, 26, 46, 50–52; police work in, 50–51, resistance in, 50, 52; white masculinist privilege in, 50; work-based identity in, 51
women, working-class: opportunities for, 64–65; white, 60–61; writings of, 10
Women Working (Feminist Press, 1979), 10
Woodroofe, Hannah, 153
workers, industrial: agency of, 17; educated offspring of, 19; expendability of, 19; self-perception of, 56; stereotypes of, 12
workers, service: internalization of blame, 44; limited agency of, 46; middle-class characteristics of, 55; resilience of, 164
work ethic, Protestant, 26
working class: admiration for, xiv; affluence in, 155; Americans identifying as, 176n2; competing loyalties in, 165; in contingent economy, 161; denigration

of, xiv; displacement of, 15, 168; diversity of, 55–56, 94; diversity of experience in, 9; economic worries of, xiv, 2; effect of economic restructuring on, 7; effects of frustration among, xviii; fragmentation of, 165; under global capitalism, 7; hard-living model of, 64–65, 78, 79, 88, 92, 164; idealized representations of, 19, 133; immigrants, 60–61; interpretation of change, 7, 8, 36; lived experiences of, 9; material realities of, 97; media stereotypes of, 55–56; memories of, 1–4, 7, 15; middle-class characteristics of, 55; under neoliberalism, 7, 60, 164; in popular culture, xiv; postindustrial difficulties for, xvi, 166–67; in postwar era, xiii, 4; public perception of, 176n7; scholarship on, 1, 2; settled-living model of, 64–65, 75, 78–79, 88, 92, 164, 167; uncertainty among, 5, 15; upward mobility for, xiv. *See also* culture, working-class; identity, working-class
working class, black: access to jobs, 17; effect of deindustrialization on, 6; industrial, 81; interracial bonds of, xvii; strikebreakers among, 82; suicide rates in, 172n3; union membership for, 80–81. *See also* African Americans; masculinity, working-class black
working class, white: addiction rates of, 68; challenges of, 6; death rates among, 60, 168, 171n1; identity of, 154–57; loss of values, xv; lost narratives of, 60–68; media treatment of, 56; millennial generation of, 77; Trump's appeal to, xiii, 168, 176n7; women, 60–61
working class, white male, 8; displacement among, 17; entitlement to jobs, 61–62; job loss among, 60; narratives of, 62–68; sense of loss, 68; threat of Equal Employment to, 61; younger, 78. *See also* masculinity, working-class white
working class, younger: in deindustrialization literature, 8, 10; low expectations among, 91; redemption for, 87–88; response to neoliberalism, 60; self-definition among, 93; sense of self, 85; white male, 78
Working Classics (newsletter, San Francisco), 10
Working Classics: Poems on Industrial Life (Coles and Oresick), 10

working-class literature: dualities of, 27; lives of workers in, 17; physicality of labor in, 16; struggle in, 9. *See also* deindustrialization literature

Working-Class Studies, xvi; cultural representations in, 168

workplace relationships, 34, 36; disruption of, 46

Wylie, John, 98, 99

Young, Gordon: on economic challenges, 158; on industrial history, 139; *Teardown*, 135, 146, 160

Youngstown (Ohio), 19; as blue-collar bohemia, 140; built environment of, 157; converted buildings of, 176n4; drug crisis in, 146; ethnic communities of, 157–58; gentrification in, 150; Henry Miller's visit to, 119, 175n6; industrial identity of, 5; job loss in, 5; local character of, 141–42, 157; metro area of, 157, 158; mob violence in, 141; past and present of, 175n6; racial boundaries of, 158; reclamation of, 157–58; Rust Belt chic writings on, 137–38; steel mill closure in, xvi, 108; Trump candidacy in, xvii; 2010 plan, 144; working class of, 55

Zadoorian, Michael, 103
—*The Lost Tiki Palaces of Detroit*, 100; deindustrialized landscapes in, 122–24; homelessness in, 123, 124; the past in, 123–24; revitalization in, 123, 124
—"Spelunkers," deindustrialized landscapes of, 100–102

Zandy, Janet: *Calling Home*, 10; on working-class literature, xvii, 9, 16

zombies, in *Horrorstör*, 42–45

Zukin, Sharon, 132; on authenticity, 147, 150, 152–53